W9-BSJ-891

News from Nowhere

News
from Nowhere

Television and the News

Edward Jay Epstein

 Vintage Books

A Division of Random House, New York

VINTAGE BOOKS EDITION, April 1974

Copyright © 1973 by Edward Jay Epstein

All rights reserved under International
and Pan-American Copyright
Conventions. Published in the United
States by Random House, Inc., New
York, and simultaneously in Canada
by Random House of Canada Limited,
Toronto. Originally published by
Random House, Inc., in 1973.

Library of Congress Cataloging in Publication Data

Epstein, Edward Jay, 1935–
News from nowhere: television and the news.

Bibliography: p.
1. Television broadcasting of news—United
States. I. Title.
[PN4888.T4E6 1974]   070.4'3   73–13708
ISBN 0-394-71998-0

Much of the material in this
book appeared originally in
The New Yorker.

Manufactured in
the United States of America

To William Shawn

"Our reporters do not cover stories from *their* point of view. They are presenting them from *nobody's* point of view."

—Richard S. Salant,
president of CBS News, in *TV Guide*

Preface

More than a half-century ago, Walter Lippmann pointed to a conspicuous gap in the study of American politics:

> Since Public Opinion is supposed to be the prime mover in democracies, one might reasonably expect to find a vast literature. One does not find it. There are excellent books on government and parties, that is, on the machinery which in theory registers public opinions after they are formed. But on the sources from which these public opinions arise, on the processes by which they are derived, there is relatively little.

More specifically, he noted, "To anyone not immersed in the routine interests of government, it is almost inexplicable that no American student of government, no American sociologist, has ever written a book on newsgathering." Since this charge was leveled, despite the fact that technological developments and increased literacy have vastly expanded the audience of news media, there have been few attempts by political scientists or sociologists to explore the processes by which news is gathered, synthesized and presented to the public. And nearly all the studies that have been undertaken deal mainly with the activities of specialized groups of newsmen, such as Washington correspondents, not with the broader question of how the various methods of selecting and organizing information into news forms may affect the final product reaching the public.

The reluctance of social scientists to grapple with this latter question is not, however, entirely inexplicable. Any systematic attempt to unravel the shaping effects of news processes from the "news" itself runs into difficulties.

For one thing, it is not possible to determine, simply by historical research or content analyses, systematic distortions in the images of events presented in the media without first independently establishing the actual course of the same events. While some social scientists have attempted this mode of analysis on a limited scale—for example, Kurt Lang and Gladys Engel Lang once posted thirty-one observers along the preannounced parade route for General Douglas MacArthur at points which television camera crews were covering to compare television coverage of a single event with that of eyewitnesses— the fast-breaking nature of news usually defies the simultaneous surveillance of news events and news reporting over extended periods of time (at least without resources that heretofore have not been available for this type of research). Coverage of ongoing events, such as wars or even election campaigns, would thus be beyond the means of most academic researchers.

Moreover, news events cannot be expected to take place under the sort of controlled circumstances which lend themselves to methodical analysis. Conditions can rarely be held constant in news events (as they can be in social science experiments), so that modes of reporting can be compared in different circumstances. For example, in analyzing varying news reports about urban riots in different cities, it would be extremely difficult to say with any sort of precision whether the differences in the reports resulted from variation in news coverage or in the actual circumstances of the disorders. To the extent that news reporting concentrates on what is atypical in events, which is the traditional focus of journalism, comparisons and generalizations have little value. To be sure, after-the-fact comparisons can be made between the way various news media cover the same event, but this still leaves the problem of determining the reality of the event—and the deviation from it.

Another problem is that up until recently, newsmen have tended to work on their own to a large extent, rather than in groups or a tightly regimented office situation. This hardly suits the more traditional forms of sociological analyses, which are mainly concerned with group behavior, or the effects of "social structures" on individuals. And to the degree that one accepts the assertion that newsmen's work, like that of authors and artists, is idiosyncratic, or entirely dependent on their individual judgments of situations, they become uninteresting subjects about which to generalize. (The few studies that have been conducted by sociologists therefore mainly deal with the problem of social control in news offices.)

Finally, serious research about the processes of news gathering has been discouraged, in no small measure, by a lack of access to news facilities. Whether to protect their competitive position in acquiring information or their credibility in presenting it, newspapers have been less than eager to open their newsrooms to social scientists. The *New York Times*, for example, refused to allow Paul Weaver to observe their news operation as "a matter of policy," even though he was then writing his doctoral dissertation on New York City newspapers.

Despite obvious problems like these, this study began as a doctoral dissertation at Harvard University in 1968. The idea that a news medium could be productively studied arose out of a seminar in Organizational Theory given that year at Harvard by Professor James Q. Wilson. The general question explored at this seminar was, briefly stated: To what extent are the directions that large organizations take, whether they are political parties, city governments, business corporations or whatever, determined by pressures to satisfy internal needs rather than by external circumstances or even long-range goals? The working assumption was that members of such organizations eventually modified their own personal values in accordance with the requisites of the organization, and that therefore the key to explaining the particular "outputs" of organizations—which could be nominations in the case of a political party, policies in the case of a city government, and product design in the case of a corporation—lay in defining the basic requirements which a given organization needs to maintain itself. In the case of news media, this suggested the approach of treating a news service as a business organization rather than as a collective faculty for highly independent newsmen—i.e., "the press." The particular output, the formulation of "news," might then be explicable in terms of what the news organization had to do to stay in business. How successful this approach would prove depends, of course, on the degree to which "news" is selected and shaped by the organization, as well as on assumptions about organization behavior.

I chose network news on television as the subject of this study for several reasons. First of all, each of the three network news services—NBC News, CBS News and ABC News—is a relatively large organization, with hundreds of employees and many tiers of executive control. Comparisons are made easier by the fact that each also has a similar set of requirements it must meet to maintain itself. The Federal Communications Commission, the agency which regulates television, requires that certain standards be met. The parent networks, which allocate money and network time to the news divisions, require that certain economic expectations be fulfilled. The independently owned affiliate stations, which provide most of the audience for national news, require that programing meet certain specifications. Newsmen and technicians require certain minimum working conditions to be effective in processing information in a credible way. And the home audience, for which each network competes, must also find the material minimally interesting.

Second, it seemed to be an important subject for political science. The three networks provide almost all the national news on television (most local stations taperecord segments of the network news and rebroadcast them as their national reports in the local news), and according to public opinion surveys, the public now relies on television as its major source of news. Indeed, given the fact that up until recently virtually all daily news organs relied on local audiences for support, network news represents a qualitatively different news form. Yet, although it had become the major national news medium in the United States, few serious studies had been done specifically on this subject. It thus seemed to deserve attention.

Finally, as a practical consideration, I was promised —and given—considerable access to the news operation by network executives and producers.

My field study began at NBC in September 1968. Reuven Frank, the president of the news division, allowed me more or less free reign of the news organization: I was able to attend, on a regular basis, the news manager meetings in the morning, which he chaired; observe the proceedings in the newsroom throughout the day; interview personnel; travel with camera crews; and examine memoranda and budget statements pertinent to the news operation. Robert J. Northshield, the executive producer of the NBC Evening News, further permitted me to observe closely the decision making involved in that program on a daily basis for a four-month period, including staff meetings, critiques, film-editing sessions, writing conferences, and the continuous discussions that went on between producers, news editors and correspondents.

The other networks presented some problems. At CBS

News, although Gordon Manning, the vice-president, co-operated in allowing me to interview correspondents and producers and also made available most material I specifically requested, the executive producer of the CBS Evening News, Leslie Midglie, did not permit me to observe the conferences and decision making on that program on a continuous basis. He explained that the presence of an outside observer over an extended period of time might interfere with or inhibit the news operation (and my experience at NBC indicated that this was, to some degree, a valid reason). I thus was given only limited access to that program.

At ABC News, there was a different problem. While Av Westin, the executive producer of the ABC Evening News, allowed me to observe decision making on his program and cooperated fully at that time, ABC News was in a state of flux. Westin, a former CBS and Public Broadcasting Laboratory producer, had just taken over the program from another producer and was then in the process of completely reorganizing it. He told me that he planned to recruit a new group of producers, editors and correspondents, and experiment with various procedures and formats until he found the most suitable one for ABC News. While this certainly provided an interesting situation, it could not be fairly compared to the established procedures at the other networks.

I therefore decided to use NBC as my main field study and attempt to determine, through interviews and limited direct observations at the other two networks, whether there were significantly different procedures for gathering and formulating news at CBS and ABC. In general, I found that the similarities at all three networks greatly outweighed differences, which is not surprising in light of the fact that all news divisions operate essentially under the same ground rules imposed by federal regulation, affiliated stations and an economic logic intrinsic to network television. The "outputs" presented no problem: all three networks gave me full access to their scripts, logs and assignment records.

The research for this study was based on five main sources: direct observation of news operations and editorial conferences for a total period of about six months; interviews with ninety-three correspondents, news editors, producers, technicians and network news executives which were "structured" in the sense that all were asked the same questions about their views on news, politics and the organization for which they worked; informal and off-the-record discussions with individuals in the peripheral organizations which help define the situation of network news, which included audience analysts and executives of the parent networks, Federal Communications Commission officials, owners and managers of affiliated stations, advertising agency executives, public relations executives, comptrollers, and attorneys for the networks and affiliates (in all, there were over one hundred such interviews); network news memoranda, the records of government investigations, and public statements by those in network news; and finally, the logs, scripts and records of news broadcasts. The only restriction placed on the study was that I agreed not to attribute direct quotations to news personnel (except where they made the statements publicly). In any case, the fragments of conversation I quote from newsroom discussions, editorial conferences, and camera crews on location were often said in the context of fast-moving news events and sometimes heated disputes about the best way of handling them, and are intended more to illustrate the climate that surrounds news gathering than as any sort of conclusive proof of the theses of this book.

Since most of the research and interviews for this book were done in 1968 and 1969, the facts and figures in the text reflect the conditions in the television industry in those years, unless otherwise noted. While there have been certain minor changes in the size of the audience that programs draw, affiliate relations and productions costs, the basic structure under which network news operates remains essentially the same.

The central problem this study addresses is the effect

of the processes of a news organization on the news product. The first chapter examines the arguments commonly made by newsmen and news executives that the news they produce is an ineluctable reproduction of reality, not shaped in any systematic way by them; and it concludes that news itself is problematic and that its final formulation is, to no small extent, a product of an organization. The next two chapters deal with the structures imposed on network news from without—by government regulation, affiliates, parent networks and economic realities. Chapters IV, V and VI analyze the effect of the internal procedures of network news—the intelligence systems used for assigning crews in advance, the techniques used by network crews to reconstruct events into "stories," and the decisional rules used for routinely eliminating possible stories from the program. The next chapter, drawn mainly from the structured interviews, discusses the values of those involved in network news, and the question of whether individuals modify their values to meet the needs of the organization or vice versa. Finally, the last two chapters inspect some composite pictures of various aspects of American society, as depicted on network news over a three-month period, and attempt to relate them to the "inputs" defined in the earlier chapters. The book does not hold that network news is entirely determined by the organizational factors. Obviously, the events reported on television take place somewhere and may be seen in different ways by different reporters. It does argue that certain consistent directions in selecting, covering and reformulating events over long-term periods are clearly related to organizational needs.

I am deeply grateful to James Q. Wilson for suggesting this subject, advising me on the research design of the project, and over the course of the past three and a half years, supervising the resulting doctoral dissertation. Without his generous assistance, time and criticism, I doubt that the study could have been completed in this form.

This study has also benefited enormously from the criticisms of friends, colleagues and teachers. I am particularly grateful to Renata Adler, Edward C. Banfield, Byron Dobell, Howard Darmstadter, Yaron Ezrari, Paul Halpern, Carol Katz, Bruce S. Kovner, Seymour Martin Lipset, Daniel Patrick Moynihan, John Rubinstein, William Shawn, William Whitworth and William Marslan Wilson for their comments on parts of the manuscript. There is no way I can express my debt to Cynthia Worswick for the research she did for me on this project over a four-year period.

Amagansett, New York   E. J. E.
June 1972

Contents

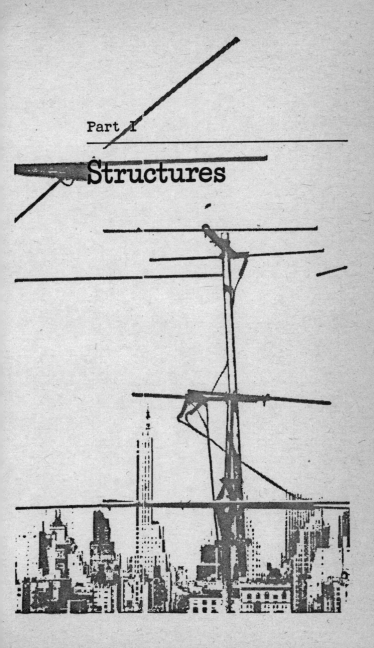

Part I
Structures

Chapter 1

Pictures from an Organization

So many different people with so many differing jobs and responsibilities have felt they wandered into the presence of a large blank canvas ... But the canvas is not blank. And none of us may fill it alone. The problem is given. The conditions for the most part are given.

—Reuven Frank, producer,
NBC Evening News

Each weekday at a fixed time in the early evening, the three national television networks—the American Broadcasting Companies, the Columbia Broadcasting System and the National Broadcasting Company— "feed" a limited number of film stories depicting national and world events through a system of closed-circuit telephone cables and microwave relays to their more than 550 local affiliated stations, which in turn broadcast these news pictures to a nationwide audience over the public airwaves. The CBS Evening News, with Walter Cronkite, broadcast by 205 local stations, is seen by an estimated 26 million viewers; the NBC Evening News, carried by 195 stations, reaches some 21 million viewers; and the ABC Evening News, relayed by 154 stations, some 10.5 million viewers. National news stories from these programs are also recorded on video tape by most local stations and are used again later in the evening, usually in truncated form, on the local news programs. In fact, with the exception of the few unaffiliated stations, which obtain their news footage from UPI syndicated news and other independent suppliers, and the noncommercial stations, virtually all the pictures of national and world news seen on television are the product of the three network news organizations.

At each network, the process by which national news is gathered, edited and presented to the public is more or less similar. A limited number of subjects, usually no more than twenty or thirty, are selected each day as possible film stories by the news executives, producers and assignment editors on the basis of some form of advance information, and camera crews are dispatched to the scene to capture the event, or a re-enactment of it, on 16-mm. color film. The filming is supervised by either a field producer, a correspondent, or in some cases, the cameraman himself. The film is then either shipped directly back to one of the network's headquarters in New York, Chicago or Los Angeles, or if time is an important consideration, processed and edited at the nearest available facilities and transmitted to New York by cable. Through editing and rearranging of the filmed scenes, a small fraction of the exposed film, usually less than 5 percent, is reconstructed into a story which has a predetermined form. Reuven Frank, then executive producer of the NBC Evening News, instructed his staff in a memorandum initiating the half-hour network news program in 1963.

> Every news story should, without any sacrifice of probity or responsibility, display the attributes of fiction, of drama. It should have structure and conflict, problem and denouement, rising action and falling action, a beginning, a middle and an end. These are

not only the essentials of drama; they are the essentials of narrative.

A sound track, using either the "live sound" recorded at the event or "canned" (previously recorded background sounds) from the network's sound-effects library, is added to the edited story. "Its symbolic truth, its power of evocation is enhanced by the supposed reality which the sounds which surround it stimulate," Reuven Frank continues in the same memorandum. Finally a narration, written either by a correspondent or by a writer, synthesizes the piece, which is introduced and integrated into the news program by the anchorman or commentator.

Network news organizations select not only which events will be portrayed as national and world news on television but which parts of the filmed portions of those events, when recombined by editing, will stand for the whole mosaic. This necessarily involves choosing symbols which will have some more general meaning to a national audience. "The picture is not a fact but a symbol," Reuven Frank notes, ". . . the real child and its real crying become symbols of all children." In the same way, a particular black may be used to symbolize the aspirations of his race, a particular student may be used to symbolize the claims of his generation, and a particular policeman must be used to symbolize, synecdochically, the concept of authority. Whether the black chosen is a Black Panther or an integrationist, whether the student is a long-haired revolutionary or Young Republican, whether the policeman is engaged in a brutal or benevolent act obviously affects the picture of the event received by the audience. If over long periods of time the same type of symbols are consistently used to depict the behavior and aspirations of groups, certain stable images, or what Walter Lippmann called a "repertory of stereotypes," can be expected in television news. Moreover, to the extent that cameramen, film editors, correspondents and producers take their cues for selecting symbols for future stories from past stories, the stereotypes tend to be self-perpetuating. Such stable images, or stereotypes, can provide not only information but, as Lippmann pointed out, "pictures in our head" for interpreting and ordering all other information on the same subject. And although the precise relation between the pictures of society seen on television and public opinion on any given issue can probably never be established with certainty, it seems reasonable to assume that the images which are continually projected of national institutions, groups and leaders—the way, metaphorically speaking, in which a nation perceives itself as a nation—are of great concern to those interested in politics.

At one level, the concern is that the networks will use their potential power to select the national news seen on television to advance their own political interests. Nicholas Johnson, a member of the Federal Communications Commission and a self-professed liberal, expressed this fear on public television, saying:

> The networks, in particular . . . are probably now beyond the check of any institution in our society. The President, the Congress of the United States, the FCC, the foundations, and universities are reluctant even to get involved. I think they may now be so powerful that they're beyond the check of anyone.

The "concentration of power" charge, which echoes from virtually all sides of the political spectrum with some frequency, takes its force not from any actual evidence suggesting that the networks have in fact controlled news for their own purposes, but from a more generalized fear of the *potential* of a few organizations to control the flow of information to the public.

At another level, the concern is that network news may systematically use its presumed power to select pictures of society that favor certain political groups and values and denigrate others. This is the thrust of the criticism of network news made by Vice-President Spiro

T. Agnew, which runs as follows: "No medium has a more profound influence over public opinion" than television, over which the three networks have "a virtual monopoly," and thus "for millions of Americans the networks are the sole source of national and world news." Network news is determined, the argument continues, "by a handful of men responsible only to their corporate employers" who "wield a free hand in selecting, presenting and interpreting the great issues in our nation" with broad "powers of choice" over which news pictures to select and which to reject. This small group of executives, producers and correspondents can, by selecting the news, "create national issues overnight," "make or break by their coverage and commentary a moratorium on the war," "elevate men from obscurity to national prominence," "reward some politicians with national exposure and ignore others," and determine "how much of each side of a great issue" will be presented to the public. Furthermore, since this "small group of men" in network news tend to share certain similar views and working conditions that proceed in part from the business, and nature, of the medium, "a narrow and distorted picture of America often emerges from the televised news." The abridged view, Agnew argued, which tends to emphasize scenes depicting the more dramatic moments of violence, lawlessness and embittered dissent, "becomes in the minds of millions the entire picture," and one that can undermine "our national search for internal peace and stability." Network news, as the creator of this truncated picture of society, is directly and ineluctably connected to politics by this analysis.

Patrick J. Buchanan, the special assistant to President Nixon who was responsible for writing this speech for Vice-President Agnew, told me that "an awareness of the problem of selected news" grew out of months of "monitoring" evening news programs on the three networks. "The policies and values of this Administration were persistently misrepresented by the networks," Buchanan said, "and a President cannot govern with the consent of the people unless he can communicate his program to them." Since the networks are the main source of news about national affairs, he continued, "it cannot help but be of the greatest concern if they give a consistently biased view against the Administration." (Lyndon Johnson held a somewhat similar if less vociferously stated view: in one political speech in Delaware in 1966 he even suggested that only two or three men determine what the country sees on network television.)

In assuming, however, that a handful of men in each network news organization are "free" to pick and choose the news as they see fit, this analysis tends to neglect seriously a number of built-in constraints which over the course of time may severely limit and shape the discretion of individuals in gathering, selecting and presenting news. For example: before any programs can reach a national audience, affiliated stations must "clear" them. Since, by law, affiliates are not obligated to carry any network programs, network news cannot in its content and presentation deviate too far, or for too long a period, from the expectations and standards of the networks' affiliated stations. Further, the very fact that broadcasting is licensed and regulated by the federal government, which makes both the affiliated stations and the networks dependent for their continuing existence on some measure of government approval, must be taken into account by the networks in their overall policies on news coverage and presentation. And the economic realities of network television, reflected in budgets and schedules, restrict the choices of stories available to news personnel. Finally, established routines and procedures for gathering information and narrowing down the list of possible stories reduce the opportunities for politically selecting news stories or modes of presentation. In short, the outputs on network news are not simply the arbitrary choices of a few men; they result from a process.

But if indeed a relatively stable process structures and

preforms the decisions of individuals engaged in news operations, what is its precise relation to the pictures of society projected on television as news? To what degree and in what ways do organizational inputs—such as economic, political and affiliative considerations—influence the news outputs? Certainly such questions also are of political concern.

Television executives and correspondents rarely doubt that news pictures have a powerful effect on public opinion, and thus on politics. On the contrary, public opinion polls, commissioned by the Television Information Office, which show that television is now both the chief source of news and the most believed source of news for most of the population, are frequently cited by network executives as evidence of the efficacy of their medium. Television news was given credit for the "success of the civil rights movement," as one NBC producer put it, and "decisively changing America's opinion of the Vietnam war," as a CBS commentator explained, in interviews I conducted with network news personnel in 1969 and 1970. The director of CBS News in Washington, William Small, wrote about television news:

> When Television covered its "first war" in Vietnam, it showed a terrible truth of war in a manner new to mass audiences. A case can be made, and certainly should be examined, that this was cardinal to the disillusionment of Americans with this war, the cynicism of many young people towards America, and the destruction of Lyndon Johnson's tenure of office. . . . When Television examined a different kind of revolution, it was singularly effective in helping bring about the Black revolution.

And few in television would dispute the claim of Reuven Frank that "there are events which exist in the American mind and recollection primarily because they were reported on regular television news programs."

But even though proponents of television generally agree with their critics about the potent effect the medium has on public opinion, or what Walter Lippmann called "the pictures in our head," they deny with equal vigor that there is any need to examine the process by which these news pictures are selected and produced. In fact, as a former president of CBS News has pointed out, news executives would probably try to discourage any research into the decision-making process. For example, when Robert K. Baker of the National Commission on the Causes and Prevention of Violence requested the cooperation of the networks in analyzing the selection of film footage dealing with racial riots, Richard C. Wald, executive vice-president of NBC News, reported in a memorandum to Reuven Frank:

> [CBS News President Richard] Salant told me in his encounter with Mr. Baker he told Baker to go to hell. Salant said that he would refuse to answer any questions about news judgments and would only agree to rerun film or tape that had already been broadcast. I said my attitude on this question would be one of attempting to explain why we do what we do but that I would not give in to showing outtakes or discussing the exact role of any individual connected with riot coverage.

News executives hold that there is no need to analyze the way in which a news organization selects material and puts together a news program because, they argue, the process has little if any effect on the end product—news is news. David Brinkley, in commenting on the role of television in the last decade in an NBC news special entitled "From Here to the Seventies," reiterated this commonly accepted notion:

> What television did in the sixties was to show the American people to the American people. . . . It did show the people places and things they had not seen before. Some they liked and some they didn't. *It was not that television produced or created any of it* [emphasis added].

And although it may be necessary to maintain the notion in the popular imagination that television does no more than "show" news events, news executives and correspondents cannot be entirely unaware of the leeway that actually exists in the production of news pictures. Consider, for example, the news story with which Brinkley concluded the NBC Evening News on the same night he suggested to the public that news was not "produced or created." Brinkley reported:

> A vastly popular song through most of the summer and fall is called, "Ruby, Don't Take Your Love to Town." It's been high on the best-seller list, sung by Kenny Rogers and the First Edition. *But it is more than a pop song; it is a social documentary, a comment on our times, and on the war* [emphasis added]. It is the lament of a Vietnam veteran, returned home gravely wounded, confined to his bed, lying there listening as his wife goes out at night, leaving him because the war has left him unable to move. Well, what the song says, and its wide popularity in this country, may tell more about the ordinary American's view of the Vietnam war than all the Gallup polls combined, and here is the song, set to film.

A three-minute film followed, supposedly illustrating the song, and showing what purported to be the room of the crippled veteran, complete with mementos, trophies, photographs and his wife "Ruby's" belongings. Interspersed with scenes of the room were scenes of the Vietnam war—flamethrowers, helicopters, tanks, casualties —and of Presidents Johnson and Nixon, all combined into a single montage. The veteran's wife can be heard leaving, the door slams, and the film ends with a funeral.

The song, although identified as a "social documentary" on the Vietnam war, was actually based on a World War II incident—a fact which the executive producer of the Huntley-Brinkley program himself subsequently apprised me of. Nor was it on the best-seller songs at the time of the broadcast. The re-creation of the popular song was, in fact, entirely fictive. The "veteran's room" was a set in Los Angeles, rented for the occasion. All the décor and war souvenirs were props which were selected, the field producer explained to me, "to create an atmosphere of futility and absurdity." The few seconds of battle scenes, intercut into the story "to show what the veteran was thinking as his wife left him," were carefully culled from ten years of stock footage in NBC and other film libraries, according to the producer. The editing suggested a definite connection between the Vietnam war and the crippled veteran. And, of course, the song itself was fictitious.

To be sure, such a news story may in its total effect imitate reality and accurately capture "the ordinary American's view of the Vietnam war," as Brinkley claimed, but it also requires a number of decisions on the part of the producer and commentator. First, a song had to be selected from literally hundreds of popular ballads which could then be identified as "a comment on our times." If, for example, "The Ballad of the Green Berets," which had been *first* for a considerable period of time on the hit parade, had been selected instead of "Ruby, Don't Take Your Love to Town," the comment might have been quite different. Second, once selected, the song could have been used to "illustrate the news," as Brinkley put it, in a number of very different ways. For example, it could have been used to suggest the continuity of popular ballads from World War II (which it actually was about) to Vietnam, instead of as an index of public opinion on the latter war. Third, it had to be decided what type of film would be used in the montage to illustrate the veteran's inner thoughts. Scenes depicting enemy atrocities would have fit the lyrics just as easily as the scenes used depicting American napalm attacks, since the song was fictitious. Finally, there was a good deal of leeway in selecting the props and décor which suggested the "mood," as the producer explained, "of the piece."

How are such decisions reached? Those involved in
network news commonly argue that the pictures of society shown on television as national news are not the
product of decisions within an organization but fixed by
some external reality. The reasons given in support of this
view, not only by news executives but also by other intelligent people both inside and outside of television, are
worth considering in some detail.

The Mirror Metaphor

One argument for believing that television news needs
no explanation is that events, not news organizations, determine the content of television news. Television news,
in this view, does no more than mirror reality. Leonard
H. Goldenson, president of the ABC television network,
thus testified before the National Commission on the
Causes and Prevention of Violence that complaints of
news distortion were due entirely to the fact that "Americans are reluctant to accept the images reflected by the
mirror we have held up to our society." Robert D. Kas-
mire, a vice-president of NBC, also told the commission,
"There is no doubt that television is, to a large degree,
a mirror of society. It is also a mirror of public attitudes
and preferences." Reuven Frank further advanced this
notion in an article entitled "The Ugly Mirror," asserting
that "individuals working in television organizations do
not make the decisive difference; the fact that television is
there makes the difference." The "mirror," Frank concluded, is being blamed for the ugly events it reflects:
"Television has become the object of what psychoanalysts
call transference." The president of NBC, Julian Goodman, putting it in more fashionable terms, told the commission, "In short, the medium is being blamed for the
message." The president of CBS, Frank Stanton, testify-
ing before a House committee, explained, "What the
media do is to hold a mirror up to society and try to report

it as faithfully as possible." Elmer W. Lower, president of ABC News, describes television as "the television mirror that reflects . . . across oceans and mountains," and suggests, "let us open the doors of parliament everywhere to the electronic mirrors." Slightly more humble about the metaphor, Harry Reasoner closed the CBS Sunday News by saying, "That's the news as we imperfectly mirror it." The imagery has even been picked up by critics of television, such as Jack Gould of the *New York Times*, who said, concerning television's coverage of racial riots, "Congress, one would hope, would not conduct an examination of a mirror because of the disquieting images it beholds."

The mirror metaphor has considerable power. If television news is assumed to be analogous to a mirror, in reflecting willy-nilly all that appears before it, questions concerning the selection and production of news become palpably irrelevant. The mirror analogy may also influence the way those in television news think about it by, as Professor Myron Abrams suggested in his discussion of poetics, tending to "focus interest on the subject matter of a work and its models in reality, to the comparative neglect of the shaping influence of artistic conventions." For example, Sig Mickelson, a former president of CBS News, recently wrote a book entitled *The Electric Mirror* which, though it sets out to examine network news, devotes little, if any, space to the processes by which news is gathered, edited and reported, and focuses instead on the major events that television reported. Conceiving of television news in mimetic terms necessarily requires a certain blindness toward the role of the organization and organizational routines in the shaping of news reports and pictures; a blindness which, from the point of view of the organization, may even be functional. But it also leads to a number of serious misconceptions about the medium.

The mirror analogy also suggests immediacy: happenings are reflected instantaneously, as they occur, as in a mirror. The image of immediate reporting is constantly reinforced by the way in which those in television news depict the process to the public. "Our directors of an actuality broadcast, like newspaper photo editors, have several pictures displayed on the monitors before them," Walter Cronkite explained in a lecture. "But they, unlike their print counterparts, do not have ten minutes, or five, or even one minute to select the picture their audience will see. Their decision is made in seconds. Theirs is a totally new craft in journalism." Given the immediacy of television, news executives can then argue that the network organization has little opportunity to intervene in news decisions, since, as Reuven Frank put it on a television program about television, "news coverage generally happens too fast for anything like that to take place." But does it? While it is true that certain events, such as space shots and political conventions, are broadcast live, virtually all of the regular news casts, with the exception of the commentator's "lead-ins" and "lead-outs" from the news stories, are prerecorded on film, which must be transported, processed, edited and projected, or on video tape, before it can be seen. In most cases, "immediacy" is thus illusory. A four-month analysis of the logs of the NBC Evening News showed that only 47 percent of the news film depicted events on the day they occurred, while 36 percent of the news film was more than two days old, and 12 percent was more than a week old. None of the news stories during that period were live, and on some days as much as 70 percent of the filmed news was more than a day old. A similar proportion of news film on the CBS and ABC Evening News was also delayed; only 50 percent on CBS and 46 percent on ABC depicted events on the day they occurred.

The notion of a "mirror of society" implies that whatever happens of significance will be reflected on television news. Network news, however, far from being omniscient, is a very limited news-gathering operation which depends on a handful of camera crews based in a few major cities for most of its filmed news. At NBC, for instance, which advertises itself as the largest news organization in the world, with "news bureaus that now ring the world," 90 percent or more of the national news shown on its evening news report actually was produced by ten film crews based in five cities in the five-month period which was examined. The other two major networks similarly rely on a limited number of film crews for the bulk of their domestic news. The idea, advanced by some network executives, that network news is the product of news coverage by hundreds of local stations, or affiliates, fails to square with the fact that only a minute fraction of network news (less than 3 percent at NBC and 5 percent at CBS and ABC) is furnished by affiliated stations. The great preponderance of network news is assigned in advance to network news crews and correspondents, and whether or not an event is covered depends, in many cases, on where it occurs and the availability of network crews. Reuven Frank, for example, explained that although "in terms of injuries and lives lost, the Miami incidents [at the 1968 Republican convention] were more serious than the Chicago incidents [at the 1968 Democratic convention]," NBC News did not cover these disturbances at Miami because "the Miami demonstrations took place far from the widely known locations of our cameras and we had no reason associated with covering convention activities for putting cameras there." What is reflected on television as national news depends, unlike a "mirror," on certain predecisions about where camera crews and correspondents will be assigned.

The mirror analogy further tends to neglect the component of "will," or decisions made in advance to cover or not to cover certain types of events. A mirror makes no decisions, it simply reflects what occurs in front of it; television coverage can, however, be controlled by predecisions or "policy." For example, during the Democratic convention in Chicago in 1968, the counsel for NBC advised the FCC that "special directives" were issued to

NBC news personnel that "no demonstrations were to be telecast live, no mobile units were to be dispatched until an event actually occurred, and demonstrations or violent confrontations were not to be telecast until properly evaluated." Explaining why few of the early demonstrations or "provocations" in Chicago were broadcast, Reuven Frank wrote: "Up until the serious violence, it was our *conscious policy* [emphasis added] to avoid covering too much of the activities of the demonstrators lest we fall into the trap of doing their advertising for them." CBS had a similar policy during the convention. Richard Salant told the National Commission on the Causes and Prevention of Violence: "We do have a policy about live coverage of disorders and potential disorders. . . . The policy is that we will not provide such coverage except in extraordinary circumstances."

Policy can determine not only whether or not a subject is seen on television but also how it is depicted. On becoming executive producer of the ABC Evening News in March 1969, Av Westin wrote to correspondents: "I have asked our Vietnam staff to alter the focus of their coverage from combat pieces to interpretive ones, pegged to the eventual pull-out of the American forces. This point should be stressed for all hands." Then in a Telex to ABC News' Saigon bureau Westin informed news personnel, and the free-lance cameramen who provide the networks with a good deal of their Vietnam footage, of what specific stories he expected the altered "focus" to produce:

> I think the time has come to shift some of our focus from the battlefield, or more specifically American military involvement with the enemy, to themes and stories under the general heading: We Are On Our Way Out of Vietnam. . . . To be more specific, a series of story ideas suggest themselves.

The prescribed list of stories included such topics as black-marketeering ("Find us that Oriental Sidney

Greenstreet, the export-import entrepreneur," the Telex suggested) ; a replaced province chief ("Is the new man doing any better than his corrupt and inefficient predecessor?") ; political opposition ("Could you single out the most representative opposition leader . . . and do a story centered about him. Preferably we would like to know about the most active opposition leader") ; medical care for civilians ("Does the granddaughter sleep under the old man's hospital bed, scrounge food for him, etc.") ; and the treatment of ex-Vietcong. Quite predictably, a radical change from combat stories to "We Are On Our Way Out"-type stories followed in ABC's coverage of the Vietnam war.

A somewhat similar decision was reached at the NBC Evening News in November 1968. After President Johnson announced a complete halt of the bombing of North Vietnam, the executive producer told the news staff that the "story" was now the negotiations, not the fighting, and although combat footage was sent to New York from Saigon virtually every day for two months following the decison, the producers of the evening news program elected to use combat film on the program only three times. The preceding year, when there were almost the same American combat deaths in the same period, combat film was shown three to four times a week. The "focus" in the content of the news coverage was thus changed, not by the amount of combat footage available (which remained about the same), but by the producer's perception of what *type* of story was called for.

Even if network news operates more like a searchlight, which seeks out and highlights subjects in preselected areas, than a mirror, it still might be supposed that it is akin to a "mirror" in the sense that it accurately reflects what it is directed at. But this more limited formulation of the mirror analogy also has problems. "Film is not reality but illusion, at best an imitation of reality," Reuven Frank perceptively wrote. This is achieved basically through film editing, a process in which a minute fraction of the exposed film taken of an event—usually less than 5 percent in network news—is selected, and then rearranged, to stand for the whole event. The edited film must also be combined with sound, which can either be "natural" sound recorded at the event itself or "canned" sound from the network's effects library, and a narration. Depending on what fragments are selected, and how they are ordered, any number of different stories can usually be edited from the same material. And the film itself may not always suggest a proper storyline.

Consider, for example, the problem of editing some film that NBC News purchased "blind" for $500 from a free-lance cameraman in Germany which purportedly showed sharp Czechoslovakian resistance to the Soviet invasion of that country in August 1968. Although the film was more than a month old, the producer of the NBC Evening News decided to buy it, he explained to me at the time, because "it is supposed to show something new—Czechs fighting Russians." But when the film arrived in New York the next day and was screened, it showed, as far as anyone could see, only a half-hour long procession of Soviet military trucks through the Czech town of Košice, and a few separate, and possibly unrelated, shots of crowds milling about. No sound accompanied the film, and all the NBC editors and producers had to go by in reconstructing the event was the free-lance cameraman's notes, which claimed that the Soviet trucks had been pelted with rocks by the Czech crowd and that the Soviet troops had fired in retaliation. According to the notes, smashed windows on the Soviet trucks indicated the extent of the resistance, but the editors could find only a few seconds of shots depicting broken windows in the half-hour of footage, and most of the trucks seemed to be intact. The producer supervising the editing of the story insisted, however, on "illustrating" the cameraman's claims, and the few shots of broken windows were thus selected and spliced together with shots of the "surging" crowd.

The story, broadcast in October 1968, when a convenient speech by Secretary of State Dean Rusk provided a "news peg" about Czechoslovakia, was introduced by Chet Huntley as follows:

What Rusk said about Czechoslovakia is under-scored by film we have obtained showing what hap-pened when Russian troops entered the city of Košice. . . . It was made by a Czechoslovakian television cameraman and then smuggled into Germany. The film makes it clear that the Russian invasion was grimmer and resulted in far more violence than was shown in earlier film reaching the West.

As Soviet tanks and trucks rolled through the streets of Košice, large numbers of Czechoslovakians began throwing rocks, and whatever else they could find, at them.

The narration, which Huntley then read over the 2 min-utes and 25 seconds of edited film, had been compiled by a news writer partly from various back issues of *Newsweek* and the *New York Times*, although neither contained specific information about the putative Košice incident, and mainly from the cameraman's sketchy notes. It continued, as the shots of trucks with broken windows were shown:

The Czechoslovakians' rocks could not stop the Russian tanks, but they did smash the windows of many Soviet trucks. The Russians were bewildered by the first show of resistance by the civilians. The invaders had been told they were liberating Czecho-slovakia from counterrevolutionaries. They did not use force immediately.

Then, some of the edited shots showing people milling about:

The faces in Košice resembled those in Paris when the Germans occupied the city in 1940. Incidents like these were reportedly common through Czechoslovakia, but few were recorded on film. The resistance in Košice continued on August 22nd, the day after the invasion.

In the city's main square, hundreds of peoples shouted insults at the invaders. Many hurled rocks and stones . . . and some broke up paving blocks to use against the invaders.

Not all of this was shown on the film; some of the more violent details were only described in the narration.

Whether or not this narrative and edited film reflected what actually happened in Košice depends primarily on the veracity of the cameraman's notes, and the accuracy with which the producer, editors and news writer followed them in editing the film, not on the "objectivity" of the film itself. If the cameraman, who was unknown to NBC News, had exaggerated his description of the violence that had occurred in Košice to enhance his chances of selling the film to NBC, the edited film would simply "mirror" this hyperbole, not reality. The half-hour of film itself, the editor who worked on it pointed out to me at the time, would lend itself to any number of stories, including one that showed the peaceful and unresisted transit of a Soviet motor convoy through the town of Košice.

Further, proverbial wisdom not withstanding, pictures do lie in the sense that they depict spurious realities. For example, the news director of CBS News in Washington noted: "One of the most impressive CBS News efforts came in 1968 with 'Hunger in America,' . . . the hour opened with film of a baby actually dying as the camera took its picture. The broadcast had tremendous impact." Over this scene, which depicted an extremely thin and malformed baby dying while being given resuscitation in a hospital, the narrator, Charles Kuralt, said: "Hunger is easy to recognize when it looks like this. The baby is dying of starvation. He was an American. Now he is dead." Millions of viewers naturally assumed that the baby died of starvation, or malnutrition. However, this was not the case. A government investigation subsequently disclosed that the dying baby, whom CBS photographed to illustrate the effects of "starvation," actually was a three-month premature child, weighing less than three pounds at birth, whose parents were neither poor nor starving. The mother, a schoolteacher, had the premature birth after an automobile accident. Thus there was no medical reason to suspect that malnutrition or starvation was in any way connected with the death of the child. In response to criticism on this point, Richard Salant said in a televised interview three years later: "In that area, at that time, and in that hospital, babies were dying of malnutrition." In other words, even though the pictures, with their "tremendous impact," turned out to be of something quite different than they purported to be, the underlying message of the program still might be true.

But this presents a dilemma: Is a network news organization justified in using, for another example, footage of a South Vietnamese base in South Vietnam as evidence of a permanent South Vietnamese base in Cambodia—as was admittedly done on the CBS Evening News on June 18, 1970—by the fact that there is reliable information that South Vietnamese bases actually existed at the time in Cambodia? In such cases it must be recognized that the validity of the story depends not on the photographs used to illustrate it—since they may turn out to be fictional—but on the reliability of the information on which it is predicated.

It still could be maintained that television news "mirrors" events metaphorically in an edited and encapsulated form when there exists sufficient information about the event and its context to reconstruct it on film. In other words, the mirror analogy is predicated not merely on "the fact of television" or the ability of the camera "to capture reality," but on the intelligence-gathering resources of network news, of which film is only one source of information. Even if, however, there is sufficient information available about an event, the filmed story still might reflect policy and predecisions more than the happening itself.

That the editing process involves something more than merely raw intelligence is illustrated by the way the NBC Evening News depicted Harlem after the assassination of Martin Luther King, Jr., on April 4, 1968. Four days after the assassination, the NBC Evening News carried a filmed report about the "relative calm" in the ghettos in New York City. Huntley introduced the story by saying: "Los Angeles and New York City, scenes of two of the first big-city racial riots, were relatively quiet over the weekend. Though there were disturbances Thursday night in Harlem, Mayor John Lindsay stepped in quickly, and his intervention has been credited with helping prevent further trouble." The film story that followed, which was edited from four days of footage taken in a half-dozen parts of the city, showed Lindsay walking through the streets, shaking hands with militants as he passed friendly crowds, conferring with community leaders and addressing a memorial service. The narration over the film concluded: "The single most important factor in keeping New York peaceful appears to have been John Lindsay."

NBC presented this picture of "relative quiet," despite the fact that it had a good deal of information from the AP and UPI wire services, the New York police teletype, newspaper accounts and news film which indicated that the "disturbances" that began on April 4 and continued through April 8 were anything but peaceful. In fact, according to the *New York Times*, these "disturbances" were on a scale which rivaled, if not surpassed, the 1964 "first big-city racial riots" (as Huntley had identified them). In the 1968 "disturbances," between April 4 and 9, the police reported "534 incidents of burglary, arson and disorderly conduct . . . directly attributed to the disorders following the assassination of Dr. King," compared to 600 similar incidents in the 1964 New York City riots (in a six-day period). In the April 1968 riots in New York City, 491 persons were arrested, compared to 465 arrested in the 1964 riots. Property damage, estimated at $5 million in the 1964 riot, was three times higher in 1968, according to the American Insurance Association.

Moreover, most of these "disturbances" occurred *after* "Lindsay stepped in quickly" on April 4. Despite the fact that the film story shows the mayor "helping prevent trouble" by walking through the ghetto, actually the mayor's tour sparked part of the trouble when one of his bodyguards became involved in a fracas with the black militant leader of "Allah's Five Percenters." The *New York Times* reported: "Mayor Lindsay, who went to Harlem to quiet the outbreaks, was caught in the midst of an unruly crowd and had to be hustled into a limousine by bodyguards." The picture rendered by the NBC Evening News did not show these moments of drama and thus presented a very different impression.

Apparently the coverage of this news story was shaped by a more general policy. An NBC memorandum on riot coverage explains that "Robert Northshield, executive producer of the Huntley-Brinkley Report, told us that he made an effort to use the minimum amount of riot footage following the assassination of King." The correspondent who narrated the story subsequently told me that he was aware of the "rioting" and "tense situation" in the "black community," but the producer had decided *before* he edited the story that it should emphasize the restoration of peace rather than continued violence (and he agreed). The producer later said that it was his responsibility to "evaluate all the information, including the social context" of a news happening and then "decide how it should be presented." In evaluating such a story, it must be decided whether the violence is "isolated incidents" or a "general trend," the producer continued. This requires a prognosis of the probable future consequences of a happening, and some idea of what is—and what is not—part of the general train of events. Unlike a mirror, which is automatic, both an informational and a value premise shape the image in television news. To describe network news as mirroring events thus necessarily involves seriously neglecting the importance of the chain of decisions made both before and after the fact by executives and newsmen, or, in a word, the organizational processes.

The Professional Analogy

Even when it is recognized that network news does not in fact automatically mirror events but is the product of a decision-making process, network executives still deny that the news pictures are the product of the organization on the grounds that the individual newsmen involved in the process are all autonomous "professionals." And as professionals, it is argued, they make their decisions about news stories independent of the needs, expectations and hierarchy of the organization for which they work. In this way they are analogous to doctors and scientists, who take their values from the standards and code of their profession, and not from any organization which employs them. This analogy also has considerable force. If newsmen, as autonomous professionals, were indeed independent of the organization which employs them—and could select and edit news according to a set of professional norms—then an examination of the decision-making process, if not entirely irrelevant, would be no more than an exercise in clarifying professional norms. And since, as Talcott Parsons has observed, "only members of the profession are treated as qualified to interpret the traditions of the profession authoritatively," even that sort of an analysis would always be held to be inconclusive.

But are newsmen in network news operations actually in a situation analogous to that of doctors and scientists in which they can act independently of the organization for which they work? Doctors and scientists are given a good deal of latitude, if not complete autonomy, in decisions concerning their subject of competence by their administrators because it is presumed that they have a virtual monopoly of knowledge in their special fields. Such a monopoly is creditable because members of the profession are assumed to have undergone an intensive and closely supervised program of formal education in their special fields, passed examinations and been certified as competent in their technical knowledge and qualifications by their professional associations. When granted, by superiors, this presumed monopoly of knowledge is tantamount to decisional autonomy, since no outsider is, by definition, assumed to have the technical competence to judge the professional. An administrator in a laboratory, for example, could not legitimately question the decisions of a microbiologist in the conduct of his experiment if he assumed that only a microbiologist had the necessary technical competence to judge the work.

Television journalists, however, have no claim to such a monopoly of knowledge in this work. Formal education, examinations and certification are not prerequisites to working in television news. In fact, few have these qualifications. Most newsmen work their way up the organizational ladder, starting as pages, copywriters, announcers and local correspondents. The suggestion, advanced by Dr. W. Walker Menninger, a member of the National Commission on the Causes and Prevention of Violence, that television newsmen should be licensed, as are doctors, by an outside authority was ridiculed by network executives. In discussing Dr. Menninger's suggestion at a colloquium at Yale, Reuven Frank argued that "here he draws false reasons for licensing. The comparison between the journalist, who never acts alone, and the doctor or lawyer, who always does, cannot hold up." Television journalists are "professionals" in a very different sense than are doctors or scientists. Indeed, Frank defines the "key to professional journalism" as the newsman remaining an "outsider": "News is change as seen by an outsider (the correspondent) on behalf of other outsiders (the audience)." Rather than being an expert in any one area, or an "insider," newsmen are expected to be "generalists" (though there are exceptions to this rule, such as space exploration and science). The networks thus make it a practice to rotate correspondents from story to story and from area to area, on the assumption that an "outsider" will perceive and report the story in terms that will be more comprehensible to a lay audience than an "insider." However, the lack of any exclusive "insider's" knowledge about subjects also tends to lessen the reporter's claim to decisional autonomy. If the producer or supervising executive can be assumed to know as much about the subject as the reporter, his judgment on how the story is to be edited and presented cannot be easily disregarded. It is not, in fact, uncommon for stories to be reshot, re-edited and rewritten at the behest of a producer or executive. During the 1968 teachers strike in New York City, for example, the NBC correspondent covering the story for the Evening News developed a story which defined the issue of the strike as the rejection of the policy of integration by black educators, who, he argued, wanted to control the schools in their own communities. Up to then, the strike had been defined as a struggle for better education, not political power. Before editing the story, the correspondent discussed the point with the producer, who decided this was "not the way to play the story," and it had to be substantially revised to adhere to the producer's decision that the strike was, after all, merely an attempt to obtain "more responsive schools." Although it is a moot point whose interpretation of the strike was correct, the correspondent, since he could not legitimately claim any special expertise in the matter, had to yield to the producer.

Intervention by the producer or assistant producers in decisions on how to play the news is the rule rather than the exception. In describing a typical day in the life of the NBC Evening News, *Newsweek* caught very clearly the relation between producer and correspondent:

> [The executive producer, Wallace W. Westfeldt] receives a call from Washington informing him that the Department of Health, Education and Welfare is about to modify its ban on cyclamates. Westfeld decides to include this in the show, and there follows in Washington a spirited discussion between correspondent Ron Nessen and deputy producer Roy Farkas as to how the story should be worded. Nessen argues that HEW's initial ban did not deny cyclamates to those who needed them medically, so in effect there has been no reversal in HEW policy. Farkas, caught between Nessen and New York, says at one point that the decision has indeed been "reversed." "That's just plain wrong," complains Nessen. Four minutes from air time, Farkas decides to go with the wording "the order is about to be changed"—and that's the way the script read. . . . There is another lively last-minute exchange between New York and Washington over the story on Judge Clemont F. Haynsworth. . . . Westfeldt puzzles the problem briefly [of footage of the Senate debate over Haynsworth's nomination to the Supreme Court failing to show support for Haynsworth] and decides to compensate by ordering the correspondent to get additional pro-Haynsworth quotes into his "voice-over" report.

Walter Cronkite drew a dramatic picture of a correspondent when he said: "When our television reporter, in the midst of the riot or the floor demonstration or the disaster dictates his story, he is not talking to a rewrite man, but directly to the audience. There is no editor standing between him and the viewer." But such moments are the exception, not the rule. Virtually all of the filmed stories on regular network news programs are essentially, as Reuven Frank described it to the National Commission on the Causes and Prevention of Violence, "a group effort." News executives decide on the deployment of correspondents and camera crews; assignment editors select what stories will be covered by whom; field producers, in constant phone contact with the producers in New York, usually supervise the preparation and filming of stories (in fact, it is not uncommon for correspondents to join a story after a substantial part of it has been filmed); editors, under the supervision of either a producer or a correspondent, reconstruct the story on film; the narration, which may be roughed out by a field producer, is usually written in its final form by the correspondent; writers then prepare the lead-in, which introduces the story on the program; and the executive producer makes the final decision of whether the story will be used on the program, re-edited or reshot, or disregarded entirely. Whatever discretion newsmen have in this group effort is mitigated by the fact that it must meet the expectation and policies of the producers if it is to get on the air. Over any sustained period of time, news personnel cannot therefore be independent of the wishes of producers who in turn are responsible to network executives for fulfilling the needs and expectations of the organization.

The analogy becomes even more strained if it is argued that even though newsmen have no distinct sphere of control over their material in the process, news decisions are still made on the basis of "professional" values—that is, standards that lie outside the organization—rather than according to the dictates of the organization. This presumes that all the members of news organizations, whether they be executives or correspondents, share certain outlooks on what constitutes news stories, and will act according to these concepts even when their actions conflict with the interests of the organization that employs them. The problem with this formulation of "professionalism" is that in fact there are sharp differences in the responsibilities of the various members of news organizations. Executives are responsible for seeing that the programs and outputs of the news divisions meet the specified budgets and expectations of the network; producers are responsible for seeing that their individual programs conform to budget, quality and policy guidelines; correspondents and other newsmen are only responsible for their own participation in the individual stories they work on. These different sets of responsibilities necessarily create some tensions between some of the more basic news values of correspondents and organizational values of executives.

The correspondents I interviewed almost all defined "news" in terms of time. "News is what is new in the world since our last broadcast" or "News is what has happened today" or "News is change" are typical of the definitions given by newsmen. When pressed, virtually all the correspondents related "news" either to the time element or change in a situation; what distinguished "news" from other forms of knowledge, such as history, was its "immediacy." It will be recalled, however, that a good deal of the film stories on network news are delayed from one day to two weeks. This arises out of certain organizational needs and policies. Reuven Frank more or less outlined these policies on "prepared" or delayed news in the memorandum he wrote when he was executive producer of the NBC Evening News: "Except for those rare days when other material becomes available, the gap will be filled by planned or prepared stories, and we are assuming the availability of two each night." These "longer pieces" were to be, he continued, "planned, executed over a longer period of time than spot news, usable and relevant any time within, say, two weeks rather than that day, receptive to the more sophisticated techniques of editing but journalism withal." Two of the four segments of filmed news, or about 50 percent of the available time, were allocated to these "little documentaries," as Frank called them. The ratio of "spot" news to delayed news suggested in the 1963 memorandum conforms, interestingly enough, to the proportions found in NBC News programs in 1968–1969, in which 47 percent was "spot," or daily, news and the balance delayed. The reason for delaying film stories, an NBC vice-president explained, "is because it gives the producer more control over his program." First, it allows the producer to control the budget, since shipping the film by plane, though it might delay the film by a day or two, is considerably less expensive than transmitting the film electronically by satellite or ground cables. Second, and perhaps more important, it gives the producer control over the content of the individual stories, since it affords an opportunity for screening the film in advance, and if necessary, re-editing it. Eliminating the delay, the same vice-president suggested, could have the "terrible" effect of reducing network news to being merely "a chronicler of events," forcing it "out of the business of making meaningful comment." Finally, it provides a "reserve" of stories which can be used to give the program "variety" and "pacing." The large percentage of delayed reporting on the other networks is at least partly explained by these organizational requisites. The high value newsmen put on immediacy is thus, to some degree, undercut by the organizational need to shoot and narrate filmed stories that can be used, as Frank suggests, up to "two weeks" later.

A second basic value that the newsmen I interviewed generally held was that of "news" as constituted by the unexpected or extraordinary event, the man-bites-dog phenomena. Network news, however, is forced by the cumbersome business of setting up cameras and shuttling camera crews between stories to seek out the *expected* event—that is, one announced sufficiently in advance for a film crew and equipment to be dispatched to the scene. For example, at NBC there was at least one day's advance warning from the "news makers" on 90 percent of the stories used on the evening news. Wholly unpredictable events, such as natural disasters, accidents and crimes accounted for less than 2 percent of the filmed stories. Assignment editors, producers and executives focus their search for news on the stories than can be depended on to materialize as "news stories" because, as one NBC assignment editor explained, "we regularly only have nine or ten crews a day assigned to domestic news, and we need a minimum of nine or ten stories to feed the news shows." This leads to the coverage of "routinized events," as the assignment editor put it, such as press conference, Senate hearings, and speeches by important news makers, which are usually conveniently located and "wired for television," and a functional neglect of events with less advance warning or of those less likely to prove sure-fire news stories. (Unexpected news, such as plane crashes, is usually covered by affiliates or local stations, but producers prefer not to use these "outside" stories on their programs if—as usually is the case—the technical quality of the piece is below network standards.) To cover the more uncertain news happenings would require additional film crews and correspondents, above the minimum necessary to produce the requisite diet of filmed stories, and would thus involve an additional cost to the organization.

In filming delayed or "prepared" stories, newsmen are expected to eliminate the elements of the unexpected so as not to destroy the illusion of immediacy. This becomes especially important when it is likely that the aberrations, or unusual developments, will be reported in other media and thus date the story. A case in point is the NBC News story about the commencement of a high-speed train service between Montreal and Toronto. While the NBC crew was filming the turbo-train on December 12, 1968, on its inaugural run to Toronto, the train unexpectedly collided with and "sliced in half" a meat trailer-truck and then suffered a complete mechanical breakdown on the return trip. Persistent "performance flaws" and subsequent breakdowns eventually led to a temporary suspension in the service.

These accidents and aberrations were not included in the film story broadcast two weeks later on the NBC Evening News. David Brinkley, keeping to the original pre-event story, introduced the film by saying: "The only high-speed train now running in North America has just begun in Canada." Four minutes of shots of the streamlined train and "ultramodern" interior followed, with the narration suggesting that this portended the future in transportation and that Canada's "new turbo might just shake American lethargy" in developing such trains. (The announcement of the suspension of the service, less than a week later, was not carried on the program.)

This practice takes on a more serious aspect in the coverage of the war in Vietnam, where most of the film stories are delayed from three days to a week. Although it is possible to transmit war films electronically by using the satellite relay in a day to the United States, the costs are considerable—a five-minute transmission costs more than $5,000, as opposed to $20 or $30 for shipping the same film by plane. So, with the exception of momentous battles, such as the Tet offensive in 1968, almost every network film is sent by plane, even though this means that it will be a few days old by the time it is broadcast. The footage is also usually shipped to New York for editing, an NBC producer pointed out, "so that the film can be more carefully evaluated before it is put on the air." To avoid the possibility of having the delayed footage dated by newspaper accounts, network correspondents are instructed to report on the routine and continuous aspects of the war, rather than on the sort of unexpected developments that might be quickly dated, according to a former NBC Saigon bureau manager. A young NBC correspondent, temporarily stationed at NBC News in New York to orient him "to the news operation" before being assigned to Vietnam, was told by producers to concentrate on "timeless pieces" such as "helicopter patrols, prisoner interviews, and artillery barrages," and to "be careful" about filming events that "might date themselves." Thus, correspondents are under some pressure to focus their reportage on the elements of stories which best fit the needs of the organization, even if it conflicts with their own news values.

A third value that newsmen stressed is originality in

reporting: that is, discovering and disclosing stories before competitors do. In their interviews, correspondents
frequently identified "scoops," "investigative reporting,"
"original reporting" and "exposés" as "the highest forms
of television journalism." Network news organizations
are not, however, set up for this form of reporting. A
limited number of film crews are assigned, basically, on
information received from newspapers, wire services and
"calendars" of news events which are circulated by the
wire services—all of which is nonexclusive or already
published information. Moreover, few crews are available to do "investigative" or original research on a possible story. Furthermore, as one NBC producer explained,
"Investigative reporting involves research, and we don't
have the researchers or time to dig, except on the most
important stories." At CBS, a producer pointed out that
the "general policy" is for "longer investigative reports"
to be done as part of news documentaries or the *60
Minutes* news magazine format, not on the regular news
program. And, in fact, there are not a great number of
exclusive disclosures in film stories on network television.
For example, of the more than seven hundred film stories
on the NBC Evening News between September 1968 and
January 1969, only three stories which were exclusively
reported on that program were subsequently reported
by the *New York Times*.

When producers of network news programs do undertake original reporting, or stories on which there is no
prior published story to cite as "a documented source,"
the costs that arise in terms of "headaches and justifica-
tions," as one executive producer put it, often outweigh
the advantages. Consider the case of the Israeli atomic
bomb, one of the few exclusive stories reported on the
NBC Evening News during my field study of that program. In January 1969, correspondent James Robinson
was told by an embassy aide in Washington that Israel
had already built a deliverable atomic bomb. This intelligence was, in turn, passed on through the Washington

producer to the executive producer of the Evening News, Robert J. Northshield. Northshield attempted to check out the report by consulting Amos Perlmutter, an Israeli political scientist doing research at the Center for International Affairs at Harvard, whom he had recently met at a cocktail party. Perlmutter subsequently informed me that he told Northshield that Israel "had the capacity but had not actually built the bomb, for political reasons," and also mentioned in the course of the phone conversation that Israel was building a factory to *service* the French-built Mirage fighter planes it had in its air force. Northshield, however, assumed at the time that the factory would be used to build fighters that could deliver the atomic bomb, and directed NBC's correspondent in Israel, Alvin Rosenfeldt, to do a film story on the putative Mirage factory. Meanwhile Robinson, looking into the story by himself, since NBC had virtually no researchers in Washington at the time, found some "confirming evidence" in the 1968 edition of *Jane's All the World's Aircraft,* a privately published assessment of military developments, which asserted that Israel could have nuclear warheads by 1970. At that point Northshield decided to report the story that night as an "NBC Exclusive."

The NBC Evening News thus began on January 8, 1969, with Chet Huntley announcing dramatically that "NBC News has learned that Israel either has built a nuclear bomb or will have one very soon. And within three years, Israel is expected to have an effective system of delivering the bombs." In the story that followed, Robinson said, "Intelligence sources here, all well placed and responsible, said that Israel embarked on a crash program to produce the bombs," which the source said would be ready for use "much sooner" than 1970. He then went on to report that Israel was now also manufacturing its own Mirage fighters to provide the means to deliver the warheads. In a follow-up film story, the "Mirage factory" turned out to be nothing more than a factory for manufacturing small, non-jet, commercial aircraft. Nevertheless, the "atom bomb" story was continued for three nights on the program. Despite denials by Israeli sources, published in the *New York Times* the next day, which characterized the story as "propaganda" and "nonsense," the episode was closed by Huntley's terse report on January 10: "For all its denunciations, though, Israel has yet to say it does not possess a nuclear bomb."

The burden of proof was, however, as far as the executives were concerned, on the producer who put the report on the air. When asked to back up the story, Northshield again called Perlmutter, who denied the substance of the story, and Robinson, who was unable to pinpoint his source any further than the account in *Jane's All the World's Aircraft* which contained a far more sketchy prediction that NBC's dramatic assertion that Israel had nuclear weapons. Robinson further cited as evidence the increase in Israel's production of plutonium, which enhances her *capacity* to build a bomb. This, however, could not be considered tantamount to building nuclear warheads for, as George H. Quester subsequently pointed out in the *Bulletin of Atomic Scientists*, "regardless of whether plutonium production in Israel is vastly expanded . . . or stays at its current lower level, a separation plant will be required before any bombs whatsoever are produced." Though Northshield maintains that he believes the report was accurate, the lack of corroborative evidence left him in a somewhat difficult position. A vice-president wanted to know "where the report came from, what the published source was, what attempts were made to corroborate it, and why it was put on the air"— all difficult questions to answer. The correspondent resigned soon afterward. Given the lack of research and investigative resources, it may in fact be far more prudent from the producers' point of view to rely on already published accounts of events than to undertake original reporting which might have to be justified to their superiors.

The fact, then, that newsmen have certain shared values about what constitutes "news" does not necessarily mean that these news values prevail when they run counter to the structural constraints and logic of the organization. And if these conflicts are consistently resolved in favor of the organizational value, it would seem that the professional analogy, which focuses attention on the norms of newsmen, begs the question of how decisions are made.

The Notion of a News Consensus

Even when it is accepted that the news pictures on television are the product of a series of decisions made within an organization, it can still be argued that these decisions are largely predetermined by a loosely defined prior "consensus" of what the news is, which is arrived at by other major media. Any attempt to explain the news pictures in terms of the internal structures and workings of news organizations is bound to be fruitless, this argument goes, because producers must conform, no matter how much discretion they theoretically have in selecting news, to this predetermined "news consensus."

To be sure, network news is reactive to other media in the sense that it depends almost wholly on them (especially the *New York Times* and AP and UPI wire services) for its basic intelligence input about the news of the day. And, in a sense, these outside sources establish a basic agenda of possible stories for the networks. Since producers are judged in their news coverage by their superiors on the basis of what the "competition" and the *New York Times* featured as leading stories that day, the "consensus" tends to some degree to be self-fulfilling.

It does not, however, necessarily follow that all, or even most, of the critical decisions about news are compelled by this "consensus," which may only include a few leading stories on any given day. In fact, there is considerable opportunity for selection. The wire services alone provide literally hundreds of possible stories a day "of film interest," and this list is not automatically narrowed down by any outside force for the network producers. This opportunity for selection is reflected in the fact that the three evening news programs select from this "agenda" different stories to cover. In a six-week period, for example, the three networks' evening news programs carried a total of 431 film stories, but only 57 of these stories appeared on all three networks. Most of the film stories, 321 out of 431, were reported by only one network. Even if the stories that are covered by all three news programs were considered to be products of the news consensus, or "mandatory stories" as one CBS producer put it, they account for only a small fraction, or about 12 percent, of the total number of stories on network news; thus the producers have a good deal of room to select the news stories in accordance with the particular needs and expectations of the organization.

Moreover, the fact that network news derives from essentially the same events as newspaper stories does not in itself mean that the coverage will be similar. Consider, for example, the way in which the Republican Governors Conference in December 1968 was reported in both media. The *New York Times* reported in great detail the various policy statements of the governors, such as Rockefeller's proposal for a federal welfare system, and in general treated the conference, the first time the Republican governors had met since Nixon's election as President, as a major political event. NBC News, however, found quite a different story in the conference. Since television was not allowed to film most of the meetings that took place at the six-day conference, the only film that NBC had to work with was obtained on the last day of the meeting, when the governors posed for the cameramen on horseback, in Western hats, and then proceeded to a barbecue, which the press attended. The NBC correspondent, Sander Vanocur, who had arrived on the next-to-the-last day of the conference, had this film edited into the story of the conference. The report, shown on the NBC Evening News the next night, opened with shots of horses neighing, governors mounting their steeds and then riding off, while Vanocur said in the voice-over-picture narration: "You are not imagining this scene; this is not the *Late Late Show*. This man is a governor . . . he wears a white hat, all the Republican governors are wearing white hats." Then, after showing the governors (and press) enjoying themselves at the barbecue, Vanocur concluded in a more serious tone:

> It is only a guess, but one has the impression that these governors, like much of the country, want a holiday from politics. Usually at these conferences there are a lot of discussions and plotting. There isn't much, if any, at this one. Nelson Rockefeller raised some important questions yesterday about medical insurance and welfare. It was as if there was no one to listen to him. This may be the result of post-election weariness. And it is understandable. This has been, after all, a brutal year. But the suspicion persists it may be something more, a wish to turn away from reality. And even in Palm Springs, where the atmosphere is somewhat artificial, the question persists: When will the holiday end and reality begin?

What was reported in the newspapers as an effort to reach political agreement on the Nixon Administration's programs appeared on television as a "holiday from politics," a "turn from reality" and an odd sort of horse opera. In this case, the film which was available determined the story, not vice versa. "Television is not expected to reproduce newspaper stories on film; it is a totally different medium," the young producer who supervised this piece later explained. The distinction had been made clear to news personnel, well before Marshall McLuhan became popular, when Reuven Frank advised in his memorandum: "The highest power of television journalism is not in the transmission of information but in the transmission of experience . . . joy, sorrow, shock, fear, these are the stuff of news."

And though there persists an occupational tendency to think of broadcasting journalism in terms of newspaper journalism, since both deal with the same subject matter —news—structurally they are very different kinds of news operations. For one thing broadcasting, unlike the print media, is a federally licensed and regulated industry. Also, the economics of both media have little in common. For example, while newspapers can increase their newsstand sales, and hence advertising revenues (which are based on "circulation"), by investing money and manpower in the editorial product—that is, scoops, exclusives, investigative reporting, features, exposés, and so forth—networks attempt to increase the "circulation" of news programs not by primarily allocating resources to the programs themselves, but by investing in preceding non-news programs to build what is called an "audience flow," on the theory that news programs inherit rather than attract the bulk of their audience. In terms of production problems, newspapers can expand their editions to cover extraordinary news by adding pages without sacrificing any advertising, while networks cannot expand programs for news developments without displacing other programs and advertising.

In terms of audience, there is also a critical difference. Producers of television news, and especially network news, must seek a level of generality in selecting and presenting news far beyond that of newspapers. As Reuven Frank explained:

> A newspaper, for example, can easily afford to print an item of conceivable interest to only a small percentage of its readers. A television news program must be put together with the assumption that each item will be of some interest to everyone that watches. Every time a newspaper includes a feature which will attract a specialized group it can assume it is adding at least a little bit to its circulation. To the degree a television news program includes an item of this sort . . . it must assume its audience will diminish.

National news on television, with a completely different set of problems and demands, cannot be adequately explained by resorting to the newspaper analogy.

Though the raw information about events may come from certain preferred sources outside the organization, or a "news consensus," the logic by which it is selected, shaped and reconstructed into news pictures is intrinsic to the organization. Thus the "news consensus" can be said to predetermine network news only in the extremely trivial sense in which it may be said that any author's work—either fiction or nonfiction—is predetermined by the information that is available to him.

In sum, constructs such as the "mirror of society," "autonomous professional" or "news consensus" have only limited power in explaining the selection of network news. On the contrary, these metaphors may only serve to discourage both insiders and outsiders—to the extent that they are assumed to be true—from attempting to intervene or purposefully influence the news outputs. To understand properly the way that network news operates, it is necessary to look inward at the producing organizations and examine the dynamics by which "news" is selected, integrated with other information and translated to visual images.

Finally, the question remains: Do news organizations lend themselves to any sort of systematic analysis? Even if it is fully accepted that the pictures of news on television are contingent upon a series of decisions made by the producing organization, it could still be maintained that the critical decisions tend to be idiosyncratic in nature—personal judgments that vary with the events, individuals and circumstances—and that therefore the search for a more general logic in the selection of news is bound to prove futile. Such a conclusion assumes, however, that the *critical* decisions are the ones made after the event has occurred, and neglects the advance decisions on coverage, rules and policies based on the needs and expectations of the organization. While any given news decision, when taken alone, may seem idiosyncratic, it is still possible, paradoxically, for the total news output of an organization to be largely determined by general rules, routines and policies.

To coordinate the efforts of hundreds of individual newsmen, technicians, editors and producers into a news product that meets certain standards and schedules, a news organization requires a set of internal rules and stable expectations. Reuven Frank began the previously cited thirty-two-page memorandum to his staff by saying:

> It is my purpose to set down as much as I can of the structure, procedures, and philosophy by which I shall try and operate this program. Some of what follows has been conveyed to me as stated instructions; some I have assumed as unstated mandate; some I have proposed to my colleagues and superiors and obtained their agreement; and some, finally, I state myself as operating rules.

Though they need not be codified or formally stated, some form of "operating rules" is necessary at every level of a news organization. Assignment editors, who select the events to be covered, must have what Walter Lippmann called "standardized routines," or a clear set of criteria and advance preferences, to reduce the virtually limitless barrage of information to manageable proportions and at the same time choose the *type* of stories which producers require for their particular programs. Correspondents require some formula for putting together their story, or what Lippmann referred to as "an apparatus and rules for naming, scoring and reporting," so that their reports can be smoothly meshed into the program. Similarly, editors, cameramen and sound technicians must have clear precepts about the requisite format of news pieces. Producers, finally, must impose guidelines on all those involved in the production of news stories so that they can meet the budgets, schedules and other standards that they are responsible for maintaining.

Although "operating rules" may not predetermine any particular stories, they do define more general characteristics of network news, such as the length of film reports (for example, whether they are three or thirty minutes long),

the amount of time and money available for individual
filmed reports (which, in turn, may define the "depth" of
news coverage), the areas which are most heavily covered
(which might be said to delineate the geography of news),
the models for dealing with controversy (whether it is a
"dialectical" model, in which two sides are presented
along with a synthesis, or the "thesis" model, which tries
to prove one side is correct), the ratio of "prepared" or
delayed news to immediate news (which determines the
time warp in the reporting and integration of stories),
and the general categories which are given preference
by producers (for example, "we-are-on-our-way-out-of-
Vietnam" rather than combat stories). And it is these
more general characteristics proceeding from the logic
and needs of the organization, not the individual choices
of one story of a certain category rather than another,
which give the picture of news on television a certain
overall consistency.

Network news thus is shaped and constrained by
certain structures imposed from without, such as government regulation of broadcasting and the economic
realities of networks; certain uniform procedures for
filtering and evaluating information and reaching decisions; and certain practices of recruiting newsmen and
producers who hold, or accept, values that are consistent
with organizational needs, and reject others—all of which
are open to analysis.

Chapter 2

The Political Ground Rules

The newspaper or magazine journalist is influenced in reporting the news primarily by the traditional canons of American journalism. . . . The broadcast journalist . . . must also keep in mind that he is working in a medium that, unlike print, operates under Federal regulation that has an impact upon what is disseminated.

—Elmer Lower, president of ABC News

Network news organizations are not independent entities; they are integral parts of the television networks, whose executives ultimately decide on the time that will be allocated for news programs, the amount of money that will be used to produce these programs, and the appointment of the top news executives. The networks, in turn, are heavily dependent on television stations they do not own or control to broadcast their programing over the airwaves. And the stations are licensed and responsible to the federal government for the programs they broadcast. Thus network news operates under conditions and rules defined by other organizations.

In this structured universe, perhaps the most basic fact that network news executives must contend with is that broadcasting, unlike other media, is a government-regulated industry. The rationale for governmental licensing and control of television stations is that the public airwaves, over which television and radio signals are transmitted from television antennas to home receivers, can be divided into only a limited number of broadcasting channels. Since the demand for channels far exceeds the supply —and no two stations can operate on the same channel at the same time without causing interference with another —the use of the airwaves require some form of allocation (although, as Milton Friedman and others have argued, such allocation does not necessarily require governmental control).

In any case, government regulation actually came at the behest of the burgeoning broadcasting industry, which was threatened by complete chaos after the courts ruled that the temporary restrictions laid down after World War I by the Secretary of Commerce on the frequencies and number of hours that stations could broadcast were unconstitutional. Soon after President Calvin Coolidge had warned that "the whole service of this most important public function has drifted into such chaos as seems likely, if not remedied, to destroy its great value," Congress passed the Radio Act of 1927, which created a Federal Radio Commission with broad licensing and regulatory powers. Then, in the more comprehensive Communications Act of 1934, Congress incorporated the powers of the earlier commission with the newly created Federal Communications Commission (FCC), whose seven members are appointed by the President. In theory this is an independent regulatory agency, funded by Congress, with full authority over the broadcasting, telephone and telegraph industries. The act empowered the FCC to license all broadcasting stations, prescribe the nature of the service in which each station could engage, make necessary regulations to prevent interference among stations and, in general, promote "the wider and more efficient use" of broadcasting. The available channels were to be allocated among localities to provide "a fair, efficient, and equitable" distribution of broadcasting service, but licenses for operating on those channels were only to be granted on a temporary and conditional basis. "The policy of the act is clear," the Supreme Court found; "no person is to have anything in the nature of a property right as the result of a granting of a license. Licenses are limited to a maximum of three years duration, may be revoked, and need not be renewed."

With this mandate, the Federal Communications Commission laid out the rules and license allocations through which the broadcasting industry developed. To achieve "a fair, efficient and equitable" broadcasting system, the available space on the public airwaves was divided into a spectrum of frequencies: the lower frequencies were assigned to AM radio broadcasters, the higher band of frequencies to FM broadcasters (FM requiring twenty times as much space on the spectrum as AM). The still-higher range, known as the very high frequency (VHF) band, was reserved for television (for which a single channel requires six times as much space as the entire AM band) and radiotelephone communications, while the highest frequency, or ultra high frequency (UHF) band, which presents a number of technical problems for broadcasting, was set aside for future developments in television. When television progressed in the 1940s, the VHF band was divided into twelve television channels (the thirteenth being set aside for land and mobile radiotelephone communications), which, when geographically assigned so that two stations using the same channel would not interfere with each other (requiring a distance of 170 miles between stations on the same channel), provided most major cities with three VHF channels. Allocation of the UHF channels had to await the solution of technical "compatibility" problems. To minimize the interference between stations, the FCC strictly specified for each individual station the frequency, power, hours and antenna height with which it could operate—in other words, regulating virtually all the engineering aspects of broadcasting.

Aside from the engineering, government regulation had a political function. The FCC was charged with determining *who* among competing interests would be given licenses to operate on the limited number of allocated channels which are, in effect, government-protected monopolies. The Supreme Court, in interpreting the Communications Act, has explained:

> The Act itself establishes that the Commission's powers are not limited to the engineering and technical aspects of the regulation of radio communications. Yet we are asked [by the plaintiff] to regard the Commission as a kind of traffic officer, policing the wave lengths to prevent stations from interfering with each other. But the Act does not restrict the Commission merely to supervision of the traffic. It puts upon the Commission the burden of determining the composition of that traffic. The facilities of radio are not large enough to accommodate all who wish to use them. Methods must be devised for choosing among the many who apply. And since Congress itself could not do this, it committed the task to the Commission.

But rather than give the FCC specific criteria for "choosing among the many," the act provided only an open-ended touchstone—"the public interest, convenience or necessity." The question of exactly what constituted the public interest, convenience or necessity in broadcasting was left to the commission to define.

The Public Interest Defined

The concept of the public interest which emerged in FCC and Court decisions rests on three central assumptions about the role of a communications medium in a free society. First, it is assumed as "axiomatic" that the "basic purpose" of broadcasting is, in the words of the commission, "the development of an informed public opinion through the public dissemination of news and ideas concerning the vital public issues of the day." The "foundation stone of the American system of broadcasting" is then the "right of the public to be informed, rather than any right on the part of the government, any broadcast licenses or any individual members of the public to broadcast his own particular views on any matter." The broadcasting of news and information on matters of public importance is thus presumed to be an indispensable element in fulfilling the "public interest."

It is assumed further that it is absolutely "essential to the welfare of the public" for these ideas and information to come from "diverse and antagonistic sources." This presupposes that "right conclusions" are more likely to be arrived at by a "multitude of tongues" competing for the public's attention than from any single authoritative source. The notion that truth is produced and tested by the unrestrained competition between news sources, if accepted, makes rational the First Amendment protection of a free, unrestrained press. "To many, this is and always will be folly," Judge Learned Hand noted, "but we have staked upon it our all." A second vital element in the public interest is thus presumed to be diversity: news and information emanating from as many different and competing stations as possible.

Finally, it is assumed that broadcasting must function preeminently as a local institution. Since it is presumed that the informational needs of different localities may be different, licenses must ascertain and attend to local needs. The Federal Radio Commission established this principle as early as 1928, holding that "a broadcasting station may be regarded as a sort of mouthpiece on the air for the community it serves, over which its public events of general interest, its political campaigns, its election results, its athletic contests, its orchestras and artists, and discussion of public issues may be broadcast." This requires "a diligent, positive and continuing effort on the part of broadcasters to discover and fulfill the tastes, needs and desires" of the communities they serve.

In theoretical terms, at least, Federal Communications Commission derived a general if somewhat conflicting goal: a broadcasting system that provides as much information as possible from diverse and competing sources which is relevant to the needs of the communities it serves. To bring the broadcasting industry into line with this goal, the FCC has very effective powers at its disposal, aside from its ultimate and little-used power to revoke and transfer licenses. For one thing, it can promulgate rules which are binding on licensees. Second, it can announce in advance that in comparative hearings, which come about if a station's license is challenged by another applicant, it will give weight to certain practices in deciding whether or not to renew the station's license. The fact that few licenses are actually revoked in a comparative hearing may indicate that licensees have in their own enlightened self-interest decided voluntarily to anticipate and conform to those practices to which the FCC gives "weight" rather than that the commission is powerless. Finally, through administrative actions, particularly by delaying the renewal of licenses until certain questions are answered, the commission gives licensees a powerful incentive to accept even its unwritten standards and guidelines. "The strength of the FCC is more in the threat it can pose than in actual action," the news director of CBS News in Washington concluded.

The rules, edicts and policies of the commission thus constitute for the broadcasting industry a set of basic guidelines and ground rules which, by defining the structure of the broadcasting industry, the relations between licensees and program sources, and the general requirements for news programing, fundamentally shapes the news operations of the networks.

The Affiliate Structure

In the hope of stimulating the "competition" and "diversity" which it believed would "best protect the public interest," the commission expressly prohibited any licensee from owning two television (or AM or FM) stations in the same market, or with overlapping signals, or from owning or controlling a total of more than seven television stations, of which no more than five could be VHF stations. (Licensees could also own up to seven radio stations.) The FCC subsequently prohibited licensees from associating with any organization that controlled more than one network, and thus, in 1941, effectively compelled NBC to divest itself of the "Blue Network," one of the two networks it owned, which then became the nucleus of a third network, ABC. Since three VHF television stations had been allocated to most major cities, this divestment opened the way for a television system dominated by three competing networks with outlets in all the major markets.

While these rules did not create the maximum possible amount of competition—apparently the FCC is unwilling to trade off the stability that comes from allowing the ownership of more than one station by a licensee for additional competition—they created an extremely fragmented ownership pattern. With no licensee owning more than five VHF stations, there was a ready market for network-produced programing, since it rarely was economically feasible for station owners to produce programs for their own group of stations.

Networks, which have been somewhat modestly described by a network president as "nothing more than programs and telephone wires," operate essentially by providing subscribing stations, or affiliates, with free programing in exchange for commercial time on the programs which could then be sold by the networks to national advertisers. The affiliate simply "plugs in" to the network, which transmits the programing and commercials from New York over private closed-circuit lines leased from the American Telephone & Telegraph Company to the stations for rebroadcast.

However, by 1938 the FCC had found that the three national networks almost completely controlled programing on radio stations which had 97 percent of the total night-time broadcasting power (a measure of potential audience). That most programs and viewpoints were being selected in New York by a few network managers rather than by hundreds of competing licensees ran directly counter to two fundamental objectives of the commission. First, it substantially reduced the competition between stations, which the FCC had hoped to induce through diversity of ownership; and second, since station owners had in effect delegated their programing function to national networks, it seriously undermined the ability of stations to serve local needs or to act as "mouthpieces" for the community. Concern "for the survival of individual licensees as decisional agents in broadcast service" led the FCC in 1940 to institute rules governing the relations between licensees and networks. And although these regulations were designed primarily to strengthen the hand of radio broadcasters in their dealings with the networks, they also later structured the crucial relations between television networks and affiliates.

Since the networks themselves do not, strictly speaking, broadcast over the public airwaves (but only relay programs to broadcasters over privately leased lines), the commission has no formal authority to regulate their operations. However, the power to prohibit licensees from entering into specified arrangements with networks is tantamount to the power to regulate networks, since each of the networks also owns five stations and are therefore licensees. The FCC, holding that "the licensee has the duty of determining what programs shall be broadcast over his station's facilities, and cannot lawfully transfer this duty or transfer control of his station directly to the networks," forbid any licensee from entering into "any contract, arrangement, or understanding with a network organization":

1) under which the station is prevented or hindered from, or penalized for, broadcasting the programs of any other network organization;

2) which prevents or hinders another station serving substantially the same area [as the affiliate] from broadcasting the network's programs not taken by the former station;

3) which provides for the affiliation of the station with the network organization for a period longer than two years;

4) which unconditionally options any segment of the station's time;

5) which prevents or hinders the station from rejecting or refusing network programs which the station reasonably believes to be unsatisfactory or unsuitable; or which, with respect to network programs so offered or *already contracted for,* prevent the station from rejecting or refusing any program which, *in its opinion* [emphasis added], is contrary to the public interest, or from substituting a program of outstanding local or national interest.

The net effect of these rules is to make it legally impossible for a network to force any affiliate to broadcast any program or series, *even if* the station has contracted in advance to do so. Affiliation contracts are thus reduced, as one network vice-president put it, to " 'one-way streets'; we are contractually bound to offer our programs first to our affiliates, and give them the right of first refusals, but they have no obligations to us."

The affiliate structure, established by the commission's rules, seriously affects the network news operation. While on the one hand it makes affiliates heavily dependent on the networks for national news—since obviously, with a limited number of stations, it does not pay to cover

events on a nationwide scale—at the same time the FCC
rules make the networks dependent on independently
owned licensees for "clearance" of each news program,
creating what network managers term "the clearance
problem." Referring to the fact that licensees have the
power to reject any program or news broadcast it prefers not to broadcast, Richard Salant noted that "whatever we do at the network has two hundred or more
bosses—every one of our affiliated stations." Although
this perhaps overestimates the actual control affiliates
have over news broadcasts—the affiliates' need for programing continuity and other broadcasting exigencies
make it impractical, if not impossible, for them to censor
portions of individual network news programs—executives and producers still must be sensitive to the "demands and vetoes," as a CBS vice-president put it, of the
affiliates' managers. For if just a small number of affiliates in key markets refuse to continue to carry a network
news program, or substitute another news program for
it, not only will the national ratings decline but advertisers attempting to reach a national audience will be
shut out of these markets. The problem of clearance is
especially acute in the case of news documentaries and
specials, since, as will be more fully discussed in the next
chapter, it is often more profitable for affiliates to substitute locally acquired programs, such as films they own,
for the network programs. Other than an altruistic desire
to serve the public interest better, the main inducement
for broadcasters to take such less profitable, or even unprofitable, news programing is fear of FCC reprisals
when the license comes up for renewal. Newton Minow,
then chairman of the FCC, was playing on just this fear
when he told broadcasters in 1961:

> Unfortunately too many television stations reject
> the public affairs programs offered by the networks
> because they can make more money rerunning old
> movies. This kind of broadcasting raises serious ques-
> tions about responsibility and the public interest. The

FCC is doing what it can to encourage what the Pilgrims called "better walking" on the part of these stations.

The relatively high value that the FCC places on the national news supplied by the networks, as contrasted to the low value the network places on locally originated movies, or even news reports, works to alleviate greatly the problem of clearance. As an NBC executive responsible for clearing programs put it: "Without the FCC, we couldn't line up enough affiliates to make a news program or documentary worthwhile." The expansion of network evening news from fifteen to thirty minutes in 1963 was reluctantly accepted by most affiliates, even though it meant sacrificing a substantial amount of advertising revenue because, as the same executive continued to explain, "They knew how the Commission, and the powers in Washington, felt about national news, and it wouldn't help matters at license renewal time if they had refused to clear the only national news program available to them." Any reversal or even reappraisal of the value of network news on the part of the commission or the vaguely defined "powers in Washington" would strike at the foundation of network news: affiliate clearance.

In this light, the charges of Vice-President Agnew that network news produces a "distorted" view of America which is in many ways detrimental to the public interest could not be lightly dismissed by network executives, especially if those charges were perceived by affiliate-owners as signaling a shift in the relative value of network and local news. An analysis of the implication of Agnew's speeches by an NBC News vice-president suggests the sensitivity of executives to the triangular relation between network, government and affiliate:

The affiliates, not the networks, may be the real targets of the Agnew speeches. A network, after all, is an abstraction. Huntley, Brinkley and Cronkite could sing, dance or strip in their New York studios, but if the affiliates don't choose to take the show in the first place, it wouldn't raise an eyebrow from here to Monterey. Each of the networks own five stations. That's fifteen among the three of them. But their affiliates add another 550 stations to the networks. Simple arithmetic will tell you that if the affiliates, out of conviction or fear, rise up in rebellion and pull the plug, then the networks are sunk.

After Agnew's speech, there was some variation in the way that affiliates reacted. But for the most part they were silent. . . . But let the Vice President stir up enough trouble; let FCC Chairman Dean Burch ask a few more searching questions about the way in which licensees are discharging their obligations to serve the interest, convenience and necessity of the public that owns the airwaves; let just one license be revoked for bias, and the affiliates' revolt will start. The networks would not be able to deal with it.

In a panel discussion analyzing the effects of the Vice-President's speech, Richard Salant said that it had already caused concern among affiliates. "One station," he added, "said it was going to black out our analysis following the President's speeches; other less candid [affiliates] would just do it without saying." (Richard W. Jencks, former president of the CBS Broadcasting Group, went further, saying that "the Vice President knew he was attacking a licensed medium of communication, and it may have been a coordinated pattern.")

That network executives believe that their leverage over affiliates varies directly with the value that high government officials put on network news, as these analyses seem to indicate, suggests that at some level, executives must concern themselves with the knotty problem of maintaining the explicit esteem of those political leaders for network news.

But even when network news is highly valued by government regulators, affiliates are still free to reject individual news programs which they believe do not further the "public interest" of their particular locality. The affiliate-owners, who have, as the FCC made mandatory, the "final decision as to what programs will best serve the public interest," constitute a prime, if select, audience for each network. "Affiliates tend to be owned by people in another business—newspapers, automobile dealers, Coke distributors—and run by salesmen or former announcers," the same vice-president noted. "Their politics is Republican, their ideals are pragmatic and their preoccupation with return on invested capital and the safety of their license to broadcast is total." Though this picture of affiliates may be too darkly drawn, network executives do make some "functional assumptions," the vice-president explained to me subsequently, about the sort of programs which affiliate-owners "will and will not clear." "It is reasonable to assume, for example," he continued, that "if the thrust of a documentary goes directly against the values of a particular community—or rather what the affiliate presume to be the values of their communities—the program probably won't be cleared in that locality." The fact that a news program is not likely to be cleared in certain markets may not in itself preclude the network from producing it, the vice-president went on to say, but it is a factor that must be reckoned with in advance decisions on the type and categories of documentaries and news specials which will be commissioned.

Moreover, producers, who understand the constraints on network programing, tend on their own to be somewhat circumspect about proposing programs on subjects that might offend certain audiences or, more important, the affiliate-owners who are the gatekeepers for those audiences. "The general rule," one producer suggested, is "the more offensive the subject, the lower the clearance rate will be." Richard Jencks pointed out to an interviewer:

> Stations are still pretty independent—a lot don't even clear high quality entertainment, to say nothing of news and public affairs. But there are some documentaries that will be cleared by a 140-odd stations (out of 200 affiliates)—the program on the Warren

> Report had a very high clearance—on the other hand,
> a program in the same series on homosexuality did
> less well; people aren't so eager for that kind of fare.

NBC had a similar problem with a documentary on mi-
gratory workers, which some affiliates that served rural
communities preferred to forgo.

This concerns producers as well as executives. Since
a program's national "audience rating," which is an average of ratings in *all* major markets, will be correspond-
ingly lower when it is not shown in key markets (even if
a relatively high percentage of the audience watches the
program in the markets in which the program is cleared),
this reflects on the producer's "track record," or standing with the network. It is not surprising, then, as an
NBC producer explained in a colloquium on television
news, that "most censorship on television is self-censorship. I have never been turned down for a program I
wanted to do for censorship reasons. On the other hand,
I am not sure I have ever asked to do one I knew management would not approve for those reasons."

To a lesser extent, clearance is also contingent on the
apparent relevance of the program to the particular needs
of the audience of the affiliates. Since the FCC has explicitly identified the "public interest" to be served by
broadcasters as the local one, a news program that is
palpably irrelevant to the informational needs of a particular locality cannot, strictly speaking, be counted as
part of a licensee's "public-service record," or the list of
programs it files as part of application for license renewal with the FCC. While affiliates might still decide to
accept such programs on purely economic grounds, networks are left in a very tenuous position in the case of
the less profitable documentaries and news specials which
are also unrelated to local problems in key markets. If,
however, news programs are "nationalized," as an NBC
executive described the process, so that they at least appear to be "relevant" to the needs of *all* areas, networks

can exert the additional leverage of license maintenance and "public-service records" on affiliates to clear even unprofitable programs. For example, while affiliates of NBC in many parts of the country had little reason to carry a not very profitable program dealing exclusively with the problems and politics of Boston, essentially the same documentary was presented as a report on "The American Urban Dilemma" through a more generalized narration, with Boston symbolically standing for all cities in America, thus making it easier to persuade affiliates to clear the program as part of their "public interest" licensing requirements.

"Network news *is* national news," an NBC executive explained. "The job of the network producer is to focus on national themes." Virtually any news occurrence can be transformed into a "national" story by editing the story around such a "theme." For instance, the producer of the NBC Evening News turned a story about the opening of a subway in Cleveland into a "national" story through the simple device of ordering two other NBC film crews to shoot some footage on subway progress in Chicago and San Francisco, where the crews happened to be; this was "packaged," or edited together, with the Cleveland story, and presented as a report on "national" transportation problems (even though, in fact, only six cities in the United States have any type of subway system). "Nationalizing" news stories is important not only to network producers and executives because it tends to facilitate clearance of network news programs but also because it is perceived to "build national audiences" for news (a consideration to be examined more fully in the next chapter).

Finally, this dependency on independently owned affiliates tends to make network executives extremely sensitive to the way in which controversial subjects are reported on news programs. Julian Goodman, president of NBC, noted in a letter to NBC affiliates that affiliate managers were expected "to react and express themselves" on the subject of network news programs. And after affiliates had voiced complaints over such matters as a "one-sided" NBC report on the National Guard shootings at Kent State (in which NBC was accused by affiliates of not interviewing National Guardsmen), the coverage of the Vietnamese war (in which NBC was accused of not fully presenting the Nixon Administration's position), and on peace demonstrations (in which NBC was accused of giving too much time to antiwar demonstrators), Goodman replied that NBC strived to maintain "a middle position," even though "errors of judgment or execution" may occur in individual news reports. To avoid such "errors" and criticism from affiliate managers, producers of network news programs are expected to take great pains to "balance" news reports on highly controversial subjects, especially ones about which affiliate managers have evidenced concern.

The Programing Structure

Government regulation has also created an artificial demand for news programing, at least in the sense that licensees must broadcast a minimum amount of news programs, as opposed to entertainment programs, to satisfy FCC requirements. Even though a number of channels are specifically reserved for educational, or "public," television, commercial broadcasters are also explicitly required by the FCC "to devote a reasonable percentage of their broadcasting time to the presentation of news and programs devoted to the consideration and discussion of public issues of interest," even though such programs may be unprofitable for the broadcaster. The reasons go back to the commission's concept of the public interest: "Since the development of an informed public opinion is our *objective* [emphasis added]," Newton Minow, then chairman of the FCC, pointed out to the National Association of Broadcasters, "we have constantly held that some allotment of time must be made to news." Minow also clearly connected news programing to license renewal, reasoning that "after all, a valuable grant to use a scarce public channel should go to those who provide more public service rather than to those who choose to provide less." The observation by a network executive that "news, for most stations, is the price of the license" may be somewhat cynical and even overstated (since, as shall be discussed in the next chapter, news programing can be profitable at times), but it is also true that news is a form of license insurance for many stations.

While the FCC seldom, if ever, resorts to measures as drastic as revoking licenses to induce broadcasters to increase the amount of time in their schedule that they allot to news and public affairs programs, it achieves the same effect by what W. Theodore Pierson, a leading communications lawyer, calls "disguised and clever leverages." In an interview, Pierson recently explained that although the commission itself does not set formal minimum quotas for news programing, the FCC staff, which actually processes the more than two thousand license renewal applications each year, must have certain guidelines or "magic numbers." If a station's proposed programing meets the "magic number," the license is "automatically" renewed; if it falls short of the "magic number," the application is held up, and a station is asked in a "letter" to justify its low proportion of news programing in terms of the informational needs of its community. Answering this request, which is legally part of the application process, may not only involve time and costly research, but may also set off a vicious circle in which each attempt to justify the proportion of news programing prompts a further letter from the FCC questioning the "justification." This bureaucratic wrangling often continues until the broadcaster increases the proposed news programing. "In acting on deferred renewals . . . ," a Senate subcommittee investigation into FCC operations found, "if an applicant's proposed service fell short on news and public affairs, his renewal would not be granted until he agreed to amend the proposals, bringing them in line with the standards."

To avoid such delays and possible complications in the renewal of their licenses, broadcasters attempt to ascertain in advance the commission's "magic number" on news programing, and then meet the expected minimum in their proposals for future broadcasting operations. Pierson, who represents many stations in their dealings with the FCC, explained that this is usually done by their Washington attorneys, who find out in their day-to-day communications with the staff what at any given time the minimum proportion of news is—in 1969, it was 5 percent news and 1 percent public affairs programs—and then apprise their clients of this fact. In this way, the attorneys make explicit the tacit guidelines of the FCC to the broadcasters.

The commission also gives broadcasters strong incentive to increase their news programing by making it abundantly clear that in comparative hearings, which come about automatically if any applicant challenges the incumbent licensee when the three-year license expires, special weight will be given to news programing: the more news carried, the better the chances that the FCC will find in favor of the licensee. Few stations, to be sure, lose their licenses in comparative hearings, but that is partly because few stations are willing to risk their extremely lucrative license, or even provide grounds for a challenge, which in itself can involve very heavy litigation costs and financial problems, by openly flaunting the commission's unwritten guidelines on news. Through such direct and indirect pressures, the FCC creates a demand for news that licensees might not otherwise find it in their interest to provide. "A substantial volume of [news and public affairs programs] have such government origins," Pierson points out in the *Federal Communications Bar Journal*. "With respect to such programs, the licensee's judgment was exercised, but not to determine what his audience wanted or needed but to determine what the *Commission* wanted or demanded. To deny this constraint exists is to indulge pure myth."

The compelling force of even the informal suggestions of the commission is made clear by an incident during the Eisenhower years which Robert E. Kintner, then president of NBC, later wrote about:

> [FCC] Chairman John Doerfer called Frank Stanton, ABC President Leonard Goldenson, and me to Washington for a private meeting. In effect, he instructed us to arrange among ourselves for each network to devote a different hour of prime evening time each week to a public affairs program. Our automatic reaction to this strongly lifted eyebrow was a statement of our belief that the antitrust laws would not permit our collusion in this manner. Chairman Doerfer then took from his desk a letter from the Justice Department explicitly granting permission for us to work together toward this end. NBC already had a one-hour public affairs program in the evening schedule. We probably would have had one in the next season, too, but Doerfer's meeting made it a certainty.

The demand that stations devote a set minimum amount of programing time to news and public affairs not only makes it mandatory that the networks, with their five stations each, be in the news business, but it also creates a ready market among independently owned affiliates for network-produced news programs. Since national news is considered by the commission to be an indispensable part of the licensees' quota—and can, according to FCC policy, be used to fulfill up to four fifths of the tacit news requirement (at least one fifth must be local), local stations, which usually cannot afford to rent special telephone cables, must obtain national coverage of such events as national conventions, presidential elections and space exploration from the networks. For this reason the FCC tends to favor license applicants who have affiliation contracts with national networks over other unaffiliated applicants. Given the strong premium the commission puts on national news, networks are obliged to devote substantial resources to maintaining a news division.

Although the FCC is prohibited by the Communications Act from engaging in any sort of censorship, it has in a more general way structured the presentation of news by its insistence that prescribed standards of "fairness" and "balance" be met by licensees. The administrative policies advanced in 1949 under the rubric of "the Fairness Doctrine" requires that a licensee present contrasting viewpoints on every controversial issue of public importance, if the issue is discussed at all over the licensee's station. A broadcaster is thus made responsible not merely for presenting the views and opinions he considers to be correct but also for the opposing views, even if he considers them to be false and injurious. This obligation on the part of licensees, although it is justified by the commission through its concept of promoting a "free market of ideas," actually represents a radical departure from the traditional concept of a free market of ideas which the Court has held to be the basis of freedom of the press.

The traditional view, which proceeds from the assumptions of John Stuart Mill and other liberal theorists, is that the free market of ideas produces right conclusions if, and only if, each individual member of the press is free to express and advocate the views or versions of events he prefers to. Biased and meretricious views will somehow, it is assumed, be balanced and corrected by the unrestricted competition of ideas. "The best test of truth," Justice Oliver Wendell Holmes wrote, "is the power of thought to get itself accepted in the competition of the market."

The modified concept of the free market of ideas, as it is applied to broadcasters by the FCC, holds that since, unlike the press, there is room on the public airwaves for only a limited number of stations to operate, each station must itself supply the competing viewpoints and ideas.

Whereas individual newspapers are assumed to be the competing parts of the market, individual broadcasters are assumed to be the market*place* itself, or a public forum in which different parties, representing different views, can be heard by the public. However, by making broadcasters responsible for airing views antithetical to their own and for achieving "overall balance in the points of view presented," the FCC has in effect restricted the freedom of broadcasters to report what they prefer, which is the cutting edge of the traditional concept of a free press. The commission's argument that "different rules and standards are appropriate for different media of expression in light of their different nature" is bitterly contested by broadcasters, who claim the same protection as newspapers under the First Amendment. But it is precisely by these rules and standards which licensees must abide.

At its most general level, the Fairness Doctrine simply requires broadcasters to present, in the course of their news and public affairs programing, "contrasting viewpoints on controversial issues of public importance." Unlike the "equal time" provisions of Section 315 of the Communications Act (which applies only to candidates running for a public office and requires that *except* for appearance on news programs, stations must grant other candidates equal time if they grant time to any one candidate), the Fairness Doctrine does not require that opposing argument be given an equal number of minutes of time, or even that it be presented on the same program, or within any specific time period. It is left up to the licensee to decide what constitutes a "controversial issue of public importance," a "fair" reply, and a "reasonable time" in which to reply. Moreover, broadcasters apparently are not expected to be equally "fair" on all issues of public importance; for example, the commission states in its "Fairness primer" that it is not "the Commission's intention to make time available to Communists or to the Communist viewpoints"—a notion which brings into question the commission's concept of "fairness." Administratively the FCC, in theory at least, only considers the question of whether or not the licensee acted in "good faith" if a fairness complaint is lodged against him. When a complaint is filed, the procedure is for the FCC to forward it to the station and request an explanation. If the broadcaster fails to convince the commission he acted in "good faith," and has or will air "contrasting viewpoints," the licensee's file is "flagged," and this is deemed a "negative factor" when the license comes up for renewal. In the event that the license is then challenged by another applicant, the unresolved fairness complaint might well be taken as evidence that the licensee "had misconstrued its duties and obligations to serve the public interest."

Although no license has ever been revoked or not renewed because of a violation of it, the Fairness Doctrine has affected the form and content of network news in a number of ways. First of all, it puts an obligation on affiliates to "balance" any network program which advances only one side of an issue by themselves providing the "other side" in the course of their own programing. Rather than risk having to fulfill such an obligation, which could prove extremely costly and bothersome, affiliates insist, virtually as a condition of taking network news, according to executives at all three networks, that the networks themselves incorporate the requisite "contrasting viewpoints" in their news reports. Networks, in turn, require as a matter of policy that opposing views be presented on any issue that could conceivably be construed as controversial. In 1968 Leonard H. Goldenson, president of ABC, explained in a letter to the Senate Subcommittee on Communications:

> To insure awareness to the Commission's fairness doctrine, ABC's operating policy with respect to controversial issue programming is included in the ABC standards and policy book which is made available to company personnel responsible for the production and review of such programs prior to broadcast. Addi-

tionally, the company retains Washington counsel who regularly distribute to individuals in various departments of the company, including the radio and television networks, memorandum bringing to their attention and explaining significant Commission rulings, including those which have involved the fairness doctrine.

Leon R. Brooks, vice-president and general counsel of CBS, also advised the same subcommittee:

> CBS's policies have in our view enabled us to achieve the goals set forth in the fairness doctrine. . . . In producing a documentary broadcast, CBS believes that basic journalistic techniques require that relevant contrasting viewpoints be brought to bear on the subject under study so that it may be put in perspective for the audience. To this end, the documentary producer strives to find spokesmen able to articulate their views.

When Robert Kintner was president of NBC he "reiterated" to news personnel, in a memorandum dated August 1, 1963, the network's policy of "balancing" viewpoints on all controversial issues. "Adherence to its own policy," NBC subsequently wrote the subcommittee, "results in compliance with the fairness doctrine."

These network policies confer clear responsibility on the producers of news programs. Elmer Lower, president of ABC News, said: "It is the job of seasoned producers and editors to decide what news goes into news broadcasts and to make *certain* [emphasis added] that the Doctrine of Fairness and Balance enunciated by the Federal Communications Commission is strictly observed." Robert Kintner wrote that "this situation is ready-made for what someone once called 'regulation by lifted eyebrow' . . . [since when] the FCC receives a complaint that a public affairs or news show was unfair, and asks us to justify ourselves, we hop to it."

To enforce these policies, producers of news and documentary programs have adopted what might be called the "dialectical" model for reporting controversial issues, in which the correspondent, after reporting the news happening, juxtaposes a contrasting viewpoint and concludes his synthesis by suggesting that the truth lies somewhere in between. If the correspondent is unable immediately to ferret out or induce a "contrasting viewpoint," producers will usually shelve the film story until an opposing view can be found to provide a balance. For example, during the previously discussed teachers strike in New York City in 1968, executives at NBC ordered a number of stories prepared for the Evening News to be reshot or canceled because the views of the black community leaders were not adequately "balanced" by filmed interviews with teachers and union officials. And it is quite common for producers to order correspondents to insert "pro" or "con" material in their voice-over narration—as, it will be recalled, the producer of the NBC Evening News did to balance the debate over the nomination of Judge Haynsworth. Further, producers as well as correspondents are "cued into" this need to achieve a near symmetry of opinions by content analysis or "word counts," as one former network vice-president explained. As an example of the "self-analysis and self-evaluation" that the networks are "constantly engaged" in, Elmer Lower gave the results of one such study, conducted in 1969, which showed such precise results as "news tending to support the administration viewpoint totaled 12 hours, 39 minutes; news likely to displease Nixon supporters, 10 hours, 18 minutes; neutral news, 8 hours, 18 minutes."

This model of "pro and con" reporting is perfectly consistent with the usual notion of objectivity—if objectivity is defined, as it is by most of the correspondents interviewed, as "telling both sides of a story." It can, however, seriously conflict with the value that journalists place on investigative reporting, the purpose of which is "getting to the bottom" of an issue or "finding the truth," as correspondents put it. Since a correspondent is required to present contrasting points of view, even if he finds the views of one side to be valid and those of the other side to be false and misleading (in the Fairness Doctrine, it will be recalled, truth is no defense), any attempt to resolve a controversial issue and find "the truth" can become self-defeating.

Robert MacNeil, then an NBC correspondent, has described the difficulties in presenting the conclusions he arrived at in an hour-long documentary on the subject of federal gun-control legislation. In the original version of the documentary he concluded that it was necessary to restrict the ownership of firearms, and that Congress had not passed such a bill because of the pressures put on it by the "well-financed lobby led by the National Rifle Association." He explains what happened next:

> Shortly after the screening [of the original version] the word came down that the program would have to be reedited. The instructions came from the NBC lawyers and were ostensibly based on the needs to observe the Fairness Doctrine. It was also mentioned that NBC representatives expected to have to testify in forthcoming congressional hearings on broadcasting and did not want to be under any cloud of disapproval when they did so. The instructions were resisted by the NBC News Department, whose president, the late William R. MacAndrews, thought the program was strong and should be aired as it was. However, the wishes of the network prevailed and the film was reedited. The effect was to soften considerably the impact of the argument and to weaken the case against the N.R.A. [National Rifle Association]. In particular, the lawyers considered that we had been too tough on Franklin Orth [executive director of the N.R.A.]. Passages embarrassing to him were cut out and passages were inserted which either put him in a better light or permitted him to filibuster. . . . In the first editing, we selected the paragraph of the letter [an N.R.A. newsletter implying that Orth opposed firearms legislation] which made it clear that the N.R.A. was deceiving its membership. In the reediting ordered by the network, the entire letter was put in. Again, the effect was to obscure the editorial point by softening the focus on the relevant part. . . . In

addition to other changes which softened the impact
of the Orth interview, an exceedingly tame ending
was concocted.

The "new" conclusion was reported by MacNeil himself
on the program, even though it ran directly contrary to
what he apparently believed to be the true findings of the
investigation—that the legislation was purposefully fore-
stalled by the gun lobby, not by "reasonable men" dis-
agreeing on the "form" of the law—which suggests that
when the values of the journalist and the organization
conflict, the journalist must modify his reporting to conform to the organization's values and policies. The producer of this program, who dealt directly with the
network's lawyers and executives on the re-editing, subsequently explained that the program was modified to
meet the network's general policy on "fairness" and "non-
advocacy," and the lawyers were primarily concerned that
if the documentary appeared to be a brief against the
National Rifle Association, NBC or its affiliates might be
forced to give the N.R.A. time for a reply.

Closely related to the Fairness Doctrine, and proceeding from the same sort of logic, is the "personal attack"
rule:

> When during the presentation of views on a con-
> troversial issue of public importance, an attack is
> made on the honesty, character, integrity or like per-
> sonal qualities of an identifiable person or group, the
> licensee shall, within a reasonable time and in no
> event later than one week after the attack, transmit
> to the person or group attacked (1) notification of
> the date, time and identification of the broadcast(s);
> (2) a script or tape (or an accurate summary if a
> script or tape is not available) of the attack; and
> (3) an offer of a reasonable opportunity to respond
> over the licensees' facilities.

Even if the allegation, or "attack," is completely and dem-
onstrably accurate, a broadcaster is still obliged to offer

air time to the offended party for a reply. Unlike the laws of libel, again truth is *not* a defense for broadcasters. Although regular newscasts and on-the-spot coverage of events are exempted from this particular rule, it applies to all other news programing, including documentaries and unscheduled or "special" news reports. If a "personal attack" complaint is made, the FCC judges not merely the good faith of the licensee but whether an attack was in fact made in connection with a controversial issue of public import, and can order a station to comply then with its rule under penalty of license revocation, fine and criminal prosecution.

As most of the network executives and producers who were interviewed agreed, the "personal attack" rule has had an inhibiting effect on news documentaries and at times, even "the way a correspondent tackles a subject," as one CBS producer put it. Indeed, in asking the Court of Appeals to nullify the "personal attack" rule, the Radio Television News Directors Association argued that if it were strictly enforced,

1) A licensee will be unwilling to broadcast personal attacks or political attacks, or to allow his facilities to be used as a vehicle for such broadcasts if he is required by the Commission's rules to incur the expense of notifying the person or group attacked, of providing a transcript of the attack, and of donating free time for a reply. This burden will be exacerbated by the potential disruptions that the necessity of airing replies will have in displacing previously scheduled programs.

2) An individual licensee affiliated with a network will be reluctant to carry a network program covered by the rules because if a response to a network program broadcast by the affiliate is required, the affiliate must either air the network's response or make independent arrangements to comply with the rules.

Network executives must take these possible effects into account in the planning and approval of projected news programs. In a panel discussion of the Fairness Doctrine, Reuven Frank said, "We can recognize the increasing strain the Fairness Doctrine can place on a vigorous news operation. . . . It seems to me that this kind of regulatory constraint must inevitably have a progressive flattening effect on news presentation, particularly in their most vital and sensitive and socially useful areas—the treatment of controversy." Leon Brooks commented that the "personal attack" rule "in the area of controversial programming, could, of course, have a damaging effect on material broadcast, since it may tend to cause many licensees to avoid the presentation of programs which could create for them serious administrative inconvenience. The result therefore may be to stifle rather than to encourage the dissemination of strong opinion on radio and television." The perception of network executives of what sort of programs might not be broadcast by affiliates can easily become self-fulfilling prophecies.

Richard Jencks noted: "If CBS were today to present its documentary on the Ku Klux Klan, the leaders of the Klan could piously avail themselves of the right to make a reply over the full network, even though, in most communities throughout the nation, it is decades since responsible news organs would turn over facilities for an uncritical presentation of the Klan's point of view." Thus, the implication is strong that such a news program could not be presented without a great deal of thought of the consequences under the FCC rules. This is more or less what happened after NBC did a scorching exposé of the unorthodox investigation of the Kennedy assassination by Jim Garrison, the district attorney of New Orleans. Garrison immediately appealed to the FCC for equal time, and NBC found it necessary to turn over a half-hour of prime time to him, in which he presented his own theories as established facts. "To say this didn't please the powers that be at NBC is to put it mildly," the producer commented. (A CBS documentary unit that reached similar conclusions about Garrison was more restrained in what they presented on the air, according to the producer, because of the intervention of CBS attorneys.)

Indirect Effects

Finally, the fact that the networks are completely vulnerable to, as well as dependent on, the rules and regulations of a political authority affects and imposes limits, albeit not always visible ones, on the operations of network news. "Reprisals no less damaging to the media and no less dangerous to our fundamental freedoms than censorship are readily available to the government—economic, legal, and psychological," Frank Stanton, president of CBS, pointed out to the International Radio and Television Society soon after Vice-President Agnew leveled his criticisms at network news. "Nor is their actual employment necessary to achieve their ends; to have them dangling like swords over the media can do harm even more irreparable than overt action."

In terms of economic sanctions, the FCC can—as it actually did in 1970—limit the number of hours of programing which licensees may receive from the networks during prime time (the evening hours which provide the networks with most of their advertising revenues), and thus effectively restrict network profits. Legally, through either commission rules or antitrust action, the government could force the networks to divest themselves of the five television and seven radio stations which each owns (and which provided 50 percent or more of the networks' income in 1969). In fact, according to Stanton, the commission's proposed "one to a customer" rule, which would eventually compel networks (and other licensees) to divest themselves of radio stations in cities where they also own television stations, would effectively bring about a drastic curtailment, if not an end, to network radio news. Since stations in New York, Chicago and Los Angeles provide the bulk of news for the network, he explained, "it does not appear possible that we could continue to maintain a radio news-gathering organization of the size and quality comparable to our current force" without the network retaining ownership in the stations in these key cities. The same principle applies, with perhaps greater force, to the networks' television news operations. And psychologically, the persistent deprecation or even questioning of the value of network news by government officials can undermine the perceived value of it to affiliates, as has already been discussed, and thereby greatly exacerbate the clearance problem for the networks.

The "dangling swords," under which the networks metaphorically live, are tied not only to the policies and values of the FCC but also to those of political persons and groups who exert influence on the regulating agency —the President, who appoints the seven members of the commission; the respective subcommittees on communications in both houses of Congress, which oversee FCC operations and hold hearings on its past and future policy; the House Appropriations Subcommittee, which approves the expenditures of the commission; and the leadership of both political parties in Congress, which can bring pressure to bear on the relevant subcommittees and initiate new legislation for regulating the broadcasting industry. Since these and other political pressures can be brought to bear on the commission, the networks must assume that, as Robert Kintner said, it "necessarily adapts itself to the political tone in Washington."

In the politics of regulation, however, the networks are at a decided disadvantage. The counsel, and chief lobbyist, for one network explained:

> We have no natural constituency in Congress. The affiliates, who own the local newspapers as well as television outlets in most big cities, can always muster some support from local congressmen and politicians. But this hardly helps the networks. In fact, the affiliates use whatever political muscle they have to get

the Commission, which is supposed to regulate them, to regulate the networks for their benefit.

The Washington lobbyist for the other major network agreed with this, adding, "The networks are caught in the middle between the affiliates, who want to restrict [the networks'] share of broadcasting time, and the politicians, who for one reason or another object to their treatment of national news." Richard Salant, who was formerly counsel for CBS, observed: "The threat is always there, and sometimes [it] is explicit—that if the Congressman or Senator doesn't like our news treatment of an issue in which he has an interest, then he will push for legislation to license the networks, or limit their profits— or some other regulatory scheme entirely irrelevant to anything but punishment for the exercise of news judgment." On the other hand, by focusing the nation's attention on events which add to the prestige of the government, such as the landings on the moon, presidential addresses and state occasions, network news can indeed enhance, as one network lobbyist put it, "the networks' standing with any Administration." Network news is thus in the unenviable position of being able either to jeopardize or bolster the precious political situation of the networks, depending on the events it chooses to cover and the way it treats issues of political concern.

The general effect of this sort of political vulnerability is to make the executives of the network—including those involved in the business side and affiliate relations— exceedingly sensitive to the operations and general direction of the news division. And although news executives claim to have some "autonomy" over news decisions, they are still responsible to network executives for the overall performance. As president of the NBC network, Robert Kintner wrote up to "35 memos . . . in a two-day period" to the head of his news division, asking why the network carried specific news stories, or otherwise commenting on the news. Executives in the news division may, as they claim, be successfully able to resist the attempts by their superiors in the network itself to influence the coverage of specific news stories which are "politically sensitive," but there still are "limits," as the president of one network's news division pointed out, "on how far we can go in upsetting the network's apple-cart." In its "Policies and Procedures" statements, NBC, for example, sets certain standards for news personnel, such as "News may never be presented in a manner which would create public alarm or panic." Usually, however, the "limits" which arise out of the network's need to placate or cooperate with the Administration are much less explicit. After the urban riots in the summer of 1968, news executives were called together for a government-sponsored "conference" in Poughkeepsie, in which members of the regulating agency sat in. The discussion centered on the need for "guidelines" in covering racial disturbances and, in general, the ways that television could help ameliorate or "cool down" the tensions in the ghettos by "better news treatment." Reuven Frank strenuously objected to such an approach, writing subsequently to Roger W. Wilkins, the Department of Justice aide who was instrumental in arranging the Poughkeepsie conference, that "the discussion was asking a medium of journalism to act as an instrument of social control. We must never accept such a request. . . . It is not for us to cooperate with government in establishing guidelines." Yet, despite the caveats of news executives, all three networks have in fact adopted guidelines for covering racial disturbances which conform to those suggested at the conference (though some policies were already in effect).

The networks also cooperate with the government in a number of positive ways. "In the case of the space program," said a CBS executive whose responsibility is special events, "we literally turn our facilities over to a government agency [NASA] which controls the whole show." He explained that since the networks could not count on advertisers to pay the full cost of covering special events, "they certainly wouldn't budget the time and money they do to cover such government-sponsored events if they didn't think it gave them some political credit with the Administration." Conversely, news coverage which undercuts this objective of building "credit" may be curtailed. For example, in covering the inauguration of President Nixon in 1969, NBC gave strict orders that there was to be no live or film coverage of the "counterinauguration," which was being held by antiwar dissidents; and NBC News relayed orders to its field producers, editors, correspondents and camera crews not to cover or film any of these protests unless they actually disrupted the official ceremonies. The demonstrations, and the few violent incidents that did occur, were thus not shown on the NBC network.

This is not to say that the "limits" imposed by the political ground rules and vulnerability of the network cannot be circumvented by correspondents reporting the news. In the short run, on any particular issue or happening, the "limits" can easily be disregarded. But over any protracted period of time, a correspondent who strays repeatedly from the norms of the organization may find himself on the "blacklist" of producers, who are responsible for the news reports on their program to network executives, and may not be assigned to politically sensitive stories by the assignment desk. The political pressures can also be brought to bear on correspondents in more subtle ways. Reuven Frank said on public television:

> There are already controls of a very insidious nature, an atmosphere is building up that concerns me a great deal, that news people, acting according to their best lights, keep feeling that their almost conditioned actions and decisions may be subject to review. And I am afraid of a process of self-censorship developing.

The political ground rules represent only one dimension of the structure of network news; and although they set the basic relations between the networks, affiliates and government, and establish the minimum conditions of existence for the networks, they do not by any means completely explain network news. To more closely define the operations of network news, another lens must be added —the economic perspective.

Chapter 3

The Economic Logic

The precise composition of the [television] audience is changing every half-hour. The point of nearly every strategy and tactic a network can devise is to get the largest possible share of that audience in each half-hour.

> —Paul Klein, NBC vice-president
> for audience analyses

Before network news can be properly analyzed as a journalistic enterprise, it is necessary to understand the business enterprise that it is an active part of, and the logic that proceeds from it. The business of network television was succinctly if somewhat brutally outlined by an NBC vice-president in his testimony before a congressional subcommittee in 1963:

Television is not only a program service but an advertising medium which operates in a framework of intense competition. The principal value television has to offer an advertiser is audience, and the rating services furnish us and our advertisers with the measurement of the audience generated by our programs. This is a business requirement of broadcasting, essential in soliciting and justifying the advertising expenditures that support our program service.

For their part, television stations "recruit" an audience for advertisers, which is not difficult since they have what amounts to a government-protected monopoly over one of a limited number of channels in an area, or "market." In turn, advertisers, who are the sole paying customers for television stations, buy minutes of time on these programs to convey messages about their products to potential customers.

The price that a station can command for its time from advertisers depends almost solely on its "circulation," or the total audience (measured in "television homes" rather than individuals) tuned to that station at any given time, which is estimated through a statistical sampling of the audience's viewing habits twice a year by the American Research Bureau, Inc., a private company specializing in such surveys for advertisers and stations. Although such ratings, based on a relatively small sample, may be imprecise, they are, as Frank Stanton testified before the above-mentioned congressional hearing, "the lifeblood of the business because they give the operator and the advertiser some index of program popularity," and he added, "I believe the advertiser makes his choice on that basis." The larger the audience a station is rated at having, the more it can charge for its time, since advertisers generally make their purchases on a "cost-per-thousand-homes-reached" basis. The potential audience that any station can reach is limited, however, by the effective range of its signal, which may vary between fifty and seventy-five miles, depending on topography and height of the station's antenna (which, as mentioned earlier, is prescribed for each station by the Federal Communications Commission). To reach a larger, or "national" audience, an advertiser requires the services of a network.

Networks are essentially in the business of selling a national audience to advertisers, which they create through the simple device of paying selected stations across the country rebates to show network programs. Transmitted over private lines leased by the networks, these programs, complete with inserted commercial messages, are then seen simultaneously by the combined audiences of the individual stations that "plug into the network." The three major networks derive virtually all their income (excluding that earned by the stations and other businesses they own) from the sale of time on these programs to advertisers.

"To achieve its national network," testified the late David Sarnoff, chairman of the board of RCA, of which NBC is a totally owned subsidiary, "NBC must be able to assure a sponsor of the minimum audience," which means that their programs must be shown in most, if not all, of the markets that are important to advertisers. Since networks themselves are permitted by the FCC to own and control only five television stations apiece, access to the vast majority of the national audience is controlled by independently owned stations. Networks must therefore form some sort of stable alliance with these stations to guarantee advertisers a "minimum" national audience. Stations agree to become "affiliates" of networks for the simple reason that it is profitable to do so; indeed, as an FCC study noted, "most stations consider network affiliation their most important single asset, next to their Commission license."

Originally, the arrangement worked something like this: networks undertook to furnish affiliates with programs during most of the time they were on the air at no cost to them, and in addition to pay affiliates a fixed percentage—usually about 30 percent—of their "rate card," or the published price per hour which stations normally charged advertisers, for the time in which they carried network programs and commercials. Furthermore, affiliates were permitted to sell one-minute or thirty-second "spot commercials" at the station break, required by law each half-hour, during network programing and to keep all the proceeds. For their part, according to the network contracts, affiliates were expected to take most, if not all, of the programs offered during "network time," which comprised three hours in the evening, three hours in the afternoon, and for NBC and CBS, three hours in the morning (ABC had no morning programing).

The 1940 FCC rules, which, it will be recalled, prohibit affiliates from making any agreements with networks that in any way limit their right to reject any network program, rendered the "option" virtually unenforceable. Legally, at least, affiliates can now reject any network program at any time and in its place show a local or independently produced program. "Affiliation contracts today aren't worth the paper they're printed on," an NBC executive dealing with affiliate relations pointed out. "Originally, stations were obliged to carry our programs unless they gave us fifty-six days' notice. Today [1969] the station has the exclusive right to decide to substitute." FCC rules also leave affiliates free to substitute the programs of a competing network. In 1969, for example, in Dayton, Ohio, the ABC Evening News was regularly shown on the NBC affiliate (because, according to the same NBC executive, ABC paid a "premium" in compensation to the station), while the NBC Evening News appeared on the competing CBS affiliate; since there are only two VHF stations in Dayton, CBS, the odd man out, was forced to put its evening news program on an unaffiliated UHF station in the area.

But though networks lack the legal authority to compel affiliates to take specific programs, they have other remedies, including the ultimate threat of not renewing the affiliate's contract (which is limited by FCC rules to a maximum duration of two years). During the 1963 congressional hearings, an exchange between Representative John B. Bennett of Michigan and James Aubrey, then president of the CBS network, illustrates both the powers and the plight of the network in this respect:

> BENNETT: Well, if they refuse to air the programs you present, what happens to them as far as your affiliation is concerned?

AUBREY: It happens to us constantly. They fill the time, then, with a program which they feel more suitable for their particular local audience.

BENNET: You have no requirement or exercise no control over stations as to whether they air, or what part of your programs they air?

AUBREY: No, sir, we do not.

BENNETT: They could air 1 per cent or 10 per cent, and still not violate their contract with you if they wanted to?

AUBREY: If they so desired.

BENNETT: Would their contract be renewed if they aired 10 per cent of your programs?

AUBREY: Not if we could find another station who would air 20 per cent.

The power of a network to jettison an affiliate, no matter how recalcitrant it is, is effectively limited by the reality that in all but a handful of cities where networks have affiliates, there are no more than three VHF licensees (not including educational stations), each being affiliated with one of the three networks. In 1969, 604 of the 644 VHF stations in the United States were affiliated with a network. If a network refused to renew an affiliate's contract in a city where no unaffiliated station exists, it would be left without an outlet in that market and thus unable to compete with the other networks in guaranteeing markets to national advertisers. The possibility of exchanging a VHF affiliation for a UHF affiliation is hardly a realistic alternative for a network, since UHF stations can reach usually only a fraction of the audience in a market (only about 5 percent of viewers tuned to UHF stations in 1969). This is partly because a large portion of television receivers cannot easily receive UHF transmissions; partly because the UHF signal, for technical reasons, has a less effective range than a VHF signal; and also, of course, because of the viewing habits of the public. In a situation where there is a fourth unaffiliated station in an area, or if the market is not a particularly significant one for advertisers, then the threat has more force behind it.

The national audience that a network amasses for its programs and commercial messages is measured bi-weekly by the A. C. Nielsen Company, which estimates on the basis of a sample of less than two thousand homes what percentage of the television sets in the United States are tuned to specific programs at given times. A difference of a few points in any program's so-called Nielsen rating—each point representing 1 percent of the total number of television households in America—can make a very significant difference in the amount of revenue that a network receives, since national advertisers are usually willing to pay more proportionately for a program with a larger audience, in accordance with their cost-per-thousand-homes-reached formula. Regardless of the size of the audience, network costs are essentially fixed, and affiliates receive a set amount of compensation per hour from the network no matter how much the network is able to sell the time for; therefore, revenues and profits can be increased through gaining a higher Nielsen rating. "It costs the same to reach thirty million as ten million," a network vice-president explained; "we just get three times as much money for the same time" if a larger audience tunes in. Networks thus have a very powerful incentive to maximize their audience, or at least their Nielsen ratings, since it involves no real diminishing returns.

Although all revenues are derived from the sale of time to advertisers, time is a limited commodity on television. The number of minutes that can be sold for commercial messages is limited by an agreement among broadcasters, which is tacitly sanctioned by the FCC, to six minutes per hour during prime time, and twelve minutes per hour at other times. (This does not include the "spot" time that can be inserted before and after the station breaks every thirty minutes.) Each of the available minutes of commercial time can be utilized either by an affiliate, which can sell it to a local advertiser, or by a network, but not by both. Whatever time affiliates use for local programing and advertisements is unavailable to the network, and vice versa. The joke "What are we fighting about; we both want the same thing" sums up the basic and unavoidable conflict between networks and affiliated stations. Essentially both want the same scarce resource: the few minutes of advertising time available each hour when most of the sets are operating. The news operation must be examined in this context.

The Scheduling of Network News

Since the early days of television, the allocation of time between the networks and their affiliates has been more or less the same. Affiliates generally turn over to the networks the prime-time period, from which the networks in 1969 derived more than half of their total revenues, while retaining for themselves the periods immediately adjacent to prime time, in which they do most, if not practically all, of their local programing, including the news and public affairs programs, which are in effect necessary for fulfilling the FCC's license requirements, and from which they in turn derive most of their advertising revenues. The balance of the broadcasting day is less of a bone of contention; since smaller audiences watch at these hours, there is less total advertising revenue involved. Daytime and late-evening programing is relinquished by affiliates for the most part to the networks, which fill it with relatively low-cost programs such as reruns of series they themselves own, quiz programs and talk shows, except for the brief intervals when the networks are not programing.

But network news does not fit into this neat division of time. In the early 1950s, when television began to become popular, the networks scheduled their fifteen-minute "news strips" in the early portion of prime time (NBC's "Camel's Caravan of News with John Cameron

Swayzee" was shown at 7:45 P.M.; CBS's "Douglas Edwards and the News" at 7:30 P.M.) because, an NBC vice-president explained, the 7:30–8 "slot" was exceedingly difficult to sell to advertisers at "prime-time prices." The reasons for this were the high percentage of children watching television then, which "frightened off many advertisers aiming to reach adults," and the sharp decline in that audience in the summer months. News was thought to be "the cheapest way of filling it." But as the total television audience rapidly increased, and prime time grew accordingly in value, network news became a problem: it consumed network time that otherwise might be used more profitably for entertainment programing. In a memorandum entitled "Research Evaluation of Network News in Prime Time," this NBC vice-president outlined the history of the problem:

> ABC [in 1954] countered both NBC and CBS News with children's or all family entertainment at 7:30 P.M. cutting in sharply to the audience of both networks. NBC was hurt most, losing some 30 to 40 per cent of its audience in one year. CBS, realizing that 7:30 P.M. [which was then network option time] must be scheduled competitively, switched their news to 7:15 P.M. in October 1955. NBC meanwhile tried to maintain its strip format at 7:30 P.M. The result was NBC slipped in audience the next two years . . . while CBS started building an audience for their news at 7:15 P.M. Not only did NBC slide in news audience but the competition was by this time bridging NBC's entertainment vehicles at 8 P.M. so that the net result was a loss of audience for both NBC News and regular entertainment vehicles.

Since network news could not profitably be retained in prime time, the network's solution was to move it to the adjacent time period, which up to then was considered— by the affiliates, at least—to be "affiliate time." This caused some problems, as the memorandum continues to explain:

> When NBC decided to move the news out of prime
> time [1957–58], they were faced with a problem of
> gathering stations. The first year in the new time
> period NBC could muster only 63 stations while CBS
> News was on 153. . . . It took NBC four years to
> build back to a lineup [of affiliates] equal to CBS.

Affiliates were reluctant to take network news because
it reduced the number of minutes of commercial time
which they themselves could sell to local advertisers
during one of the most valuable time periods available to
them. In actual cost, taking the fifteen-minute network
program meant a loss of two and a half minutes of commercial time for affiliates and a gain of the same amount
of time for the network. Although affiliates were paid
"compensation" by the network amounting to about 30
percent of what they normally could have sold the two
and a half minutes to local advertisers for, it still would
have been more profitable for most of them in the
larger markets to continue showing a local news program during the fifteen-minute period, especially since
in any case, a local news operation was deemed necessary
to satisfy FCC requirements.

Naturally, with a local news program, affiliates retain
for themselves the full advertising revenues derived
from that time period, and though they have to pay the
costs of programing those fifteen minutes, an affiliate
executive explained that the extra cost for expanding
local news programing is "very little once a news program is operating anyhow," since stories can be edited
"longer," and interviews and weather reports extended
with very little difficulty. Moreover, contrary to some of
the more popular notions of news, network news does not
necessarily attract a larger audience to a station than
local news; indeed, audience studies indicate the reverse
is more probably true. In the top twenty markets in
1969, local news programs on CBS affiliates drew a larger
share of the audience in all but three markets (Washington, D.C., Seattle and Houston) than did the "CBS

Evening News with Walter Cronkite," which immediately followed them. The ABC Evening News surpassed the preceding local news programs in popularity in only two markets (Chicago and Seattle) ; while NBC's evening news, "The Huntley-Brinkley Report" (which had replaced the "Camel's Caravan" in 1957) attracted a larger share of the audience than did the local news programs in less than half of the twenty markets (though the pattern was more mixed here). In most markets, then, network news was greeted by a decreased share of the audience.

Nevertheless, affiliates accepted fifteen minutes of network news in their "time market," along with the loss of two and a half minutes of commercial time, partly because of direct pressures from the networks (especially in the markets where they had the opportunity to change affiliates), partly because of the value that the FCC put on network news as opposed to local programing, and partly because affiliate-owners believed, as one put it, that "network news did a job we couldn't possibly do."

But when NBC and CBS expanded network news to a half-hour in 1963—ABC did not follow suit until 1967 —in what had been the affiliates' choice time market, many stations resisted the move at first, though gradually they gave in to network pressures. One affiliate executive said quite frankly, "The networks used their news programs as a wedge to expand prime time." And the networks did, in fact, increase their share of evening advertising time by five minutes through the expansion of network news, with the affiliates losing a like amount of commercial time.

Those extra minutes made network news profitable. For instance, the five minutes of commercial time on the CBS Evening News, which could be sold for upwards of $28,000 a minute in the peak season in 1969, brought in about $36 million a year in revenues for the network. At that time it cost the CBS network about $7 million a year to produce the Evening News program, $9 million in "compensation" paid to affiliates for carrying the program, and $5.4 million in rebates to advertising agencies (which receive 15 percent of the price advertisers pay the networks)—which left a profit of about $13 million a year. So it is not surprising that network executives have advocated the idea of expanding network news to an hour, from 6:30 to 7:30 P.M., since this would double the revenues—assuming the time could be sold—while the additional cost of producing the extra half-hour of news programing would be considerably less. In 1969 a financial officer of CBS estimated that if the network were to double the number of hours of news programing, "the utilization of the facilities would be fuller per hour" and consequently the average "cost of programing would drop by 40 percent." The actual possibility of expanding network news to an hour, though no doubt profitable for the networks, remains remote because of opposition from the affiliates. One network news president explained: "You have to remember that this time period is gold to the local guys. We paid a price [in clearances] for moving to a half-hour. The affiliates didn't really want a half-hour." Another network news executive put it more bluntly: "The affiliates would simply revolt if we tried to expand on their time, no matter how we tried to rationalize it."

The rationales most often given for the need to expand network news are worth considering. A longer network news broadcast was necessary, one network executive argued, because "world and national events can no longer be covered in 15 minutes." The additional fifteen minutes of network news was not used, however, to cover more daily news events and stories, but for feature-type stories. Reuven Frank explained this in the previously cited memorandum to his staff just before the program was expanded to a half-hour:

The proper formula for a half-hour news program is not doubling the length of the quarter-hour pro-

> gram but adding to it the functions, subject and technique of the half-hour once-weekly programs. . . . [In other words,] the expansion of our news program to double its length will be accomplished by the use of longer film stories. . . . For a while, among ourselves, we referred to these as features, to the people we hired to do them as a features department. Please do not use the word.

These films were designed to be less topical so that they could be kept on the shelf up to two weeks, and thus fill the fifteen-minute news "gap." (Ironically, NBC returned to a format very much like the original "strip format"—fifteen minutes of news and fifteen minutes of entertainment—that it began with.) Indeed, all three evening network news programs used most of the extra fifteen minutes taken from affiliates for the same sort of less timely filmed stories—"magazine pieces," as they are called at CBS, and "features" and "fillers" at ABC. According to a comparison of network logs in December 1962 and 1968, the increase in network news time led to an almost 100 percent increase in the proportion of old or dated news on the programs. It would seem that the expansion of network news to a half-hour, and the scheduling of it in what had been the affiliates' time—6:30–7 or 7–7:30—fulfilled an economic rather than the stated journalistic need.

Similarly, the location of less profitable five-minute-long newscasts on the networks' schedule seems to be based directly on economic considerations. For example, the decision by CBS to shift the "Morning News with Mike Wallace" from 10 A.M., which was network time, to 7:30 A.M., when only 5 percent of the television sets were in use, though explained at the time by CBS as an effort to establish an early-morning news service, was attributed by Fred W. Friendly, former president of CBS News, to "a sales study [which] indicated that by inserting *I Love Lucy* reruns in that spot [formerly occupied by the news] the company's revenue would increase by $1,000,000 a year." Friendly subsequently explained to me that scheduling was all a matter of "opportunity costs"; analyses were constantly made at CBS of what kind of program would "bring in the highest price," and news was relegated to "whatever time slots they would least damage."

The scheduling of newscasts shapes the news operation in a number of general ways. For one thing, the scheduling of the newscast determines the number of hours the news staff will have to prepare, edit and "package" the news program. With a news program that is broadcast at 6:30 EST, the staff has only about eight and a half hours from the time they arrive in the morning until air time (and because of the time differential, news from the West Coast must be closed by 3:30 P.M. Pacific Standard Time). Using what is called a dual-feed arrangement, NBC and CBS go on the air live with their evening news at 6:30 EST, and then rebroadcast it on tape at 7 P.M., while ABC broadcasts live at 6 P.M. and rebroadcasts on tape at 6:30 and 7 P.M. As will be discussed later, this tends to limit the hard-news part of the operation to a range of events that is conveniently scheduled around midday.

Perhaps more important, fixing the hours of the news broadcast to a large extent determines the audience. Those viewers who can be counted on to watch a news program are not all drawn to their set from their various pursuits by the appeal of the program; for the main part they are already watching television at that hour, or disposed to watch it then, according to the audience-research studies that networks have conducted over the years. In the early afternoon, for example, the television audience is predominantly made up of housewives, preschool children and the retired elderly; it changes, of course, with the hour as children return from school, workers return from their jobs, and preschool children are put to sleep. When the network news is shown at the dinner hour, it tends, according to an ABC analysis, to draw its audience "from the older, smaller family groups, and quite contrary to what most people think, from lower-income groups." CBS executive Richard Jencks also pointed out to an interviewer that "preliminary indications of a survey we're currently involved in seem to show . . . the audience for hard news seems to be less sophisticated, educated, affluent than the average audience," which again apparently proceeds from the fact that the dinner-time news audience is older and therefore statistically likely to have fewer years of formal education.

These assumptions about the audience are important to the producers of news programs scheduled at dinner time, since they are responsible for maintaining the audience.

The Logic of Audience Maintenance

Since network television is in the business of attracting and holding large audiences, the news operation is also expected to maintain, if not attract, as large an audience as possible. But unlike other news media, drawing and holding an audience does not depend simply on its news product. To a large extent its audience hinges on two outside factors: affiliates and the "audience flow" it inherits from preceding entertainment programs.

A network audience is no more than the sum of the separate audiences of its affiliated stations (including the ones it owns and operates). This means that network programs must be "cleared" on affiliated stations. If affiliates refuse to take or "clear" programs they cannot possibly achieve a high audience rating, it will be recalled, because the Nielsen ratings measure the percentage of the nation's population exposed to a program, not the program's popularity in the areas in which it is shown. And William R. McAndrew, former president of NBC News, pointed out as early as 1962 that "available statistics do indicate that, on the average, regularly scheduled news and information programs receive somewhat lower station clearance than entertainment programs."

To some extent, affiliates also control when a network program is shown in their area. The hour a program is shown affects its rating, since the number of sets in use at any given time is determined more by the routines and timetables of the population than by the appeal of the program—at least that is the way network executives tend to look at the situation. If it were to be pictured on a graph, the potential audience would follow the contours of a bell-shaped curve: the television sets in use gradually increasing from 5 percent at 7 A.M. to 30 percent at 4 P.M. (as students begin returning from school), reaching 50 percent sometime shortly after 6 P.M. (as people begin returning home from work), jumping to 60 percent by 7:30 (after dinner), hitting its peak of about 66 percent shortly before 9, then declining to 60 percent shortly before 11 (as the older and younger parts of the audience begin retiring for the night), abruptly dropping to 30 percent after midnight, and back to 5 percent again by 2 A.M. Except for seasonal fluctuations—television sets are in use substantially more in the winter than in the summer—this pattern remains remarkably constant.

The same program will obviously get twice as high a Nielsen audience rating if it is shown at an hour when 60 percent of the potential audience is watching television as it would were it shown at a time when only 30 percent of the television sets are in use, all other factors being equal. Similarly, affiliates can increase the overall ratings of news programs if they show them in more favorable time periods. Even a half-hour difference, between 6:30 and 7 P.M., can make an appreciable difference in the ratings.

A less controllable factor that affects the potential audience is the location and broadcasting quality of a networks' affiliated stations. If some affiliates have overlapping or weak signals, which fail to reach effectively significant numbers of television households, ratings will be diminished, no matter how great the appeal of the program. In 1968 the ABC network covered only 94 percent of television households through its affiliates, while the other two networks covered 99 percent. This disparity resulted in a constant struggle on the part of the networks, especially ABC, to improve their affiliates.

But even if programs are available through affiliates to most television households in the important markets, it is not presumed by executives that the audience a program draws will be entirely determined by the appeal of that program. On the contrary, network executives and advertisers believe that a significant portion of the audience for any program is "inherited" from the preceding program. In this "audience-flow" theory, the audience is viewed as a river that continues to flow until it is somehow diverted. A network vice-president responsible for audience studies said:

> I wish that everyone chose to watch the program that most appealed to them from among the competing programs; it would make my job much easier. Unfortunately that is not the way it works; the viewing habits of a large portion of the audience—at least the audience that Nielsen measures—is governed more by the laws of inertia than by free choice. Unless they have a very definite reason to switch, like a ball game, they continue to watch the programs on the channel they are tuned in to.

Frank Stanton, who aside from being president of CBS is a leading authority on audience studies, explained the practical implications of the theory to a House subcommittee as follows:

> Both the overall schedule and the program which precedes and which follows the time period which an advertiser has under consideration are important to him, for he *knows* that audiences are built up and retained through an appropriate flow in sequence of programing.

... When two or more good programs are presented at the same hour over different stations in the same area, a large part of the audience of one station may never know that a good program is on the other station if their attention has already been attracted to the first station by a preceding program on that station, which they enjoyed watching.

As an example of "the phenomena of audience flow," he cited:

"Stage 7" had only a 32.1 percent of the audience when it was preceded by the "Fred Waring Show" with a 32.8 percent share of the audience. When the "Fred Waring Show" was replaced with "General Electric Theatre," which attracted 54.6 percent of the audience, the audience for "Stage 7" increased to 45.1 percent, a 40-percent increase.

If, as this theory suggests, a program derives a significant portion of its audience from a preceding program, networks must build audiences by attracting viewers early in the evening—the regress "going back sometimes to children's programs," the vice-president quoted earlier pointed out.

The audience-flow theory is especially important to network news, since it is generally assumed by executives that national news is less likely to attract viewers than entertainment programs or even local newscasts which feature reports on local sports and weather. Richard Salant explained to an interviewer that "you'll find a general correlation between the audience ratings of network news broadcasts and local news broadcasts—and probably the local news is the decisive thing." A comparison of the percentages of the viewing audience attracted by local and network news programs in the ten leading markets in 1969 seems to bear out this conclusion (Table I). It can readily be seen that the popularity of network news programs varies sharply from city to city and tends to match, within a few percentage points, the popularity of

TABLE I

Share of the Market—1969	CBS		NBC		ABC	
	Local	Network	Local	Network	Local	Network
New York City	20%	21%	23%	21%	13%	9%
Los Angeles	32	28	19	17	19	20
Chicago	16*	18	29	32	11	13
Philadelphia	37	37	23	21	12	11
Boston	47	44	25	25	10	—
San Francisco	22	22	39	38	12	11
Detroit	29	32	33	32	14	13
Cleveland	22	31	30	23	18	—
Washington, D.C.	28	29	25	28	11*	7
Pittsburgh	14*	11	46	40	26*	23

* Indicates non-news program.

the preceding program. Why, for instance, does NBC's national news in Chicago draw almost twice as large a share of the audience as the competing CBS news and almost thrice that of ABC, whereas in Los Angeles it draws only a little more than half of the audience against same CBS program and is even exceeded by ABC? The answer that network executives have found is that, as one vice-president put it, "the great majority of the viewers simply don't change channels for network news," and the share of the audience that network news gets in any given market is governed primarily by the popularity of the preceding program, or even channel, in a particular locale—which in the above instance was the local news. The "lead-in" (i.e., the audience already tuned into a channel) "is most important" in achieving audience ratings for network news, according to the vice-president for audience analyses at NBC. "The bulk of the audience watch news to find out about local weather, sports or events, or because they are tuned into that channel anyhow. Unfortunately, network news is able to add to that audience only when there is a real national crisis, which doesn't happen every day, and even then only slightly," he explained. Richard Salant postulated that "the audience is tuning in the channel mostly for entertainment, and what we do is salt our [news] programs in."

Although there may still be a considerable number of viewers who seek out network news programs rather than accepting willy-nilly what is "salted" in, there are also some popular misconceptions about this audience, as an NBC audience study indicates:

> One of the most cherished thoughts about News and Public Affairs (particularly public affairs) is that the lighter viewer of TV (who presumably has rejected the run-of-the-mill entertainment) will tend to watch quality public affairs programs. We have found that the people who watch the "quality" (and like the "quality") also watch and like the run of the mill as well. There is no indication that public affairs programs are seen to any great extent in the lighter viewing homes any more than normal entertainment programs are. In fact in one attempt to prove this cherished thought to a client we found that our public affairs programs were poorer in attracting light viewing homes than the entertainment fare.

In other words, the more sophisticated audience that watches television only selectively—that is, "the lighter viewing homes"—is not the primary news audience.

But what of the selective viewer, who does change channels for network news? Relying on both audience studies and personal intuition, network executives generally assume, first, that there is not a significant number of such viewers; second, that most of these selective viewers choose particular news programs on the basis of the personalities of the commentators rather than the extent of the news coverage—an assumption reflected in the six-figure salaries anchormen often receive; and third, that it would be difficult for any but the most informed viewers to know what stories are *not* being covered. Further, even though the exact relation is somewhat elusive, the fact that most executives assume that there is little if any relation between news coverage and audience ratings is in itself significant. For it is the network executives who, in the final analysis, make the decisions concerning what resources will be allocated for news coverage, and according to the audience-flow theory, money invested in the news programs themselves might not be the best way to attract and hold audiences.

In fact, networks have a number of more effective strategies at their disposal to increase the audience ratings of network news programs, as a vice-president at NBC News explained. First, a network can attempt to improve its "line-up" of affiliates. ABC's Evening News, for example, was not cleared by one third of its affiliates in 1969, including such major stations as Boston, Houston and Miami, and thus could not achieve a comparable rating with NBC's and CBS's Evening News programs, which were cleared in all major markets. The clearance problem is most acute in cities which have only two VHF channels and three competing networks offering news programs. The main incentive for affiliates either to clear network news programs or to carry the news of one network instead of another's is money. A network can pay recalcitrant or "shared" affiliates "premium compensation," the NBC executive continued, which "comes very close to outright bribery."

A second way that a network can boost its audience ratings is to have affiliates carry the news program at a later time. As all three networks use the dual-feed arrangement, affiliates have the choice of scheduling network news at an earlier or later time. Since more people are usually watching television in the later time period, the program will probably get a somewhat higher rating if it is shown then, all other things being equal. (The tape is also repeated three hours later, sometimes with a local "up date," in the Pacific Coast time zones.) A network can usually persuade an affiliate to yield the more favorable time period again through some sort of financial compensation.

Since the size of the audience for network news is presumed to be strongly correlated to that of the preceding programs, a third method of improving ratings is to attempt to attract a larger audience to the channel earlier in the day. For example, to increase the ratings of the NBC Evening News in Los Angeles, the third largest market, a vice-president responsible for audience analysis suggested to the president of NBC in March 1968 that the "only sure-fire way" involved putting on the then popular *Mike Douglas Show* at 3:30 in the afternoon, which would increase the audience for the local news, then:

> Coming out of this increased lead-in—and a *news* lead-in at that—I believe that Huntley-Brinkley at 6 P.M. will get a couple of rating points more. . . .

Rather than considering putting more money into the national news program itself, which the vice-president explained to me "would never increase our ratings," the proposed solutions centered on scheduling the Mike Douglas entertainment program (produced independently by Westinghouse Broadcasting Company) two and a half hours before the actual news program.

Similarly, a network can also "invest" in the local news programs in the five stations they own that precede the network news. From a detailed study that it commissioned of the Chicago audience, NBC concluded that local news ratings, unlike network news, which attracts audience only in times of calumnious news, can be increased by the improved weather, sports and local events coverage. The study, for example, recommended that the network hire a more popular local weatherman in Chicago, since "almost as many viewers look forward to seeing the weather as the news itself." Also, to assist affiliates in improving their audience ratings for their local news programs, the networks provide a news syndication service, which supplies subscribing stations with sports and news stories through a half-hour closed-circuit feed, from which the stations can record the particular stories they want and then rebroadcast them as part of their own news programs.

(A more dubious way of attempting to increase ratings of local programs is to advertise heavily in local newspapers the broadcasting of a report on a sensational subject, such as WBBM-TV, the CBS-owned and operated affiliate in Chicago, did in regard to a "pot party" that was specially arranged for the television cameras. A congressional investigation of this incident noted: "The record of the hearings before the special subcommittee indicates that the licensee contrived and staged the filming of Pot Party, so as to enhance its news ratings for the time period involved." Whether or not this conclusion is well-founded, such means of "enhancing" ratings are quite rare, according to network executives.)

Finally, a network can invest in "stars, like Huntley and Brinkley," who can attract a personal following to news programs, which, the NBC News vice-president continued, is in fact what the network did to counteract the "natural lead" CBS derived from its more popular daytime programing. "Our policy has been to put Huntley and Brinkley at the center of every important event from political conventions to space shots so that they would be identified in the public's mind with news events," Reuven Frank explained. "We have a saying around here: Enhance Huntley-Brinkley." At best, however, the star system can only marginally increase audience ratings as selective viewers who change channels for news or personalities comprise only a minor portion of the audience rated by Nielsen. "If David Brinkley moved over to ABC, it might increase their ratings by a [Nielsen] point or two," an NBC executive surmised, "but I doubt it would have much of an effect; they just don't have the affiliates and lead-in to pull a high rating." The NBC executive thus explained the dramatic rise in the ABC

Evening News ratings between 1968 and 1972 almost entirely in terms of two factors: "First of all, they increased their clearances in major cities. Secondly, they increased the lead-ins for network news through a very flashy local news operation in New York and other major cities."

The idea that the audience for network news can best be maintained through investing in "outside factors," as one NBC vice-president put it, has consequences for the news operation.

The Logic of a Network News Operation

While it might make economic sense for a newspaper to invest resources in increased news coverage on the assumption that it would produce exclusive and sensational stories which in turn would lead to a higher newsstand circulation, it does not make economic sense for a network to maintain anything more than the minimum number of camera crews necessary to fill the available news-programing time, if one accepts the prevailing theories about audience. Additional camera crews might well improve the quality of the news coverage, but they would not, at least according to the assumptions of network executives, significantly increase the Nielsen ratings of network news or the advertising revenues derived from it.

The costs for gathering and producing news programing is controlled mainly by the deployment of camera crews and correspondents. Aside from costing about $100,000 a year to maintain in salaries and overtime, each camera crew generates a prodigious amount of film —about twenty times as much as is used in final stories —and this has to be transported, processed, edited and narrated. NBC accountants, in using a rule-of-thumb gauge of $14 in service cost for every foot of film used in the final story (or $504 a minute), have estimated that in 1968 each film crew accounted for about $500,000 annually of the budget of NBC News. In other words, if NBC decided to hire another twenty camera crews, it would add roughly $10 million in salaries, film costs, editorial services, and so forth, to the total budget. Of course, a minimum number of crews is necessary to provide enough news film to fill the networks' news-programing time. But aside from this bare minimum, the actual number of film crews deployed, and their whereabouts, is not only a critical budgetary decision but one which defines the scope of the entire news-gathering operation. "The news you present is actually the news you cover," a network news vice-president said; "the question is how far do you fling your net."

From a journalistic point of view, the more camera crews deployed, the better, since the more news beats and potential happenings that can be covered by camera crews, the greater the chances are to capture the significant news of the day. A large number of film accounts might also lead to a more interesting program, since the producer would have more stories from which to select. But even if it produced a program with greater appeal to viewers, a wide-flung net of camera crews would make little sense from an economic point of view, given the paradox of audience flow, since it is not the appeal of the program that mainly garners the audience.

Answering his own question somewhat circuitously, the vice-president continued: "We use practically everything . . . everything that's done results in practically some use," and added, "There aren't enough crews, so we can only cover the top stories." In other words, the number of crews deployed is expected by network executives to be related to the number of hours of programing rather than the number of possible news events. Reuven Frank noted this as one of the main budgetary controls on the news division: "Like everyone else my indices are money, but my goals aren't money. . . . I'm asked questions [by network executives] like why it is [that] with no increase in total hours [of news programing] the use of film stock is up 15 percent from last year."

In fact, NBC relies mainly on only ten regular camera crews in the five cities where it owns television stations (New York, Chicago, Los Angeles, Washington and Cleveland), and three staff cameramen (who can assemble camera crews) in Boston, Houston and Dallas, to cover the entire country. In 1968, more than 80 percent of all domestic stories shown on the NBC Evening News were produced by the ten NBC camera crews and three staff cameramen. (In comparison, to cover the news of *one* city, Los Angeles, NBC's local news operation used twelve camera crews, according to their news director, to fill local news-programing needs, which ran two hours.) CBS used a similar number of crews—located at its own stations in New York, Chicago and Los Angeles, as well as in Atlanta and Washington—for the bulk of its domestic news stories. ABC, which had considerably less news programing in 1968 because it produced no morning news, was able to get most of its national news stories from eight full-time crews, in New York, Chicago, Los Angeles, Washington, Atlanta and Miami. All three networks also maintained regular camera crews in nine cities overseas, including London, Paris, Bonn, Rome, Tokyo, Saigon and Hong Kong.

To be sure, in the event of a momentous news happening, the networks can quickly mobilize additional crews regularly assigned to news documentaries, sports and local news at network stations, or the camera crews of affiliated stations. But the net which is cast for national news on a day-to-day basis is essentially defined by the ten or so crews that are routinely available for network assignments, a number which proceeds directly from the economic logic of news coverage.

The Logic of Network News Production

Even though the scope of news coverage is not assumed to be important in attracting an audience for network news programs, the appearance of a truly national news service must be projected for two independent reasons. First, affiliates clear network news, it will be recalled, not only for economic reasons but also because it is presumed to be in the "public interest" (as defined by the FCC) to carry national as well as local news. However, if network news were perceived to be no more than local news from a handful of cities, affiliates would have a less compelling reason to yield some of their most valuable time for it, especially when the time could be used for its own news and advertising sales. Second, to hold the maximum possible audience throughout the program, producers work on the theory that each story should have some "national" appeal.

Network news producers thus have the problem of creating the illusion of truly national coverage, a world literally ringed with news cameras, and of "national stories," which are of interest everywhere, with the reality of a minimal number of film crews based in a few cities. To meet this demand, network producers have adopted the strategy of commissioning the national, or trend, stories they need well in advance of the actual happening (very much in the same way that magazines commission timely articles), so that they can attain the maximum use out of the available camera crews. Av Westin summed up this policy in a memorandum to correspondents when he took over as executive producer of the ABC Evening News in 1969: "I am operating on the theory that a producer should be aggressive and 'produce' a broadcast, not waiting for news to happen in order to scramble after it. Anticipating events is most important." For example, he asked correspondents the next week for the "future production" of stories on "medical, consumer, geriatric and pediatric reports, as well as ombudsman reports"—subjects which he subsequently explained to me were "chosen with an eye towards the demographics of the news audience."

Westin also applied the policy of "anticipating events"

to overseas news, explaining it in some detail to correspondents:

> I want to point out to correspondents and Bureaus, particularly overseas, that the same pre-thought which we are engaging in here, before sending a cabled assignment, ought to be exhibited where you are. A specific example. Rote assignments to cover May Day in *every* capital. Unnecessary. They arrive too late for air, and unless there is major news anticipated, I am willing to take the risk and not cover. The off-chance that some "beleaguered" Berliners, Diffident Englishmen, Unemotional Japanese, or War-weary flower children in Saigon will do something is not enough reason to spend your time, Bureau energy, and our money on coverage....
>
> It is possible that in previous years, no one in New York ever expressed these thoughts and since no one ever said "Do Not Cover," the tradition of blanket coverage has grown up. Please consult New York before you assign these "annual" stories. Stringers and crews cost money. And I'd rather spend these funds on having Dunsmore in Beirut, when the Lebanese Government fell [and other stories]. . . . In short, we're spending correspondent's time and crew resources where it counts, and not for some two-day late electronic feed. I am not trying to usurp correspondent's prerogatives to assign coverage of news stories in their areas, but I am suggesting a re-evaluation of judgments based on the criteria now operative on the evening news.

This strategy of preselecting stories was well adumbrated for network news by Reuven Frank, who wrote in 1963 when NBC expanded the evening news from fifteen minutes to a half-hour:

> The picture of the producer frustrated at what he has to leave out is less accurate than the picture of the producer canvassing the nooks and crannies of the cutting room for 45 seconds more [film]. We cannot do the same for fifteen more minutes. . . . Except for those rare days when other material becomes avail-

able, the gap will be filled by planned and prepared film stories, and we are assuming the availability of two each night.

The deficit in day-to-day news coverage can thus be compensated for by producers anticipating and "producing" the desirable stories, which would be free of daily news contingencies. "We simply couldn't find the type stories we need for balance and pacing," an NBC producer pointed out, "if we had to rely on the news film that comes from general coverage every day." To implement this strategy, the CBS Evening News divided the responsibility between two producers. One is in charge of daily news stories; the other is responsible for commissioning and developing film stories, called "enterprise pieces" or "magazine stories," for future use. The latter explained that "local news, which has much less area to cover, can set up a camera at City Hall, and whatever it records is shown that night. We have the whole country to cover, and we can't just set up cameras and wait for news to happen somewhere. We have to plan it out in advance." For example, the Charles Kuralt "On the Road" series he produces "covers the nostalgia of small-town life in America" which "could never be found in day-to-day news coverage."

However necessary it may be to project an image of a national news service, the process by which the networks "produce news" involves more than simply "mirroring" news events: decisions must be made about which stories will be "anticipated" and sought out.

The Geography of News

The quest of attaining the appearance of truly national news programs is further complicated by the simple but intriguing fact that it costs a good deal more to transmit stories from some places than it does from others.

While the fixed costs and overhead of the news operation, such as salaries of camera crews, correspondents and executives, are subsumed in the general budget of the news division at each network, the more incremental costs that news programs add to the general overhead are charged directly against their budgets. At the beginning of each year, the network allocates each news program a budget to which the producer is expected to conform (unless it is subsequently adjusted because of extraordinary events, such as the invasion of Czechoslovakia in 1968). The single most flexible item, and one which comprises from 30 to 40 percent of the total program's budget, is the outlay for transmitting stories over telephone cables from "remote" locations—that is, any place outside the networks' facilities in New York and Washington—to the networks' broadcasting centers in New York City. The closed-circuit lines that interconnect networks with their affiliates across the country normally can only be used to transmit programs in one direction: from the network's nerve center in New York to affiliates. Therefore, to transmit news reports electronically from any "remote" location to the network for rebroadcast, a news program must order special "long lines," or closed-circuit connection, between the two points from the American Telephone & Telegraph Company. In 1969 the charge for the "remote" was $1.60 per mile for up to an hour's use of the long lines, and from $800 to $1,500 for the "loop," which is what the package of electronic equipment that connects the transmission point (usually an affiliated station) with the AT&T's long lines is called. Such costs make a considerable dent in the producers' budgets.

Although the NBC Evening News had a total budget of about $160,000 a week in 1969, and the CBS Evening News one of about $100,000 a week for seven nightly half-hour programs, most of the budget was actually committed in advance for the salaries and expenses of the producers, editors, writers, and other members of the unit, and for the studio and other overhead costs which were automatically billed to the program. (The difference in these accounting charges is responsible for most of the difference in the budgets of the NBC and CBS Evening News.) Only about $49,000 a week, or $7,000 a program, was left over in the budget for "remotes." Since a news program needs six to eight film stories a night, and some remote charges can be as high as $5,000 apiece, the budget in effect limits the number of "remote" stories that can be transmitted each week or month. Indeed, as Fred W. Friendly, former president of CBS News, wrote: "The cost of long lines is so high that often television fails to take advantage of one of its greatest assets."

In weighing the value of individual stories against the costs of transporting them to New York, producers must consider such questions as: Is the story a "mandatory" one, which will be on competing programs (and thus seen by both network and affiliate executives who "use the competition as a scorecard")? Can the story be delayed and the film shipped by airplane (which might involve a few days if the film is from Vietnam), without "dating" the material? Is the program running ahead or behind its budgetary schedule?

While mandatory stories—those stories of moment in all the headlines—are rarely eliminated from the program, "optional" stories, which are defined by one producer as "stories which will never be missed" by the executives or the audience, are not infrequently dropped to save the long-line costs, especially when the budget is "running tight." For example, when an NBC executive unexpectedly inquired why a news story about the unveiling of a new Boeing 707 passenger plane was not carried on the NBC Evening News, a producer replied, "I just didn't think it was worth four thousand dollars [for a long line] to go to Seattle." He later explained to me that the unveiling would probably have been included on the program if it had occurred in New York City instead of Seattle. The budget officer added that "there were enough other good stories to choose from without ordering a spe-

cial [long line] to Seattle when we are running over
budget."

While news stories from some cities like Seattle are
relatively expensive for network news programs to obtain, news stories from a few cities are "free" (at least
in terms of the bookkeeping charges) because they can
be fed to New York over permanently leased network
cables that connect Chicago and Washington, as well as
cities en route, to New York, during the hour between
5:30 and 6:30 P.M. EST when these closed-circuit lines
are not otherwise being used by the network to transmit
programs to affiliates. Thus at NBC a news story can be
fed from Chicago during this time period over the "round
robin," as the circuit is called, at no cost to the program's
budget, and to get stories from points farther west, a producer need only pay out of his budget for a special long
line from the remote location to Chicago (or Washington,
or any other point on the round robin), from where it can
be relayed to New York "free." Furthermore, the networks themselves maintain permanent loops connecting
stations they themselves own to the AT&T transmission
point, which means that network news programs can
send stories from these stations without having the cost
of renting loops from the telephone company charged
against their budget. This leads to some sharp variations
in the cost of obtaining news in different parts of the
country.

Because of these cost differences, producers have a
positive incentive to take news stories, at least "nonman-
datory" ones, from some cities rather than others, especially if their budget is strained for other reasons. The
fact that networks base most of their camera crews and
correspondents in New York, Washington, Chicago and
Los Angeles further reinforces the advantage of using
news stories from these cities, as will be discussed in
the next chapter. So it is not surprising that most of
the film stories shown on the national news originate
from these cities, according to an analysis of film logs

in 1968–1969. Although the geographical distribution of film stories varies greatly from day to day, over any sustained period of time it leans in the direction of these few large cities. This also means that certain types of stories that occur in these areas are more likely to be covered by network news. For example, the business manager of NBC news pointed out that "civil rights is very expensive" to cover in the South because it is an "out-of-town story," meaning that loops and long lines had to be installed.

On the other hand, covering confrontations between black militants and police in cities connected by the round robin is much less expensive for network news. It is therefore economically more efficient to consign news of small town America and remote cities to such timeless features as the CBS series "On the Road with Charles Kuralt." This suggests that if network news tends to focus on the problems of a few large urban centers, it is not because, as Vice-President Agnew argued, that an "enclosed fraternity" of "commentators and producers live and work in the geographical and intellectual confines of Washington, D.C., or New York City" and "draw their political and social views from the same sources," but because the fundamental economic structure compels producers to select a large share of their film stories from a few locations.

The high cost of transmitting stories electronically also affects the distribution of stories over time as well as space. Since none of the network news programs are given sufficient budgetary allocations to transmit film stories regularly back to New York from overseas bureaus by satellite relays, all but momentous foreign news stories must be shipped back by airplane, which means that they seldom can be shown to an American audience on the day they happen. Because of the almost certain delay on foreign news, producers are virtually compelled to commission timeless stories from overseas bureaus, especially ones that can easily be "pegged" to likely future news bulletins. And if the satellite costs are to be avoided, stories that are tied to a definite news happening, such as a battle in Vietnam or civil disturbance in some country, must be detached from the dated event and re-cast, through editing and narration, in vaguer terms. For example, NBC News obtained "excellent footage" from the BBC of a riot that flared up between Protestants and Catholics in Northern Ireland in late September 1968, but since there was not time to ship the film to New York by plane while the event was still in the headlines, the pro-ducer of the Evening News requested his London bureau to do a "backgrounder" on the confrontation in which the BBC film could be used. The next week an NBC film crew went to Londonderry and shot footage of boarded-up windows, riot damage and a protest march, which was edited together as "a civil rights story," ending with, as the script describes it, "various shots of cops and kids sitting down in the street" and the narrator concluding: "Still, youth may break down the cruel walls separating Ulster's two communities." Since the story described a general phenomena (youth resolving conflict), rather than a specific one (that is, a riot in Londonderry), it could be shown more than a month later without appear-ing to be dated.

Moreover, Fred Friendly claims that the "excessive charges" for relaying stories electronically back to New York substantially "discourage competition and are re-sponsible for the networks' use of the 'pool' system on space stories and other big news events." Confronted with an extraordinary news event overseas, such as a President's visit to Europe, which is expected to be broadcast on the same day as it occurs, a network pro-ducer can defray part of the expense of sending the story via satellite by entering into a "pool" with one or both of the other networks. The programs in the pool get the same footage, though they may edit it differently, but divide the satellite charges between themselves. President Nixon's trip to Europe in 1968 was handled this way. Occasionally a pool arrangement can also make a satellite transmission unnecessary, since it guarantees that a story will not be shown first by a competing network, and thus can be shipped by plane. For instance, when the Soviet press agency Tass made film available in March 1969 depicting the fighting between Soviet and Chinese troops on the Ussabi River frontier in the Far East, an NBC producer called his counterparts at CBS and ABC and arranged a pool for the film, which CBS at least up to that time was considering relaying back to New York by satellite. But the pool made such an expenditure unnecessary, since the film would not be shown on any other network before CBS had access to it, and it was shipped back by airplane and shown the next day. However, such arrangements tend to be relatively infrequent, if only because there are not many stories from overseas that producers consider to be worth the cost of covering as a major event.

To be sure, one can find sufficient incidents in which network news covered costly events that could have been avoided without any repercussions in terms of a diminished audience or executive disapproval to make it clear that news decisions cannot be entirely explained in terms of weighing immediate costs, benefits and budgetary pressures. The argument given here is not, however, that individual news decisions are made with a budget in hand, but that the economic logic—which effectively denies that any benefits in revenue will come from an increase in the quality of the news content of newscasts, yet at the same time demands that the illusion of national coverage be maintained—affects the news operation in very fundamental ways.

A different sort of economic interpretation of network news, suggested by Nicholas Johnson, FCC commissioner and frequent critic of television, is that advertisers apply pressure to news programs to withhold information that might deprecate their products or undercut their corporate policies. The immediate problem with such an analysis is that the evidence presented in Commissioner

Johnson's book *How to Talk Back to Your Television Set* was refuted by the president of CBS News, Richard Salant, who published an itemized and impressive list of newscasts on subjects which Johnson suggested would not be aired on television. Moreover, none of the hundreds of correspondents and production personnel I interviewed could give any examples of a sponsor interfering in regular network news broadcasts—though such suspicions were voiced in the case of news documentaries, special events and local news. Nor have any outside observers of the process of assembling network newscasts reported any such interference to my knowledge. This does not mean that sponsors do not at times intervene through executives at the network level; for instance, in his book, *Due to Circumstances Beyond Our Control*, Fred Friendly reported that as a condition of sponsoring a segment of the CBS Evening News, a major advertiser demanded that that segment be devoted to sports or other soft news. It simply means that such sponsor influence, if it exists at all, is not obvious to those engaged in putting together news programs. Aside from the empirical evidence that Salant could gather, demonstrating that a number of news reports directly conflicted with the interests of major network sponsors, the fact is that time on the regular news broadcasts is now sold, rather than to any one sponsor, in one-minute or thirty-second spots. According to advertising agency executives, advertisers generally buy these as part of a general plan to reach a large share of the audience at the minimum cost. Again according to advertising agency executives, this situation does not afford the advertiser any control of the content of the programs in which their "spots" appear.

Unscheduled News

Whereas regular news programming tends to be profitable for networks, since it adds valuable time to the advertising schedules and involves only a problem of controlling production costs, unscheduled news, which displaces regular network programing, presents an entirely different set of problems that brings the news divisions into conflict with other network values.

Although news executives at any of the three networks generally describe, at least to an outsider, the news division as being "autonomous" from the rest of the network, in a number of important respects it must operate within the economic matrix of the networks. For one thing, news divisions are not financially independent. The revenues from the sale of commercial time on news programs is returned directly to the network, and it allocates funds to the news division. Julian Goodman, the president of NBC, explained the relation between network and news division to an interviewer as follows:

> Reuven [Frank] isn't the head of a profit center, but he does have his own allocated budget. He knows what he can spend in a year, including what he has for contingencies. All the [network] divisions are equal—News isn't a supplicant to the television network—and if Reuven and the network have opposing points of view, I decide. He reports to me. And since his division is the equivalent of the others, he's budgeted like the others. We meet quarterly and he tells me what he needs for whatever is upcoming— say X million dollars for the primary and elections. . . . I say "Try to stay within the budget," and if he doesn't I determine whether I think it's worth the money.

The news divisions of CBS and ABC have similar budgetary constraints.

An even more important allocation than money for network news is time in the networks' schedules. When confronted with an extraordinary flow of news, newspapers can add extra pages without sacrificing advertising space or revenues. But network news is not in an analogous situation, as Richard Jencks, former president of the

CBS Broadcasting Group (under which both the network and news division operate) explains: "They [the news division] always want to do more news—but while a newspaper or magazine can expand an issue if it wants to do more news, we can't; we can only expand news at the expense of some other value." In other words, since there are only a limited number of broadcasting hours in the networks' schedules, other programing, as well as the advertisements it carries, must be canceled to make room for additional news. "The power to pre-empt is the power to destroy," Reuven Frank explained to me. "The president of a news division simply can't be given the right to unilaterally pre-empt the programs of the network and destroy its revenues; that must ultimately be a network decision." Frank added that in practice he is seldom "turned down by Goodman" when he requests the pre-emption of an entertainment program for an extraordinary news broadcast, and most other news executives take this position. But if, in fact, news executives are rarely "turned down" in such requests, it may be simply because they are aware of a basic economic situation which makes some types of programs extremely costly to pre-empt and other types profitable—or at least much less costly—rather than because they are "autonomous."

In theory, when a program is pre-empted the advertisements scheduled for it are not shown; consequently the network is not paid for the time and incurs a dead loss. Hence it is assumed by many knowledgeable people, even critics of television, that the networks lose millions of dollars covering momentous events, as network public relations executives claim. In fact, however, according to both network and advertising agency executives, rather than asking for their money back if a program is pre-empted, the advertising agencies almost always grant the networks a "make-good" on the commercial minutes pre-empted. A "make-good" requires that the network reschedule the commercial time lost in an "equivalent time period" at a later date.

Advertising agencies are customarily flexible in interpreting what is an "equivalent time period," since if the advertisement is actually canceled and not "made good," they lose the 15 percent rebate from the network on the advertisement (their only source of income, since clients don't themselves pay their advertising agencies), after having done all the work on it. To the contrary, according to a network vice-president, even if a network has a full schedule toward the end of the year, advertising agencies have been known "to tell us to say that we ran their minutes this year, so they can get their rebate, and run them next year or whenever we want." Moreover, he continued, if an advertiser "tells his agency in advance that he wants his money back if his time is pre-empted, the agency puts an asterisk next to that minute on the schedule they send to us and we avoid pre-empting it, if we have any choice." In short, advertising agencies have a vested interest in allowing networks to "make good" on pre-empted commercial time at their own convenience.

As long as a network has some slack in its schedule—that is, unsold time where an extra commercial can be "squeezed in" (the limits on the number of commercials an hour, it will be recalled, are not legal restrictions but a self-enforced code which can be shaded at times), pre-emptions do not necessarily cost the networks any loss of revenue. Past this point, of course, every minute of commercial time deleted represents a dead loss.

The profitability of pre-emptions depends not only on the amount of slack in the schedule but also on what program is pre-empted. If a filmed series is pre-empted, the network can save the production costs by canceling a later segment in the series, yet eventually earn the advertising revenues through a "make-good." "Suppose we pre-empt *Adam-12* for a speech by the President," an NBC vice-president explained to me. "It's a money loser, anyhow; we simply cancel the last chapter in the series, which we have a right to do, save ninety thousand dollars in production costs, and move the three minutes of commercials, at thirty thousand dollars a minute, to some unsalable spot. We don't have to pay the stations any compensation for carrying [an unsponsored] presidential speech, and we've made a clear profit."

On the other hand, if a live program is pre-empted in which the production costs cannot be recouped, such as a daytime soap opera, or a rerun of a series the network already owns, there are no savings, except for the residual fees that otherwise would be paid performers on these programs. Moreover, executives point out, while there may be slack on the daytime or early-evening schedule, when a program is canceled in a time period for which advertisers pay a "premium rate" (say, a football game or a popular program in prime time), it is much more difficult, if in fact possible at all, to find acceptable "equivalent time" in the schedule.

To be sure, the news broadcast which replaces a pre-empted program may involve substantial production costs for the network (though in some cases, such as a presidential speech or news conference, it involves little additional costs). For momentous news happenings it may be necessary to rent additional video-camera units for live coverage, to order special long lines directly to the event from AT&T and to pay employees overtime. But these figures can also be grossly inflated by bookkeeping charges. For example, although NBC estimated that it cost $800,000 to cover the shooting, hospitalization and funeral of Robert F. Kennedy in 1968, at least $500,000 of this sum was for the salaries of correspondents, news crews and technicians already employed on an annual basis by NBC, and for "general overhead," which would have been the same in any circumstances, according to one NBC vice-president. In other words, the real cost to the network was less than $300,000 for three days of news programing. Entertainment programing can easily cost $200,000 an hour, so, as a network vice-president pointed out, "We didn't exactly lose any money on the [Kennedy] funeral train." He explained that most, if not all, of the pre-empted commercial time was "made good" at later dates without unduly interfering with the network's sales schedule, and hundreds of thousands of dollars were saved in production costs by canceling future segments of filmed series. As the president of NBC frankly said, when asked about the cost of the news operation, "When you total up what was spent and what you get back, it isn't truly an expensive way of doing business. We don't throw money away profligately."

The Resignation of Fred W. Friendly: The Question of Autonomy

The way that these economic considerations define the rules of the game for network news executives can be derived from the dramatic account Fred W. Friendly has given of his resignation as president of CBS News in 1966. Since it illustrates, albeit inadvertently, the limits of the concept of the "autonomy" of network news, it is worth considering in some detail.

In January 1966 the Senate Foreign Relations Committee held open hearings on a supplementary appropriations bill to fund the war in Vietnam, and its chairman, Senator J. William Fulbright, permitted a pool television camera to cover the hearings for all three networks. The networks could either show the proceedings live or use edited portions of them on their regular news programs. During the first week of the hearings, when Secretary of State Dean Rusk testified, none of the networks elected to broadcast the event live. However, on February 3 Friendly learned from the CBS Washington bureau chief, William Small, that NBC planned to pre-empt regular programing to televise the testimony of David Bell, administrator of the Agency for International Development, the next day, beginning at 8:30 A.M.

As Friendly fully realized, NBC could pre-empt network programs in the morning much more easily than CBS. Since CBS's programing drew the lion's share of the morning audience at the time, its advertising rates were more than twice those of NBC; moreover, unlike NBC, most of its late-morning advertising schedule was sold out. (In fact, according to an NBC executive, since NBC was then losing money on its morning programing, it was actually "profitable to pre-empt money losers" for news.) CBS, on the other hand, would have to displace highly profitable programs, which were for the most part network-owned reruns; canceling them would not result in any savings in production costs.

Despite the unfavorable economics of the situation, Friendly called John Reynolds, the CBS Broadcasting Group vice-president, under whose jurisdiction the news division operated, and asked permission to pre-empt a half-hour or more of programs to broadcast the Fulbright hearings live. According to Friendly, Reynolds replied that he should use his own judgment but "Try to keep it to a half-hour if you can." This suggestion was based on the fact that during the first half-hour, from 8:30 to 9 A.M., only a minimal number of television sets are in use, and that the period earns only $3,000 in advertising revenues; however, these rise rapidly until they reach $30,000 a half-hour by noon. (By contrast, NBC could simply integrate the first half-hour into its morning news program, the *Today* show, and then pre-empt programs carrying much less advertising, from $2,000 to $12,000 per half-hour.)

As the questioning of Bell by the members of the Senate committee continued throughout the morning, Friendly decided that the testimony was "too important" to cut off, and despite persistent calls from network executives advising him of the cost of the pre-emptions, he continued live broadcasts of the hearing. In the afternoon NBC returned to its regular entertainment programming, which then commanded a much higher share of the audience, but Friendly tenaciously maintained his coverage of Bell's testimony, forcing the network to cancel live game shows and soap operas from which it could not recoup production costs. "At the end of the day," Friendly notes, "I was told that we had cost the television network some $175,000 in lost revenue (though I believe much of this money was recaptured in 'make-goods' at later dates)."

Nevertheless, Friendly considered the coverage to be a "splendid job," and informed Frank Stanton, who seemed to be considerably less enthusiastic about it, that he would also like to televise the scheduled testimony of Lieutenant General James Gavin. A few days later, on February 8, Stanton explicitly warned Friendly of the dangers of "getting 'boxed in,' as we had with Bell's testimony," and further asked him to consider seriously "the financial damage that another all-day session" would cause the network. Though Friendly said he "would monitor the hearing closely and use no more air time than necessary," Stanton refused to authorize the pre-emption, and asked him to discuss it further with John A. Schneider, then the executive vice-president of CBS Broadcasting.

Unable to get a "clear-cut answer" from Schneider, Friendly went over Schneider's head and again asked Stanton for permission to pre-empt time for the hearings. Instead, Stanton suggested that the Gavin testimony be edited into a special report and shown in place of another CBS news documentary scheduled for the night of Gavin's appearance. Friendly, however, persisted in his demands for live coverage, and finally assumed that what he "considered reluctant permission to go ahead" was given by Stanton. Another full day of CBS's schedule was thus pre-empted at a cost, Friendly was later told, of another $175,000, though he considered it "brilliant television."

When Friendly asked Stanton for permission to televise the testimony of George F. Kennan, he was told in no uncertain terms that henceforth Schneider would be the "decision-maker" on what programs would be pre-empted for news. Friendly then sent a memorandum to Schneider requesting that the testimony of Kennan, as well as that of General Maxwell Taylor and a further appearance by Secretary of State Rusk, be carried live instead of the regular programing on those three days.

As he might have expected, Friendly was turned down flatly. Schneider called him and said, "We are not going to carry the Kennan hearings," giving as his reasons the high costs of pre-emptions, the fact that most opinion leaders were not at home in the daytime, and that the audience, primarily housewives, was not interested in the hearings. (Less than half of the CBS affiliates cleared the Gavin or Bell hearings, a CBS executive subsequently told me.)

"Jack, I find this situation untenable," Friendly replied. "You are making a news judgment but basing it on business criteria, and I can't do this job under these circumstances. . . ." After Stanton refused to intervene, Friendly resigned.

The issue at stake was not, however, as Friendly suggests in the letter of resignation he released to the press, "the concept of an autonomous news organization." For Friendly himself, in explaining "why we had cut back on unlimited space coverage," wrote: "Certainly CBS News knew it could never have an open-end claim on air time with no constraints." The constraints were not only on network time. During his two-year tenure as president of the news division, Friendly took considerable pride in keeping news-gathering expenditures in line with the budget allocated by the network; in this respect he even cites his own "remarkable record in numbers." Moreover, he notes, the scheduling of news programs was controlled by the network, not the news division: "If *I Love Lucy* reruns meant an increase in the ratings over the CBS morning news at 10," he notes, "then the news was moved to 7:05 A.M."

Friendly also gives sufficient examples in his book to cast doubt on the notion that the news division was ever completely autonomous from the network, even in matters concerning the content of news programing. To wit: Concerning the incident in which Walter Cronkite was replaced as the anchorman in the 1964 political conventions, he writes: "When my superiors suggested that we replace Cronkite with a new team, Roger Mudd and Bob Trout, it struck me as a debatable solution [to the problem of competing in audience ratings with NBC] . . . At subsequent meetings I realized that it was not so much a suggestion as a command." While in response to a request by network sales executives to conclude the "CBS Evening News with Walter Cronkite" (which had a total of twenty-three minutes of news time in it) with a five-minute "sports package," because an automobile manufacturer wanted to buy commercial time on a sports, or "soft-news," feature, Friendly reluctantly agreed "to try to program the last five minutes of Cronkite with so-called 'back-of-the-book' news, which would include sports when the story warranted it," though he "refused to hire a sports announcer to do it." (However, Heywood Hale Broun, the sports reporter, then began doing frequent sports stories on the program.) Finally, when network executives objected to some portions of a news documentary on student unrest at the Berkeley campus of the University of California, Friendly noted: ". . . I ordered many changes in the final editing of 'The Berkeley Rebels' and removed some of the cinema techniques to which the mangement objected."

Nor did the fact that Schneider, who was Stanton's vice-president and executive officer, was the "decision-maker" rather than Stanton himself have any real bearing on the question of an autonomous news division—though it may well have made Friendly's personal position at CBS untenable. Indeed, he states:

Never for a moment have I believed that the decision not to televise the Kennan hearings was Schneider's alone . . . The system had made the decision; Schneider was merely in charge of the stop light. He would not always say no, but when that answer had to be given for financial reasons, he would be the villain to the news division, the press and the public.

Thus Schneider, as Friendly told me, was simply "standing in for Stanton" and making the decisions the "system dictated." Therefore the contention that Schneider made a "news judgment" on "business criteria" begs the question. How can network executives allocate the scarce resources, as Salant put it, other than by asking, "Is the story worth it?" To some extent, even news executives must rely on business criteria in making news judgments. For example, Friendly notes that CBS News did not broadcast live the speech by Ambassador Arthur Goldberg on the war in Vietnam in 1965 because "my colleagues [in the news division, operating under *his* authority] were so conditioned not to spend the $80,000 per half-day it costs to throw the switch that the courage of their news convictions failed them." More to the point, Friendly himself decided not to televise the UN debates, "when faced with the costs of all-day coverage." Schneider's decision, it would seem, was based on precisely the same logic.

In any case, a "news judgment" could not have been made on the basis of the news by Friendly, Schneider or anyone else, since the decision had to be made before there actually *was* any news—that is, before Kennan testified. Friendly had a purpose that went beyond reporting whatever "news" Kennan's testimony might contain. Revealingly, he told Stanton, "I want to use television to illuminate, to stimulate debates. The fact that we are on during the day with hearings that may bore some housewives will alert the nation that broadcasting isn't doing business as usual." In other words, interrupting regular programs was in itself the message —not what might be said at the hearings.

What was really in dispute was not the preservation of an autonomy that never existed, but the basic concept that network news was an integral part of the network, operating under a set of rules and constraints imposed by executives with an overview of the network's problems. After adhering to these ground rules up until the

Fulbright hearings, Friendly suddenly challenged them. Instead of pre-empting unprofitable time, he insisted on eliminating the entire daytime schedule. Instead of restricting the number of hours of pre-emptions to the amount of slack in the schedule, he demanded as much time as the hearings might take, even though this would mean unrecoverable losses for the network. "He broke all the rules," a CBS former vice-president commented.

When Stanton suggested that "the testimony could be best handled in the form of a succinct summary and important excerpts in later news and special broadcasts," he was expressing the basic premise of network news. The principal assumptions are: 1) news is *not* perishable and therefore it can be delayed on film until a regularly scheduled broadcast without losing any of its immediacy; 2) no matter how many hours it lasts, a news event can be encapsulated into a five-minute segment on a news program, without any loss of vital information; and 3) a news report can be edited or expurgated without distorting it in any way.

In demanding that the Kennan testimony be presented live, unexpurgated and unedited, Friendly was undermining all these assumptions. If the important testimony could not be adequately summarized on the evening news program, how could it be reasonably maintained that the testimony of other important public figures before other congressional committees could be so summarized? To present news events in their entirety, whenever they occurred, would involve a radically different concept of television programing, one in which the entertainment schedule would be contingent on the news of the day—as interpreted by the news division. Obviously, under the existing system of advertiser-supported television, this was not a change that a network could accept or implement. Whether for quixotic or pragmatic reasons, Friendly demonstrated, therefore, that even the president of a network news division cannot consistently buck the economic logic under which the network operates and survive.

The Channeling of Unexpected News

Confronted with the general unpredictability of news developments, which can happen at any time and persist for indeterminate periods, and with the more or less predictable value of the different periods of time in the networks' schedules, the most rational way of handling news developments economically is simply to route them to the parts of the schedule in which they displace the least profitable programing.

Most news can easily be channeled into regular news programs, but when extraordinary events demand special coverage, network executives must decide, as Reuven Frank explained to me, "what commercial time to kick out of the schedule." The decision at all three networks is predicated on the relative value of different time periods. "Every month the finance people prepare a schedule for [Julian] Goodman—it shows all the programs and a number for each," an NBC vice-president explained. "That figure is the pre-emption cost to the network. He carries it around in his pocket. So the decision to pre-empt isn't made without an awareness of how much revenue will be affected." At CBS, Friendly followed the same procedure: "I always carried in my pocket a weekly summary of the network's schedule which pinpointed its 'soft' rating spots; in an emergency these could be pre-empted for news extras or specials." A time period may be "soft" because of the relatively low number of television sets in use at that hour, or because of the popularity of programs on competing networks, or because of a combination of these factors. "The trick is to fill time that isn't worth anything anyhow with news," an NBC executive explained.

Unlike Friendly's approach, the pre-emption of network time for President Nixon's trip to Europe in February 1969 is a case which illustrates that unexpected news can be dealt with in an economically compatible way. The President's communications aide, Herbert Klein, informed the networks that the President's first trip to Europe was to be a major event, and the networks would be expected to give it special coverage. This meant pre-empting time, but at ABC, rather than displacing prime-time programs, Julian Goodman came up with the "very efficient idea" of expanding the NBC Evening News from a half-hour to an hour during the week of the President's trip and using the additional time for the requisite special coverage. Since the extra half-hour of network news—including five additional minutes of commercials—would displace local news programs rather than network programing, affiliates had the Hobson's choice of refusing to clear the President's activities or of giving up local programing time. (Affiliates were, however, allowed to sell the commercial time on the extra half-hour in lieu of network compensation.) The balance of the coverage was "routed" into a one-hour news special presented in a "soft spot" on the Sunday evening of the President's return. Thus very little, if any, network time was lost. The president of CBS News commented to an interviewer:

> NBC confined itself to 6:30–7:30—which was a hell of a good idea, and if I thought we could get away with it we might have done it . . . When you take away from 6:30–7 P.M. [as NBC did] you're taking away the affiliates' most valuable time, when they do their most important job. And there's also the thing called sweep week—there are two weeks each year when the local stations are rated [for audience]—this past week was such a week and it was felt by the network and group vice president that to tear out of an affiliate's schedule its local news . . . would be unfair.

The solution that CBS found, one of its news vice-presidents explained, was to digest its coverage into a series of half-hour news specials, most of which were presented in "soft spots," generally from 11:30 to midnight, which was not network time.

Rather than open-ended coverage of extraordinary

events, the networks have recently tended to use the "news special" format, which not only "locks" unscheduled news into a definite time period, but can also be sold in advance to sponsors who want to identify their product with momentous news happenings. NBC initiated the concept of sponsored and "pre-packaged" news specials with the Gulf Oil Company, according to a former executive who helped arrange the deal. For its part, Gulf, which was seeking "a stronger identification with public service," agreed to pay NBC for the network time preempted, though not for the programing costs, on any of the news specials it accepted. In return, NBC displayed the corporate symbol of Gulf on the commentator's desk during the news report, and inserted Gulf commercials, supplied in advance, at "convenient breaks." CBS made a similar "instant sponsorship" arrangement with the Western Electric Company, a subsidiary of AT&T, except that it did not allow the company's symbol to be displayed during the program. The purpose of the news special, an NBC executive suggested, is "to turn unscheduled news into scheduled news."

The News Documentary

Although the news documentary, which is produced over a longer period of time than news specials—usually months rather than days—may serve the journalistic functions of "providing greater depth in news coverage," as one network commentator suggested, it also serves the economic function of allowing networks to substitute relatively inexpensive news programing for unprofitable entertainment programs in the more-difficult-to-sell portions of the networks' schedule. For example, during the early 1960s, when the CBS program *Gunsmoke* garnered the lion's share of the Saturday night audience, NBC could sell time opposite it to advertisers only at greatly reduced prices. To fill this ineradicable soft spot, Reuven

Frank explained, "Kintner hit on the brilliant idea of counter-programing news documentaries against *Gunsmoke*. If advertisers didn't buy time on them, we could avoid paying compensation to the affiliates; and in any case, they were cheaper to produce than entertainment programs."

Frank further observed that "the prime-time documentary was invented so that we could stay on the air at the least possible cost when we had only a very small share of the audience." Although the budgets for a news documentary usually sound impressive, ranging from $60,000 to $150,000 for a one-hour program, a substantial part of the budget is actually only bookkeeping charges for studio space, office overhead, correspondents, camera crews and other network facilities which are part of the networks' fixed costs and would otherwise not be fully utilized. In fact, Fred Friendly estimated that almost half of the expenditures charged against the news division for the coverage of a space shot were directly "traceable to the excessively high prices the television network charged us" for the use of network facilities. The out-of-pocket expenses of an NBC documentary were estimated by an NBC news vice-president to be only 60 percent of the budgeted costs for the program; the remaining 40 percent were internal bookkeeping charges. Even if the higher NBC figure is accepted, the real cost of documentaries to networks—varying between $36,000 and $90,000 an hour—is impressively cheap compared to evening entertainment programs, which cost between $100,000 and $250,000 to acquire.

Selling time on documentaries to advertisers, however, presents a more difficult problem. Unlike entertainment programs—which draw a more or less predictable audience and therefore can be sold to various advertisers on a cost-per-thousand-households-reached basis—news documentaries, which a considerable portion of the regular audience may be expected to switch off, are essentially unpredictable in terms of audience. Therefore, they must generally be pre-sold to sponsors looking primarily for identification with a particular news message, rather than on a businesslike cost-per-thousand basis.

The process of pre-selling news documentaries by the ABC Network to an institutional sponsor, Minnesota Mining and Manufacturing, is described in considerable detail in the trade paper *Variety*:

> About 120 subject ideas are thrown into the pot. The network news division then sifts through that list and comes up with about 30 titles which are ready for submission to sponsor Minnesota Mining (3M) via sales presentations. Each summer the pilgrimage by top ABC news executives to 3M is made, and the company chooses those titles among the 30 in which it is interested. Production then proceeds on the [documentaries] 3M has chosen.

In 1969, for example, thirty proposed ABC news documentaries were divided into three categories: "Concern for Fellow Man," which included such subjects as the American cowboy, American heroines, the Peace Corps, the Teachers Corps, the hospital ship *Hope,* and "Footsteps of Tom Dooley" (concerning the efforts to follow in Dr. Dooley's tradition in Vietnam) ; "Americana," which included such titles as "Smalltown USA" and "The Death of the Iron Horse"; and a miscellaneous category embracing such topics as Medicare, earthquakes, famine, "The Unseen World" (about microscopic life in a pond) and "The Revolution in Sex Education."

In deciding among possible subjects, "a process of self-censorship is at work," *Variety* suggested, since the news executives and documentary producers generally assume that the sponsor prefers "soft subjects" that may be expected to hold a larger proportion of the network's regular audience at that hour than "hard," or controversial, programs, which a large portion of the audience is expected to switch off. Moreover, even if a controversial subject, such as "The Revolution in Sex Education," is presented to the sponsor, it is generally not accepted. In point of fact, Minnesota Mining and Manufacturing picked such titles as "The Westerners" and "The Unseen World," and "The Death of the Iron Horse," which was retitled "The Golden Age of Railroads."

After selecting subjects from the ABC list, *Variety* continued, "the documentary sponsors have kept in close touch during production, and at times have examined rough cuts and seen scripts. Further, the sponsor involvement has on occasion led to alteration of a program's content."

The other two networks pre-sell a smaller proportion of their documentaries to sponsors than does ABC, and consequently have less sponsor involvement with the content of the programs. Nevertheless, as an NBC producer of *White Paper* documentaries pointed out at a colloquium:

> This is a real pressure: to fill the time available with programs that can be sold and that will attract many viewers. This does not mean that the networks won't do programs that can't be sold on subjects that are not popular. It means the network won't do *many* such programs.

Again, many exceptions can be found that are purely journalistic enterprises, but most news documentaries owe their origins to economic considerations: low out-of-pocket production costs, and if not pre-sold, the strong probability that the subject will appeal to sponsors. Unlike regular news programs, news documentaries are usually selected and designed to fit the expectations, if not the demands, of advertisers.

In fine, despite the highly unpredictable and contingent nature of news itself, network news is a much more economically rational and systematic operation than it is generally assumed to be by knowledgeable persons, including even a number of newsmen involved in it. While FCC ground rules and other political imperatives set the minimum level of news programing, as well as certain conditions it must fulfill, it is primarily the economic logic that determines when the news will be scheduled, and thus, to a large extent, what type of audience will see it. This logic also dictates the amount of money and resources that can be used for seeking out, covering and producing news stories, which in turn structures in no small measure the time and space that can be routinely covered. Economics further effectively limit the range of choice of news executives and correspondents in selecting subjects. Where political and economic objectives coincide—as, for example, in the selection of noncontroversial subjects for news documentaries (which simultaneously satisfies the political requisites of the FCC's Fairness Doctrine, clearance by politically concerned affiliates, and the economic requisite of maintaining an audience flow for the benefit of advertisers)—the news strategy is clearly defined for executives.

However, in cases in which the political and economic values conflict, an intermediary strategy must be found which at least minimally meets the political ground rule with the least possible economic loss. For instance, confronted with the demand for prime-time news programing by FCC commissioners and members of influential congressional committees, NBC and CBS each reserved two hours a month in their schedule for prime-time "news magazines"—NBC's *First Tuesday* and CBS's *60 Minutes*. But news programs almost always draw lower audience ratings than entertainment programs—"as sure as queens beat jacks at poker," as one executive put it. According to the vice-president in charge of audience analysis, NBC scheduled its news magazine opposite CBS's so that both major networks would "divide the news audience and both suffer an equal loss of ratings that night" thus maintaining "the rating parity." In one way or another, then, political and economic ground rules (and the logic proceeding from them) shape, structure and confine the process in which newsmen gather and report the news.

Part II

The Selection Process

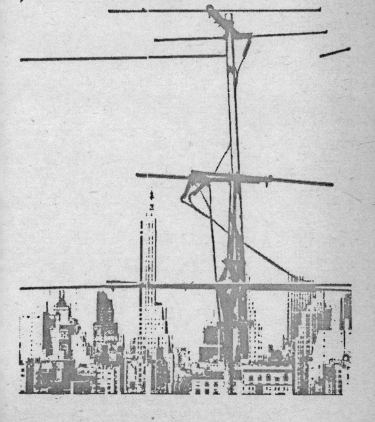

Chapter 4

The Intelligence Function

The desk tells me that Ike is going to look out the window of Walter Reed today for the cameras at 2:30 P.M.

> —*Drew Phillips, national news editor of the NBC Nightly News, advising the producer on future events*

The search for news requires not only a reliable flow of information about events in the immediate past but also advance intelligence about those scheduled for the foreseeable future. Though no doubt a part of any news operation, this latter function is of critical importance to network news. For unlike newspaper and radio news, which literally can put together a news story in a matter of minutes through the expedient of telephone interviews or wire-service dispatches, a network needs usually hours, if not days, of lead time to realize a film story of even a minute's duration. The appropriate camera crew and correspondent must be dispatched to the scene of the event, equipment set up, the story photographed; then the film must be processed, edited, narrated and returned for projection.

In practice, this means network news must usually commit its crews to stories at least six hours before they occur—and considerably longer if they take place in cities in which the networks do not have camera crews readily available. Since the economic logic of network news dictates against operating with more camera crews than is necessary to produce the number of stories required to fill the news programs each day, the available crews must be assigned in a highly efficient manner. This means, in effect, that crews must be dispatched to those happenings which are sure to yield stories, regardless of the vagaries of news developments.

The most common types of such stories are those that are especially planned for the convenience of the news media—press conferences, briefings, interviews and the like—which Daniel J. Boorstin has called "pseudo-events," and which by definition are scheduled well in advance and certain to be "newsworthy," if only in a self-fulfilling sense. Other news events, such as congressional hearings, trials and speeches, though they may not be induced for the sole purpose of creating news, can also be predicted far in advance. In either case, it is this sort of pre-scheduled event which network news seeks out and operates on. "The whole trick in television news is anticipating stories six or more hours before they happen," a network executive explained. The way in which this trick is routinely managed is by means of various procedures for gathering, screening and assigning value to information about future events which, to the degree that they systematically influence the coverage of news, may be considered a basic input of network news.

While each network news division organizes its own search procedures, and may be influenced by individual preferences and styles of reporting on the part of news executives, all network news divisions operate under economic and political structures which impose a similar set of requisites and restraints on them. The search for suitable stories is thus conducted along similar lines, and at all the networks it is based on five organizing principles.

First, network news is centrally assigned. Rather than having leeway to seek out their own stories, correspondents are generally assigned stories selected by an assignment editor in New York (or an editor under his supervision in Washington, Chicago or Los Angeles). This fact of life for network correspondents proceeds from the nature of film stories, where the movements of camera crews, film couriers and equipment must be carefully coordinated with those of the correspondent. As Reuven Frank has noted, television news is, by its very nature, "group journalism." To ease this problem of coordination, all information concerning possible stories, as well as the locations of correspondents and crews, and programing needs, is funneled through the "assignment desk," the focus of the intelligence effort, which is manned by assignment editors on a round-the-clock basis. It is the job of the assignment editor to screen the incoming intelligence, matching available camera crews and correspondents to possible stories, so as to satisfy most closely the needs of the producers for the particular type of stories they require for their particular news programs. In preparing the line-up of stories each morning, generally before 8 A.M., the assignment desk more or less fixes the agenda of available news stories for the producers. This policy not only lessens the possibility of a film crew being wasted by covering an event that is not suited for a news program but also allows news executives "to exercise firm control, and take responsibility for, news coverage," as one NBC News vice-president explained.

Second, rather than maintaining regular "beats" where correspondents stay in contact with the same set of news makers over an extended period of time, network news coverage is ad hoc. Correspondents are shunted from story to story, depending on their availability, logistical convenience and producer's preferences, after the event is selected for news coverage by the assignment editor.

Often a correspondent may be assigned to five different subjects in five different cities in a single week, each assignment lasting only as long as it takes to film the story. To be sure, there are a number of more or less conventional beats in Washington, such as the White House, but these are the exceptions rather than the rule. Quite simply, the alternative of permanent assignments, or beats, would not satisfy the networks' basic problem of creating "national" news; since network news, unlike local news media, is expected to cover the nation, if not the entire world, hundreds of camera crews would be needed to cover even the most prominent sources of potential news. Yet networks need only a limited number of stories—usually no more than a dozen or so—to fill programing requirements. Inevitably, in a beat system, most of the camera crews' film could not be used and would represent a waste of resources. "It would be important to be able to have a beat system," one NBC vice-president observed, "but you can't unless you have a spare camera crew." Spare camera crews obviously cannot be economically justified, since this would entail increased costs without any compensatory gain in advertising revenues.

Third, network news relies mainly on the general correspondent, who can be expected to cover any subject he is assigned to with equal facility, rather than specialists who are expert in a single field. Even in the cases where networks do employ specialists, such as sports and space exploration, better-known general correspondents may be called on to report a major story in their field. The "generalist" is not expected to be a jack-of-all-trades, but simply to be able to apply general rules of fair inquiry to any subject.

In part, the preference for generalists over specialists is based on audience considerations. Since the news audience has fewer years of formal education than the population at large, according to previously cited network studies, it is presumed by most of the network executives interviewed that a generalist who, like most of the audience, is an outsider to a subject, will make it more interesting and comprehensible for most viewers. Indeed, Reuven Frank went so far as to define news as "change seen by an outsider in behalf of other outsiders," noting that "these are the people the reporter reports for, the viewers, the hearers. . . . an insider in one situation is an outsider in all others, and in those outside situations the news he gets is about as much as he wants or is interested in. Otherwise, we should not stay in business." In one specific application of this precept, Frank, rejecting a suggestion put forth by Roger W. Wilkins, director of the Community Relations Service of the Department of Justice, that networks should use correspondents with special knowledge of ghetto problems to cover racial disturbances, noted: "Any good journalist should be able to cover a riot in an unfamiliar setting . . . a veneer of knowledgeability in a situation like this could be less than useless."

Network executives also tend to prefer generalists on the grounds that they are less likely "to become involved in a story to the point of advocacy," as one NBC vice-president suggested. Specialists, it is feared, because of their intimate knowledge about a situation, might be prone to advocate what they believed was the correct side of a controversy, and this might directly conflict with the political ground rules, such as the Fairness Doctrine, and cause unnecessary "headaches" with some of the affiliated stations, a CBS executive pointed out. To prevent correspondents from becoming "overly involved" in news situations, a news executive explained, NBC has a policy of rotating correspondents covering major candidates for political office. Though not admitting to an iron-clad policy rule, the other networks also usually rotate correspondents in situations where they might become involved.

Specialists also present a problem of control. Since they can claim to know more about their field of competence than an executive producer or assignment editor, they tend, as one CBS producer put it, "to resist the news judgments of others" on questions concerning the assignment, scheduling and editing of news stories in their areas.

But perhaps the most important reason is that generalists lend themselves to a far more efficient use of manpower than specialists. Since it is possible to dispatch any available generalist to the nearest or most convenient happening, the news staff can be fully utilized—assuming stories can be found in areas proximate to the correspondents. On the other hand, by being restricted to a single field of competence, specialists cannot always cover nearby stories; nor would the distribution of possible stories necessarily coincide each day with the available specialists. Consequently, to produce a set number of stories a day, a network would have to employ many more specialists than generalists.

A fourth feature of the intelligence system of network news, made possible by the use of centrally assigned ad hoc coverage and generalists, is that a relatively small number of correspondents are constantly used on camera. A six-week analysis of evening-news broadcast logs shows that ten correspondents reported 68 percent of the film news stories at NBC, 56 percent at ABC, and 51 percent at CBS (excluding those reported by the anchormen). An NBC assignment editor suggested that a small group of correspondents are relied on for most of the stories "more for reasons of audience identification than economy." This leads, he continued, to a "star system" in which producers request that certain leading correspondents cover major stories, no matter what the subject matter, and lesser correspondents, who for one reason or another do not fit the image the producer is attempting to project, are "blacklisted." While assignment editors and producers at the other networks claim to be less concerned with developing star correspondents, the fact remains that at all three networks a handful of correspondents are kept fully occupied reporting most of the film stories.

The number of stories produced are also kept to a near minimum. Unlike newspapers, which generally produce more stories than can be used so that editors have room for selection, television news generally cannot afford the luxury of "overset." Because of the high costs involved in producing a film story—by an NBC rule-of-thumb measure, it runs $500 a minute—and the limited number of crews available, the general practice in network news is to send crews and correspondents to happenings only if there is a very high probability that the result can be used in the programing schedule. This leads to the practice of commissioning, or pre-producing, stories, in which the assignment editor gets the advance agreement of a producer to use a story on his program. Usually this arrangement entails choosing a correspondent for the story.

Finally, network news is not, as one news division president frankly put it, "a record-keeping organization." The video tapes of news broadcasts are routinely erased the next day at NBC and ABC, and kept for only a limited period of time at CBS. After a week or so films used in stories are shipped to storage depots, from which producers of news programs find it difficult, if not impossible, to retrieve them on short notice. Up to 1969, NBC did not even retain complete transcripts of its news broadcasts for "budgetary reasons" (although presently all three networks obtain transcripts from a private firm, Radio-Television Reports, Inc.). Nor does NBC or ABC retain any sort of a "news morgue," where stories are filed according to subject matter. Robert MacNeil, the former NBC correspondent and anchorman, described the situation at the time of his departure in 1967:

> At NBC News . . . there have been no adequate facilities for backgrounding a story. An index or morgue or clipping service which collects and files information from day to day for instant retrieval is the most elemental part of a news organization.

Broadcasters, however, have to rely on their memories, on what recent newspapers they can find, or on what makeshift files they are able to patch together in the midst of very busy lives. NBC's own product is not filed for convenient reference because there is no house respect for it as a source of background information.

Even in the case of CBS, which has the most extensive news library of any of the three networks, a former CBS research director pointed out its inadequacy in a memorandum:

> There are virtually no research facilities for any of our general news broadcasts except the Evening News. On weekends the research blackout is complete. . . . The Evening News, our network flagship, has only one researcher to handle queries on everything from Viet Nam to multiple birth. And for the hectic, final half-hour before air, our main CBS News reference library is closed. The fact that the CBS News reference library is closed as *every one* of the major CBS News television broadcasts prepares for air is not only astonishing in itself. It is, I believe, symptomatic of what is wrong with our whole research effort: it is simply not geared to our news effort.

Although the particular problems referred to in this memorandum were in part remedied, the scope of the whole research effort remains necessarily limited by the previously discussed logic of audience, which holds that the size of the audience that a network news program draws, and hence its advertising revenues, is determined chiefly by the audience flow or lead-in it receives from preceding programs instead of from its own news content. Only in cases in which research might yield a competitive advantage to a network, such as enhancing its ability to predict the outcome of national elections, does it have a concrete value to networks.

What are the consequences of the type of intelligence system employed by network news? In the same way that questions can pre-fit answers, the lines along which the search for news is organized tend to structure the resulting news outputs in a number of systematic ways. For one thing, assignment editors cannot depend on their own personnel to alert them to impending news happenings. Correspondents are not usually expected to maintain beats, or to keep regular contact with the same news makers or institutional spokesmen for the purpose of gathering information, except possibly in the case of continuing stories. Generalists typically perceive their job more in terms of "reporting news stories than finding them," as one NBC correspondent put it. Besides, the low ratio of correspondents to stories tends to keep the leading correspondents fully occupied either in piecing together film stories or traveling from story to story (ABC advertised that its Asian correspondent traveled 100,000 miles a month, or an average of some 3,333 miles a day), leaving little time left to ferret out impending stories.

While producers of individual news programs are in a position to suggest feature or timeless stories to assignment editors, they are of less help in suggesting hard-news stories, since the crews for these often must be assigned before 8 A.M., which is before the producers even arrive at work. In any case, assignment editors readily acknowledge that they rely heavily on the wire services for information about possible stories. Hence, it is not surprising to find that at NBC, for example, the AP and UPI wire services were the proximate source for more than two thirds of the assigned domestic stories, and that less than 15 percent of the assignments were predicated on in-house sources. (See Table II.)

The other networks are equally reliant on the wire services to alert them to news happenings. As one ABC national editor put it, "Without the wire services, we'd be dead."

Furthermore, the intelligence system imposes severe limitations on the possibility of evaluating the content

TABLE II

ASSIGNMENT SOURCES: DOMESTIC FILM STORIES
NBC, DECEMBER 1968

Proximate source	No. of stories	Percent
AP and UPI wire services	308	70.0
Producers, news programs	45	11.0
Public relation agencies	28	6.5
Newspaper clippings	20	4.5
Affiliates and local TV	14	3.2
Staff cameramen and free-lancers	8	1.8
Correspondents	7	1.0
Others	10	2.0
Total	440	100%

of a scheduled news happening before a commitment to cover it is made. Since the wire services and other outside sources provide a plethora of potential stories each day, the critical problem of network news is not expanding the search but reducing it to manageable proportions. For the assignment of editors this means, in effect, routinely narrowing down the wire services' list, or "daybook," of scheduled events to the number that can be handled by the available camera crews and correspondents. Naturally, the problem is complicated by the need of network news to select and reject stories for coverage hours, and sometimes days, before they are scheduled to happen.

In preselecting the scheduled happenings for coverage, the assignment editors cannot expect ready guidance from their correspondents, since most are not presumed to have inside information on any single subject. As a practical matter in fact, assignment editors (at least according to the assignment editors interviewed) rarely ask or receive advice from correspondents on the future news value of scheduled events, except in the case of continuing stories or the few Washington "beats" where newsmen are presumed to have some advance knowledge.

Nor are there adequate research facilities or time for assignment editors themselves to appraise the relative consequences of future events. Noting the lack of in-house research facilities at NBC, Robert MacNeil termed "the dependence on the wires . . . almost total."

Producers provide guidance of a different sort to assignment editors by "ordering" specific stories in advance, and by defining general categories of stories they prefer for their programs. For example, in a single week in 1968 one NBC producer "ordered" a story on a school for clowns in Saratoga, Florida, and asked for "any good stories on student demos [demonstrations] or urban crises." Further complicating the task of sorting out news situations, the assignment editor is responsible not only for filling producers' shopping lists but also for efficiently matching news crews to stories so as not to strain the news organization's budget.

Since the wire services provide only a minimal amount of information about the context of an event, and since the decisions concerning which stories are to be assigned coverage are made under time pressure, assignment editors must rely to some extent on relatively stable criteria, routines and operating rules for quickly dispatching correspondents and camera crews. The criteria for narrowing down the range of possibilities do not apply to the few stories of extraordinary moment—those which cause bells on the wire-service teletype machines to ring and newspapers to reset their front pages. Of course these stories are assigned coverage automatically. But in the case of more routine events, which are not fixed in time and place by newspaper headlines, and where the assignment editor must choose between various happenings in a general category, the selection criteria tend to pattern the long-term pictures of events seen on television. For in selecting items to fill a producer's shopping list—for instance, choosing a confrontation at Columbia University to provide a requested student riot—the routines tend to favor some areas and types of stories to the neglect of others.

In 1969, through interviews and observations of the assignment desk of NBC News and attendance at the daily news-manager's meetings, I attempted to delineate some of the more stable criteria used by the assignment desk. While such criteria no doubt vary with the networks—and even with changes in the news managers' preferences—they must constantly meet the problem of maintaining the appearance of national coverage with a staff not much larger than that of a local news operation, and therefore it is pertinent to examine the criteria used by NBC at one point in time.

1. *Newsworthiness.* Because there is generally little contextual information about a scheduled news happening at the time a decision must be made, the assignment editor uses the relative importance of the personalities involved as an index of newsworthiness. The question asked is "Who is involved?" rather than the less predictable question "What is going to happen?" At any one time, assignment editors claim to have "a mental list" of the ranking of news makers, which they infer from producer and executive preferences. At the top of the list are those involved in one way or another in presidential politics. For example, the President is automatically assigned coverage, so one NBC film crew is permanently stationed at the White House—the only full-time beat. "We are in the business of supplying national news, and whatever the President says or does is by definition national news," one NBC assignment editor explained.

Assignment editors at NBC also gave a high priority, though not automatic coverage, to public statements by anyone presumed to be a serious candidate for the presidency. "If there's a choice, producers would rather that we cover Kennedy, Muskie, McGovern or some other senator who might be the next President, rather than a subcommittee chairman with no political future," the same editor added, referring to possibilities for the Democratic nomination in 1972. Under this criterion, Governor George Wallace received national coverage, even though he was not assumed to have much chance of being elected President. (Richard Salant, president of CBS News, noted in a memorandum: "We have been working for some time on a documentary on George Wallace. Obviously, he is newsworthy and can significantly affect the outcome of the 1968 election.")

Cabinet members and other Administration heads were usually assigned coverage only if it was presumed that they would elaborate on some presidential policy. For the same reasons, any public official who contradicts or attacks the President is also considered "newsworthy." In cases in which senators are not directly involved in presidential politics, assignment priorities depend on his position in the Senate. An NBC vice-president explained to an interviewer:

> That we haven't enough crews results in situations like the one in Washington where the deskman decided that any investigation involving a full committee was to be covered, or a sub-committee if there was someone recognizable chairing it, . . . the way it worked out we'd be covering the Post Office but not the Foreign Relations Subcommittee.

In general, senators who were perceived to have "a national constituency" were given assignment priority over congressmen—who, in any case, rarely received network coverage. Recognized spokesmen for national organizations, like civil rights groups, were also assigned coverage "if producers showed some interest in them," an NBC editor said. Conversely, spokesmen for groups could be "blacklisted," or routinely excluded from coverage, if executives suggested that they had become "overexposed" or "didn't really represent their group"; this happened, for example, in the case of Stokely Carmichael, then head of SNCC, according to NBC assignment editors. Also, local officials such as mayors and governors are usually excluded from coverage—unless, like John V. Lindsay, they happen to be involved in presidential politics—since it is assumed that local news programs, which have independent assignment desks, will cover them if the happening they are involved in has any special import.

2. *Predictability.* Since there is a daily demand for film stories from the news programs and only a limited number of network film crews available to meet it, camera crews must be assigned to scheduled events that will almost certainly materialize on schedule. All other things being equal, in choosing among possible stories, assignment editors at NBC therefore tended to give preference to happenings planned in advance for the press, since these were virtually sure to take place on schedule, rather than those happenings which are contingent on less controllable factors. News conferences, interviews and public statements are, as one editor pointed out, far more likely to receive coverage than unplanned confrontations, unexpected policy changes and off-the-cuff remarks, even if there is good reason for expecting such moves. The more predictable the event, the more likely it will be covered. In August 1969, for example, network crews were assigned to cover the movements of the train carrying poison gas from an army arsenal to a chemical firm in Lockport, New York, where it was to be destroyed in accordance with President Nixon's orders. The "poison-gas train" was shown going through various cities, without event. Meanwhile, in Cambridge Springs, Pennsylvania, a few miles away from where network crews were stationed for the scheduled passing of the army train, an Erie-Lackawanna tank car carrying dead acrylonitrile fuel overturned, spewing out poisonous fumes, and requiring that a dike be built around the tank car. This

unexpected event was not covered by any of the networks.

3. *Film value.* Since assignment editors generally assume that "good pictures" are indispensable for "holding audience interest," as one editor suggested, priority is naturally given to the story in a given category that promises to yield the most dramatic or visual film footage, other considerations being equal. This means, in effect, that political institutions with rules that restrict television cameras from filming the more dramatic parts of their proceedings are not routinely assigned coverage. For example, since the rules of the House of Representatives prohibit filming of committee meetings or floor actions—although reporters are permitted inside and cameras can be stationed outside in the corridors—assignment editors prefer not to assign a valuable camera crew to "corridor duty," as it is called, unless an exceptional news maker is involved and can be interviewed on camera afterward. On the other hand, camera crews are frequently assigned to Senate hearings, which, at the discretion of the chairman, may be fully televised. The same generally holds true of the Supreme Court, which traditionally neither allows its proceedings to be filmed nor the Justices to be interviewed on cases before it. In short, organizations that seek and accommodate publicity tend to be covered more than those that shun exposure of their proceedings.

4. *Geographic balance.* To maintain the appearance of national coverage of news events and thus satisfy the requirement of affiliated stations for a national news service, assignment editors are expected to distribute stories between different regions of the country. At the same time, they are supposed to stay within a budget which allows for only a limited number of film crews in a few cities. This dilemma is routinely solved by allocating assignments geographically, according to the whereabouts of the crews. NBC stations five network crews in Wash-

ington; therefore five stories a day are expected to be "Washington" stories, and are assigned by a Washington assignment editor working under the supervision of New York. Similarly, since there are three full-time network news crews in Los Angeles, Chicago and New York, and one on a part-time basis in Cleveland, an equivalent number of stories are usually assigned in these cities. In momentous circumstances, additional crews can be mobilized, and crews are dispatched outside of the city in which they are based when a major new story presents itself, but to a large degree the basic pattern is predetermined by the development of crews in these five cities in which NBC owns and operates television stations.

In choosing among equivalent stories in different cities, assignment editors therefore tend to select the ones that can be most easily reached by crews—or at least the ones that require no additional resources being expended. An assignment editor explained: "If we have to choose between covering a student demonstration in Chicago or Little Rock, and we can't tell from our advance information which will be more significant, we'd probably choose the one in Chicago, where we already have a crew."

5. *Time considerations.* Since the main demand for film stories comes from the evening news programs, which originates at 6:30 P.M. EST, and since, it will be recalled, it normally takes about six hours to film an interview, process the film, and edit and integrate it into a news program, assignment editors prefer, again all other things being equal, to select stories scheduled to take place, as one put it, "early in the day rather than late." This in turn tends to favor organizations and news makers who are more aware of the needs of network news and schedule their news conferences, speeches and hearings accordingly, over those whose proceedings are not primarily set to accommodate the media. This is an especially important consideration in the case of California news, where there is a three-hour difference in the time zone,

and in the case of overseas stories, which, unless they are of extraordinary importance, are assigned only if "they are not likely to be dated" and have great interest to an American audience, an assignment editor explained.

6. *Correspondent preferences.* Finally, assignment editors at NBC made an effort to choose stories that could be covered by star correspondents, who were highly favored by the producers, and to avoid stories which could only be covered by correspondents for whom producers showed a low preference. A standard joke on the assignment desk was "Cover it only if ———— is *un*available"—the blank being any correspondent who was in disfavor with the producers. Since the star correspondents at that time tended either to be with news makers involved in presidential politics, or in New York, Washington or Los Angeles, this criterion tended to dovetail with the more general news-maker and geographical preferences.

Whereas the search procedures that take place at the level of the assignment desk can be concretely defined, since essentially they aim merely at finding the logistically feasible story that fits a general category of news events, the intelligence system which leads to the choice of general categories cannot be so easily explained. In early 1969, for example, why was the assignment desk at NBC asked for "ecology" stories, while the requests for "black militant stories" seemed, at least to assignment editors, to markedly decrease? The producers who immediately define the categories are responsible for maintaining the audience of their program, but according to the audience theories discussed in the last chapter, the general categories—or even the content of news stories—has little to do with audience viewing patterns, so long as the presentation of the news is not offensive or "above the heads" of the general viewers. Indeed, most producers operate under the assumption the audience "doesn't miss what it doesn't see," as one producer repeatedly said in the newsroom at NBC.

On the other hand, most producers showed a great deal of concern about the reaction of certain select audiences —network executives, affiliate managers (who often spoke through network executives), peers in the news division, and their own circle of friends. Network executives would show interest only on rare occasions, but then it was usually taken seriously. For example, in December 1968 an NBC vice-president asked the producer of the Evening News for an analysis showing the amount of time the program had given to black militant leaders during a three-month period. (It later turned out that the study was requested in conjunction with testimony to be given before the National Advisory Commission on Civil Disorders by network executives, but of course the producer was not told this at the time.) Coincidentally, an affiliate-owner bitterly complained about "unbalanced coverage" favoring black leaders in the New York City teachers strike, and a news division vice-president asked the producer "to handle the complaint." A few days later, after a long story on blacks in the Florida schools was shown on the program, the producer openly told the assignment editor, in front of the news staff, that "the audience is becoming bored with Negro stories, and it isn't helping them." In the month that followed, there were no stories concerning blacks on the NBC Evening News, except for two concerning presidential appointments of blacks to jobs in the incoming Nixon Administration.

It is impossible to say how new categories of news emerge. Producers claim they have a "news sense" which identifies important general topics; they also constantly attempt to survey the press—notably the *New York Times*, especially the Sunday "Review of the Week" section, *Time*, *Newsweek* and the Washington *Post*—for "new trends." It was also clear from my personal observations that producers spend a good deal of time discussing news with newsmen and watching "the competition." But as one producer suggested facetiously, any attempt to identify more precisely the factors that define or alter general categories of news would require "intensive psychoanalysis of the producer."

All that can be definitely stated is that there are two intelligence operations in network news: one that takes place at the assignment desk and follows relatively stable criteria in selecting stories to be covered by camera crews; and a less well defined system, centered around the producers of individual news programs, which chooses the general trends and categories that are to be illustrated by examples chosen by the assignment desk.

Chapter 5

The Resurrection of Reality

The essence of journalism is the editing process.
—Elmer Lower, president of ABC News

Almost by definition, news events are short-lived phenomena. Except for rare instances, what is seen on network news is not the event itself unfolding before the live camera, or even a filmed record, but a story about the event reconstructed on film from selected fragments of it (or even from re-enactments of it). Despite the hackneyed maxim that television news "tells it like it is," presenting events exactly as they occur does not fit in with the requisites of network news. For one thing, the camera is not always in a position to capture events live or on film as they happen. In some cases, news events are unexpected and occur before a camera crew can be dispatched to the scene. Others cannot be filmed direct because of unfavorable weather and lighting conditions (especially if artificial lighting is unavailable or restricted), or simply because decision-making bodies such as committees of the House of Representatives, the Senate and the Supreme Court prohibit news crews from filming their proceedings. Even when such institutions as political conventions permit television to record their formal proceedings, the significant decisions still may take place outside the permitted purview of the camera.

But even when coverage presents no insurmountable problems, given the requirement that a network news story have definite order, time and logic, it would be insufficient in most cases to record from beginning to end the natural sequence of events, with all the digressions, confusions and inconsistencies that more often than not constitute reality. When Reuven Frank, as producer of the NBC Evening News, wrote in the previously cited memorandum to his staff that "every news story should have structure and conflict, problem and denouement, rising action and falling action, a beginning, a middle and an end," he was outlining a basic formula for news stories on his program, one in which stories could not be expected to unfold naturally. Moreover, although events can last hours or be over in a brief moment, a network news story is expected by producers to be of a prescribed length—from one to seven minutes, depending on the program and segment it is to be shown in. Even in terms of content, controversial stories are supposed to follow a definite order in the presentation of views, despite the fact that actual arguments may have followed a different order.

It therefore becomes necessary in network news to reorganize the film into a story. An NBC producer succinctly describes the process as involving "shooting twenty to thirty times as much film as is actually needed for a story, preparing a tight story line, then editing the film to fit the story line." In other words, according to the ratio commonly used at all three networks, a three-minute news story must be boiled down from an hour or more of film, which requires three separate operations. First, to obtain the excess footage, camera crews—who may film a story either on their own or, more often, under the direction of producers or correspondents—need to have some general guidelines on which parts of a happening should be filmed, since filming often takes place *before* the story is written. Second, to prepare a narrative "story line," correspondents or producers require some general idea of the "formulas" that stories are expected to follow, especially since these may vary from program to program. Third, to edit the film and sound track into a final product, editors must have some general criteria for filling out a story line.

In each case, "standard operating practices" are needed to coordinate individual technical skills—especially since the cameramen, reporters, editors, writers and producers are not always in a situation where they can consult. And in all cases, they are dependent not only on network policies but also on more deep-rooted technological limitations of network television. To the extent, then, that these procedures for "bringing stories to life," as one editor described the process, remain consistent, they can be looked at as a secondary input in the selection of news on network television.

Generating Film

In producing most news stories, the first problem is generating sufficient film, so that the editor and writer can be assured of finding the material they need for the final story. Perhaps the most commonly used device for producing this flow of film is the interview. Reuven Frank points out in his memorandum that "the interview is a basic tool of our business and we could not survive without it."

Although it is simply an arrangement whereby a correspondent questions another person in front of a camera, the television interview serves several important purposes for network news. For one thing, it makes it possible for a news crew to obtain film footage about an event which they did not attend or which they were not permitted to film. By finding individuals who either participated in the event or at least have an apparent connection with it, the correspondent can re-create the event through the eyes of those interviewed. And if the questions are worded so that the answers will reflect an "immediate presence," as is the customary practice in network news, the presentation will appear to the audience to be of the event itself rather than a vicarious reconstruction of it.

Second, the interview assures that the subject will be filmed under favorable circumstances—an important technical consideration. In the memorandum Reuven Frank advises his staff:

> By definition, an interview is at least somewhat controllable. It must be arranged; it must be agreed to ... Try not to interview in harsh sunlight. Try not to interview in so noisy a setting that words cannot be heard. Let subjects be lit. If lights bother your subject, talk to him, discuss the weather, gentle him, involve his interests and his emotions so that he forgets or ignores the lights. It takes longer, but speed is poor justification for a piece of scrapped film.

To make subjects appear even more dignified and articulate, it is the customary practice to repeat the same question a number of times, allowing the respondent to "sharpen his answer," as one correspondent suggested. At times the interviewees are permitted to compose their own questions for the interviewer, or at least rephrase them. For example, when Chet Huntley interviewed Senator Edward Kennedy before the 1968 elections, Kennedy suggested a number of questions (while the camera was still running) which Huntley then conveniently asked him. The answers, minus the senator's stage directions, were used in the final version, which was aired in October 1968 on the NBC Evening News. Rehearsals are also quite common. ABC policy, in fact, calls for the correspondent to "do your rehearsing before the camera rolls, and not do 'wet' dry runs [i.e., rehearsing while the camera is running]." The correspondent may also add to the appearance of a logical dialogue by rephrasing his own questions after the interview has ended and having them reshot—a technique which produces a wider range of articulate answers from which the editor can select for the final story.

Third, interviews provide an easy means by which an abstract or difficult-to-film concept can be presented in human terms. Reuven Frank explains in the same memo:

> The best interviews are of people reacting—not people expounding. . . . No important story is without them. They can be recorded and transmitted tastefully. Integration, Algeria, Skybolt, nuclear disarmament, flood, automation, name me a recent news story without its human involvement.

While it is visually effective to show complex concepts through the reactions of an individual involved, the technique often leads to hyperbole. For example, in illustrating the concept of inflation, based on a news item about a fraction of a percent rise in the cost-of-living index, NBC News presented an interview in which an unemployed itinerant dramatically described how he had to scavenge leftovers from fine restaurants at which he had formerly dined. In this case, the abstract problem of inflation was brought to earth in the form of one individual's problem—an ironic change of life style, but one that exaggerated the effect of a minute rise in the cost index. Moreover, since the views of an individual stand symbolically for a national range of issues in this technique, unrepresentative views or reactions can result in major distortions. For instance, to portray the pre-election mood of the black voters in 1968, John Chancellor of NBC interviewed a single black voter, Lou Smith, an extremely articulate and original thinker, who argued that some degree of black separation from white America was prerequisite to black progress. But was this representative of the black voter in 1968? Chancellor later explained to me that he had selected Lou Smith as a "profile" of the black voter because his point of view was "the most interesting and provocative of the seven or eight possibilities considered." The individuals selected to represent Wallace, Nixon and Humphrey voters were selected, he continued, on the same criteria of "what most interested me." No sampling procedures were used to ascertain whether those selected even approximately represented the views of the electorate for whom they were symbolically standing.

Finally, the interviewing device is probably the easiest way of satisfying the Fairness Doctrine, which requires, it will be recalled, that if one viewpoint is presented on a controversial topic, an opposing one will be presented in the course of a reasonable period of time. Network executives can assure that correspondents comply with this standard, and also avoid any problems with affiliate managers who might be particularly sensitive to one-sided presentations, by simply requiring interviewers to seek a balance on all subjects that are to be treated seriously. In some cases, producers will even hold stories in abeyance until the correspondent obtains an interview with a "con" viewpoint for the story. In most cases, however, correspondents almost automatically seek out the opposing viewpoint, which is considered to be, as one explained it, "a basic part of the job of putting together a story." If correspondents, for one reason or another, cannot produce such "balancing" interviews, the story may have to be reported as an unserious one, as will be discussed shortly.

In general, the interviewing device tends to favor the articulate over the inarticulate person. As Reuven Frank shrewdly noted, "Most people are dull. That is, they communicate ineptly. If they are dull, their description of interesting events will be dull." Therefore, network news must rely for interviews on those who can make events seem interesting, but this too presents a problem. "Those who communicate eptly—politicians, actors and the like —tend to be self-serving," therefore "too many of the best interviews are achieved at the expense of integrity. An interesting, important, articulate subject can often command his own ground rules as the price of granting the interview, and if we don't pay the price, the competition will." Moreover, when the balancing interview is mechanically inserted into political arguments, it tends to reinforce the impression that at the root of political controversy is an intelligent argument between evenly matched opponents—an impression fostered by the articulateness of the interviews.

Another commonly used device for generating film about an event to which television cameras are not privy is re-enacting the happening. This usually involves having participants act out for the cameras after the fact the part they played in a news event. In this practice, however, the line between what constitutes "staged" news as opposed to a legitimate reconstruction is not always clear. For example, in its documentary on "The Selling of the Pentagon," CBS criticized the Department of Defense for staging the landings of South Vietnamese river patrols for conveniently placed cameramen (since it was known that there were no enemy troops in the vicinity). Yet a former Saigon bureau chief pointed out that "it is considered standard operating procedure for troops to fire their weapons for the benefit of cameramen. If our cameramen had to wait until a fire fight with the Vietcong broke out, we'd have much less footage—and perhaps, cameramen."

This sort of "reconstructed" news is not limited to combat situations. ABC News producer Bruce Cohn stated in 1972 to a House subcommittee: "A feature story must be 'set up' by a journalist if it is to be transformed into usable information. . . . By its very nature, a feature story may be nothing but what the Subcommittee negatively refers to as 'staging.' But it can, and should, be honest staging—not altering any facts or circumstances." Attempting to evaluate charges of "staged news" concerning the networks' coverage of the 1968 Democratic convention, the Federal Communications Commission noted:

> In a sense, every televised press conference may be said to be staged to some extent; depictions of scenes in a television documentary—on how the poor live on a typical day in the ghetto, for example—also necessarily involve camera directions, lights, action instructions, etc. The term "pseudo-event" describes a whole class of such activities that constitute much of what journalists treat as "news." Few would question the professional propriety of asking public officials to smile again or to repeat handshakes, while the cameras are focused upon them.

The FCC concluded that such re-enactments and supervised news happenings were an integral part of television news. According to the FCC, such stage management raises questions of license abuse if, and *only* if, "a purported significant 'event' did not in fact occur but rather is 'acted out' at the behest of news personnel." In other words, a television station is not inhibited by its license obligation from restaging an event that did actually occur at some time in the past, out of range of cameras, even if the audience is not informed that they are seeing something other than the authentic event. At the 1968 Democratic convention, for example, it was alleged that a CBS news crew arranged for a "girl hippie," wearing a bandage across her head, to approach a line of National Guard troops shouting, on cue, "Don't hit me." So long as the purported event occurred at some time—as it could be reasonably maintained in this case—such a re-enactment is considered legitimate by the FCC.

Up to a point, enacting news events is generally regarded by correspondents as simply an efficient means of "pre-editing a story," as one CBS newsman suggested. Rather than shooting endless amounts of film until those actions naturally occur which the correspondent or producer believe represents the "real" story, individuals may simply be asked to enact them. For instance, a candidate may be asked to wave to a crowd, real or imaginary, on cue. An extreme case was the previously referred to enactment of the pot party for the cameras of the CBS owned-and-operated station in Chicago, WBBM-TV. Following a newspaper story in the Chicago *Daily News* which suggested that marijuana was being smoked by middle-class as well as hippie students, the CBS reporter, John Missett, discussed with several students at Northwestern University the possibility of arranging a "pot party" which could be filmed by television cameras. The reporter suggested the type of students that should be invited to the party—"clean-cut people, no beatniks"—and the general format, according to the students who had arranged the party for WBBM-TV. The students who attended knew that the party was being enacted purposefully for television, arrived after the camera crew had set up their equipment in one of the students' apartments, and followed the explicit instructions of the news crew in lighting up joints and answering questions. The cost of the party was in part subsidized by the reporter through his purchase of some of the marijuana. Presumably it could argue that the story was essentially true, despite the enactment: the reporter could have achieved the same story by surreptitiously filming a large number of scenes of marijuana smokers and then editing out the undesired types of students and conflicting elements. The prearranged party was simply more efficient in terms of television's resources.

To be sure, when interviewed, network news executives and producers generally look askance at such contrived enactments. An NBC producer explained that "all re-enactments must exactly duplicate an actual event, and one which it is otherwise impossible to film." The same producer, in fact, reprimanded a correspondent when it later came to his attention that the man had requested a number of people to remain in their seats after a speech by Richard Nixon, then a presidential candidate, for the purpose of shooting additional footage, which understandably showed the "audience" appearing restless and confused. This film was then intercut with the candidate's speech, creating the effect that it was not well received. A CBS producer summed up the problem by saying, "Some direction is almost always needed to film a news event, but here we ultimately must rely on the integrity of the news crew."

A third basic technique of creating film for editing purposes involves shooting additional silent footage of the principal actors and background settings from various angles. The silent footage then can be intercut with the second film, according to the demands of the story line.

A mandatory type of such silent footage, required by all three networks, is known as the "cutaway shot." Essentially this is a view of an audience's reaction while the news subject is speaking. Most sound pieces, such as press conferences, hearings, speeches and interviews require such cutaway shots if they are to be smoothly edited. This is because they provide the editor with flexibility in matching film to story lines. A CBS News Manual explains:

> Because of time limits and in order to heighten impact, television must shorten speeches. . . . This is difficult to do unless the cameraman furnishes a visual "meanwhile," or cutaway. For example, in shooting a speech, be sure to make several shots of audience reaction. If there's no audience, shoot other newsmen or your own sound camera. These clips will furnish the second-and-a-half cutaways which the film editor can insert to avoid a "jump cut" if he wants to clip a sentence from the middle of one lens "take." Otherwise, the speaker's head would seem to jump. . . . In this connection, it often helps to shoot a roll or two of stock cutaways for editing use—various shots of the film crew, close-ups of a hand writing on a pad, reporters' faces, etc.

More generally, the cutaway shot allows action to be compressed, as Reuven Frank demonstrates in an example:

> A man walks a block. It takes him one minute. We show him starting his walk. We show a cutaway of a policeman watching. We show him ending his walk. Total edited film time: 8 seconds. If we cut the walk [directly to 8 seconds] but did not use the cutaway, it would appear that after four seconds he had miraculously covered most of the block by ectoplasmic transference.

To maintain the illusion that an actual event is being witnessed, cutaways always need only conform to one rule: they must *appear* to be directly related to the story. The cameraman is usually responsible for finding cutaways that match the angles, lighting and background of the main subject. In doing so, however, he is supposed to select only "neutral" cutaways, in which the audience is not shown expressing any clear point of view, according to producers at all three networks. By selecting a part of the audience that is smiling, yawning, grimacing or otherwise providing cues on how the sound portion should be appreciated, cutaways can be used to make editorial points. This, however, cannot be done at the discretion of the cameraman. Such editorial cutaways, almost all newsmen interviewed agreed, must be "ordered" by the producer—and are a rarity.

Silent footage is also important for establishing the atmosphere of a news story. "The aim of news film should be less to record one event than to bring the audience into its presence," Reuven Frank advised in his memorandum. The most direct way of accomplishing this is through an "establishing shot," which is merely an overall view of the setting from a relatively distant perspective. CBS News advises in its manual:

> An established shot "places" a story in its proper setting and atmosphere. In a real sense, it is the equivalent of exposition in text. Include street signs,

building exteriors, signs on office doors, wide shots of nearby activities and of the subject itself.

Reuven Frank also suggests that cameramen use "signposts and artifacts and the like which, while having no relevancy to the event itself, hint interestingly at where it happened."

Of course, it is not necessary for such establishing footage to be taken at the time of the event. The CBS News Manual states that "an objective of television news is to bring you to the scene of the news," even though the film used to illustrate a story "may be months old." And no matter how remote establishing film may be from the actual event, it can always be directly connected to it by means of the voice-over narration in which a commentator tells the story as the silent footage is being shown.

While the bulk of network news stories are sound pieces—speeches, press conferences, testimony, and the like—spliced together with cutaways, there is also a category of stories mainly concerned with visual action, such as riots, demonstrations and disasters, in which the pictures need not be synchronized with words spoken at the time. In the case of these action stories, the establishing footage becomes the story itself, with the simple addition of a voice-over narration. In these stories, cameramen are usually given free rein and are expected to seek out the most violent or exciting moments of the event. One NBC cameraman explained, "What the producers want on the film is as much blood and violence as we can find. That's the name of the game, and every cameraman knows it." Robert MacNeil claimed in his book that cameramen in Vietnam at the height of the war were ordered by the networks to "shoot bloody"—and this produced a strong focus on military action at the expense of the less visible political considerations.

Although in filming action footage as well as establishing shots, cameramen are generally given a great deal of discretion, they are still expected to seek out scenes that are consistent with the predetermined theme of the story. Footage that contradicts the story line is usually unacceptable. For example, during a youth congress in Moscow in 1964, Nikita Khrushchev made one of his rare public appearances at which he was supposedly snubbed by young delegates. ABC News decided to do a story on that subject, the theme being that Khrushchev was being embarrassed. The establishing shots, however, showed a large number of people in the hall and an ABC executive complained that the appearance of a "packed hall" did "not play with the narration of Khrushchev being snubbed." The correspondent on this story later said that he was often asked to have cameramen re-shoot scenes that did not "jibe with what New York thought the story was." According to the correspondents interviewed, the problem is usually avoided by making clear to the cameramen in advance exactly what the story is supposed to show. "The shooting of such a report must be carefully planned by the reporter and cameraman," Reuven Frank notes. "All such planning should begin by agreeing on why the reporting is being done." The film of an event is thus defined, to a large extent, by the prior expectation of it.

The Story Line

More than fifty years ago Walter Lippmann suggested that newspaper reporting was in large part a process of filling out an established "repertory of stereotypes" with current news. In a similar way, network news is involved with illustrating a limited repertory of story lines with appropriate pictures. One NBC commentator, Sander Vanocur, observed that "network news is a continuous loop: there are only a limited number of plots— 'Black versus White,' 'War is Hell,' 'America is falling apart,' 'Man against the elements,' 'The Generation Gap,' etc.—which we seem to be constantly redoing with different casts of characters." Many of the correspondents interviewed complained about the need to fit news developments into developed molds or formulas, and to order stories along predetermined lines; at the same time, most accepted it as a practical necessity. Again, the fact that a film story requires the coordinated efforts of a large number of individuals—reporters, cameramen, sound men, writers, producer, editor and commentator —working on the product at different times, makes it necessary that there be a stable set of expectations of what constitutes a proper story. Moreover, producers generally assume that a given audience will have certain preferences in terms of both the form and the content of news stories. "Every program has certain requirements and guidelines for its filmed reports," an ABC executive explained. "Eventually these might harden into formulas and clichéd plots, but when they fail to hold the audiences' attention, the producer or the program is usually changed."

The ABC News "Correspondent's Handbook" gives some idea of how specific program requirements can be. For example, the producer of the ABC Evening News in 1965, Wally Pfister, clearly prescribed the form the news was to take on his program (which was then only fifteen minutes long).

We are trying to give a new fresh look to television news. We are a fifteen-minute news show and therefore our needs are different than those of our competitors who are doing spots for the half-hour shows. We want well-produced, visual, succinct, punchy film stories.

. . . Plan your spots in advance. If possible, survey before you shoot and unless it is the most extreme emergency, NEVER ad lib a double chain [i.e., a sound piece]. Look at the story visually and get as many production values in as possible. . . . but never let "gimmicks" get in the way of your telling the story.

In planning the story don't automatically out-date yourself. We are the victim of far too many lost spots because they are "old stuff" by the time they reach us. If you are "one or two days away from show time" and are doing a spot that could become obsolete . . . do another one that won't be . . . alternate possibilities or a backgrounder.

Time: About tops for us is 1 minute 15 seconds. Unless the story is monumental, we don't want spots longer than that. . . . DON'T give us long uncuttable stories.

Half of television is sound. When at all possible give us natural sound-on-film.

Keep in touch. On major stories when decisions must be made immediately . . . phone us. And, when you are to embark on a story or a trip and you are unsure of what we want or expect, call us. Even overseas calls are cheaper than discarded film stories!

Analysis Spots: This is a new approach to telling the story from the field and could be really effective. When you are out on a story, do your regular "double-chain" sound piece to be used under film. AFTER you have done that please give us a straight stand-up piece (with the best and most interesting background) which is strictly ANALYSIS. The spot should be between 45 and 50 seconds . . . no longer than 50 seconds. It should be truly an interpretive piece, the "why" of the story . . . the little analysis that puts the story in perspective. . . . If you have a little anecdote or personal experience that gives the foreign story some meaning or brings it home, do that . . . Here is how we plan to use them. [The commentator] will give the hard news, incorporating some of the silent film sent on by you in the same shipment. Then, under the film he will say something like "And now for the story behind Prime Minister Wilson's resignation, here's ABC's Bill Sheehan reporting from London." We will then broadcast Bill Sheehan's news analysis of his commentary.

Props, objects from locations. Another way we can look different is to relate the story more closely to the viewer. By now he is pretty well jaded by the constant stream of film from remote and exotic locations in the news. If you can send us (for the lack of a better word) "props" from the story you are covering,

[the commentator] can use them to introduce your spot and stimulate interest in the story.
. . . Whenever you have an opportunity, ask your cameraman to shoot 20 or 30 feet of silent film of you at the scene for use in our headline section. I don't want a picture of you standing erect with a mike in your hand. . . . I'd want you running towards the scene, talking with a demonstrator, picking up a discarded sign (if covering demonstration).

Other ABC News programs, with different audiences and time requisites, ordered different sorts of news stories. The producer for a five-minute news program (with Marlene Sanders) shown in the afternoon to an audience that was predominantly housewives, noted in the same handbook: "We do lean towards the feature, towards the HUMAN story. This is our bow to women." It also detailed the news requirements:

Our problem is getting into the show all the things we want to say. We have only 2:55 minutes for news content. The Sanders feature runs in the neighborhood of a minute. . . . Often, one of the stories comes from Washington—LBJ, Secretary McNamara, or any of the newsmaking politicoes. If we can cut a short piece of sound, we do. Otherwise, we use it silent with Marlene (or a Washington correspondent) doing voice-over. For the remaining piece of film, I like to use a dateline . . . Saigon, Moscow, Paris, London, Tokyo, any of those places. . . . Between them, the two film pieces—other than the Marlene feature —total about a minute. They are as short as 17 seconds, as long as 45.

The producer for DEF (Daily Electronic Feed), the ABC syndicated news which sells "a quota of about a dozen visual news stories a day to affiliated stations" that they can incorporate into their local news programs, requested still different sorts of news, including:

SPORTS: DEF tries to deliver one sports story every day and our subscribers are extremely enthu-

siastic about this. . . . Most take the form of advances
—workouts, interviews about forthcoming big sports
events.

REGIONALS: These are stories of interest in only
one area. Washington is a fountainhead for this type
story but other correspondents should be alert. Military honors or feature interviews with war heroes,
for example, are good for regional stories in any of
the 70-odd cities we cover. Touring governors, Senators or Mayors of big cities are natural subjects.

DEF clients want silent stories of 30 to 45 seconds;
sound stories of 1 minute or 1:30 at most. Sports can
go to 2:30. . . . DEF clients don't like stand-up reports
or analysis. When that's the only way you can cover
an important story, be sure to plant yourself in a good
location with some natural action. We can only use
stories that are exclusive enough to hold up for the
necessary travel time.

NBC and CBS news programs have similar requisites for
film stories, which specify the desired length, format and
particular focus for news.

In terms of content, however, the producers' unwritten
but generally known preferences for certain types of
stories are of much more importance to correspondents,
who generally find it necessary to "sell themselves" to
producers of the news programs by the kind of stories
they do. These preferences, in turn, are predicated on
certain assumptions about what types of news stories are
most likely to interest, and least likely to disconcert, the
special audiences that producers are most concerned
about: network executives, affiliate managers and news
directors, other newsmen, and in a general way, the home
viewing audience.

The Dialectical Model. A prime concern of network
executives, as perceived by the producers interviewed, is
that news stories appear to be balanced and nonpolitical
so as not to conflict with the FCC's Fairness Doctrine.
"Executives simply don't want the headaches of answering complaints about one-sided news or news that advo-

cates a definite position," one NBC producer explained. To avoid such headaches, producers order correspondents, field producers and writers to include in their story lines opposing views as a matter of policy. Not surprisingly, then, story lines tend to follow a point-counterpoint format, with correspondents providing some sort of synthesis of, though not necessarily an answer to, the opposing views in a final comment. Most correspondents assume that they are expected by executives to take a completely neutral position, and to identify with the audiences as far as possible. "In this country play it down the middle," William S. Paley, chairman of the board of CBS, is quoted as saying.

The Ironic Model. If correspondents cannot find plausible balancing views, producers generally prefer that they present the story ironically, rather than as a one-sided polemic. This involves a straight exposition of some unexpected turn of events. The attempt by an NBC field producer to do a story in 1969 for the Evening News about the urban-refuse problem in California is a case in point. The producer came across a story in the San Francisco *Chronicle* which reported that the city of San Francisco proposed to ship its garbage 200 miles away by train to the desert on the Nevada border, and bury it in trenches alongside the railroad tracks. While this would relieve San Francisco's disposal problem, the newspaper story suggested, it was causing a great deal of anguish among local residents in the area of the proposed dumping grounds, since it would defile the landscape and desecrate an Indian burial ground. With sufficient possibilities for pictorial conflict—"Indians protesting the arrival of a garbage train," as one NBC producer put it—the suggested story was quickly approved by the New York producers, and a camera crew was dispatched to Reno, Nevada, to film it.

The story turned out to be quite different: the proposed site was in fact located in an uninhabited salt desert, used only as a government ammunition depot, with no Indians or burial grounds in the immediate vicinity. Moreover, the local residents seemed exceedingly pleased rather than resentful about the project, since the county, which was an economically depressed area, would receive a relatively high income from allowing the railroad the use of its deserts. Although the NBC producer called the Sierra Club and local ecology groups in the hope of finding some opposing viewpoints, none could be found, since the solid wastes involved were to be used to reclaim the desert.

With no balancing views to be found, the story was given a jocular tone, the producer explained to me at the time. The theme of the story thus became irony: a county actually wanted someone else's garbage. Tongue-in-cheek interviews, a background sound track of cowboy and Indian music, comic shots of garbage being amassed in San Francisco, a moving train (shot elsewhere) and an introduction stressing Indian place names were used to stress the unserious nature of the piece.

The joking news story, which uses zany photography, nostalgic music and commentators' wry smiles as its cues to the audience, have increasingly become the only viable alternative for producers faced with stories that do not fit into the point-counterpoint model. One NBC producer said, "The president of this company wants us to end with a light piece and leave the audience smiling, which means there is always a demand for a news joke." Indeed, NBC even went so far as to use a comedienne from *Laugh-In* to "act out," as the producer put it, a news story concerning the women's liberation movement. (CBS, it will be recalled, also has a policy of ending the program with light news.)

The National News Package. A second audience that must be taken into consideration by network producers is the affiliate managers, who determine when and if network news will be shown on their station. As mentioned earlier, one main demand of affiliate managers is that network news stories concern "national" rather than local events. As one CBS affiliate manager put it: "We don't expect the network news to be simply a replay of various local stories; it must be something different."

While there are always stories on such national institutions as Congress, the Presidency and the Supreme Court, as well as international events, which easily qualify as "national news," it is more difficult to fit stories that occur outside Washington, D.C. (and which are likely to be reported by some affiliates as local stories) into a network news program. Yet such local happenings might hold substantial interest for a national audience, or be needed to give the program geographic balance. Hence, a key problem for network news producers is to transform news stories about local events into a national story.

A commonly used solution is "nationalizing news stories" by fusing together two or more local stories into a "package" which purports to show a national trend. The process involves shooting parallel stories in different cities related to some essentially local story which for one reason or another the producer wants to use. Then a commentator will do an introduction which describes the national trend, which the film stories are presented, in sequence, as illustrations of. For example, to illustrate the problems of blacks in the cities in February 1969, five separate stories on this theme were commissioned in the five cities in which NBC owns television stations. As described in the evaluation report, they were "Lem Tucker on slums and welfare in New York; Valeriana with crime, using Washington as an example; Bill Matney in Chicago with urban blight and Negro discontent over housing; Mark Landsman in Cleveland on black politics; also Perkins [in Los Angeles] on Negro job opportunities; . . . and Tucker wrap-up. Each segment had appropriate illustrative footage." None of these reports involved a news happening that day; all were commissioned in advance so that the package could be presented as a report on a national trend on the first anniversary of the National Commission on the Causes and Prevention of Violence on February 27. (The same sort of "nationalization" can be accomplished without commissioning or finding a second similar story by having the reporter simply comment on the national significance of the event in his on-camera remarks.)

No matter how this imperative is achieved, according to Reuven Frank, ideally network news subjects should be microcosms of national problems. The format for a network news story must therefore provide a way of linking a local (or even unique) happening with a more general trend. Many of the trend stories—transportation, urban decay, national crime problems and so on—derive from the need to nationalize local stories.

The Action Story. A third critical, though less well defined audience is the home viewers that determine the Nielsen ratings of news programs. While it is presumed that network news does not *attract* an audience, it can reduce the already existing audience. To satisfy this requisite, the producers interviewed generally assumed that the home audience is more likely to be engrossed by visual action than a filmed discussion of issues, or "talking heads," and so they placed a high value on action film. Each producer has his own style for an action story. Some prefer to begin with a "news bite," or dramatic film, continue with the correspondent's comments, and then go on to the unfolding drama; others prefer to build a story, beginning with the correspondent's introduction, followed by the rising drama leading to some climax of action. However, virtually all the stories given high marks for action at NBC involved violence toward humans: "head-busting" (i.e., police charging groups of demonstrators), "bang-bang stuff" (i.e., shoot-outs or combat) and "rioting" were the terms in which such action pieces were favorably described to the executive producers. Terms which denoted a dearth of action included "talking heads" (i.e., conversation), "nothing happened," or a "quiet walk" (i.e., an unopposed demonstration).

The one ingredient most producers interviewed claimed was necessary for a good action story was visually identifiable opponents clashing violently. This, in turn, requires some form of stereotype: military troops, fighting civilians, black versus white students, workers wearing hardhats manhandling bearded peace demonstrators were cited by producers as examples of the components for such stories. Demonstrations or violence involving less clearly identifiable groups make less effective stories, since, as one CBS producer put it, "it would be hard to tell the good guys from the bad guys."

The scenarios for action stories are thus organized on the principle of stressing the presumed claims and differences of opposed groups. Interviews and narration that define these distinctions and prepare the audience for the ensuing action are preferred over discussions that point to a more complex relationship between and within the groups. In the case of the student strike at Harvard in 1968, for example, interviews with student leaders which suggested the existence of numerous factions, with objectives that were not always consistent, were not used in the network reports. Instead, students were shown as a more or less united and monolithic group. "We tried to show what the students had in common," an NBC producer explained to me, "not what the petty differences were."

The Nostalgia Model. As Reuven Frank pointed out, attempts to reach specialized audiences through specialized news subjects generally result in the loss of more members of the audience than are gained, since the propensity for existing viewers to turn off uninteresting news is greater than that of new viewers to be attracted by news of special interest to them. It follows, then, that special audiences must be reached through a treatment of the news that is general enough to interest *all* members of the audience. To reach the rural audiences (which for technical reasons are disproportionately important in maintaining good Nielsen ratings) therefore requires an approach which is still of general interest to urban viewers. One device, used at all three networks for satisfying these audience demands, is the "nostalgia" format, which in its most elemental form focuses on a traditional value threatened or replaced by a modern value. The chief requisite of this type of story, according to correspondents interviewed, is "pretty pictures," as one put it. By either narration, interviews or juxtaposition of images, the story is told in terms of the conflicting values. (As was discussed in Chapter 2, this kind of story also has the economic advantage of being timeless.)

To be sure, all network news stories do not fit neatly in the various pigeonholes described above. Some momentous events fit no preconceived story line; some more specialized subjects fit in less well defined models; and still others require elements from more than one model. Moreover, the repertory itself changes from time to time and network to network. Nevertheless, at any given time, the requisites of network news make it necessary to have some preformed story lines for containing the chaotic flow of news.

The Editing Process

Editing involves selecting certain fragments of a film of a given subject and arranging them in an order which appears to represent a coherent view of the event. The same set of pictures can, however, yield different coherent views, depending on how they are edited. "Given at random, say, half a dozen shots of different nature and subject, there are any number of possible combinations of the six that, with the right twist of commentary, could make film sense," a leading film editor suggested. In network news, the meaning is prescribed by the story line. Film editors in network news typically defined their role as being noncreative: "Our job is simply to put together the story ordered by the producer in a professional way," one chief film editor for NBC observed.

In editing a news story with sound, the film editor usually works closely with a field producer or correspondent, who at times literally stands over his shoulder. First the footage is viewed in its entirety, and the producer or correspondent designates which of the newsmakers' sentences are to be pulled out and used in the final piece. Whatever sound portions are chosen are transferred to magnetic tape and "laid out" according to the sequence dictated by the story line. Historical continuity is not required; on the contrary, often a sentence used toward the end of a news conference will be used as the beginning of the film, and vice versa. Then the film editor chooses cutaways of the correspondents and suitable establishing shots, and uses them to create the illusion that there was continuity to the sound portions.

In the case of silent footage, film editors have considerably more discretion. Usually the story line calls for some general effect, such as "crowds milling" or "street fighting," and it is left to the editor to achieve this scene.

Producers have definite expectations as to what constitutes a visually effective editing job. First of all, according to the editors interviewed, they are supposed to eliminate all technically inferior film footage (unless otherwise instructed by a producer) and reduce visual noise or disconcerting elements. The CBS News Manual states, for example:

> A convincing realism demands that only the best-quality scenes should be selected. Avoid using scenes that are poorly exposed. . . . Be sure the sound quality is distinct and easily grasped. Distorted sound or low-level audio will most certainly destroy the realism of the news story.

Paradoxically, carefully prepared or even rehearsed news scenes are far more likely to satisfy these criteria for a "convincing reality" than spontaneous news scenes which, by their very nature, have unpredictable lighting and sound conditions.

A second editing norm, which all the editors interviewed accepted without qualification, is the desirability of concentrating scenes of action so as to heighten the visual effect. "Our job is to cut out all the deadwood and dull moments," one NBC editor commented. The procedure involves routinely eliminating the intervals in which little of visual interest occurs, and compressing the remaining fragments into one continuous montage of unceasing visual action. For instance, an attempt by the SDS faction at Columbia University to block the registration of students in September of 1968 involved, according to my observations, a few speeches by SDS leaders, hours of milling about, in which the protest more or less dissipated for lack of interest, and about one minute of violence when five SDS leaders attempted to push their way past two campus patrolmen at the registration hall. The half-hour of film taken that day by an NBC camera crew recorded various views of the crowd from 9 A.M. until the violence at about 2 P.M., and the minute or so of violent confrontation. However, when the happening was reduced to a two-minute news story for the NBC Evening News, the editors routinely retained the violent scenes, building up to them with quick cuts of speeches and crowd scenes. The correspondent, who was not himself present at the demonstration that day, simply narrated the scenes of concentrated violence in the accepted formula used for campus violence at the time—which juxtaposed the demands and violence of the students with the enlightened negotiating efforts of the university administration. The process of distilling action from preponderantly inactive scenes was not perceived as any sort of distortion by any of the editors interviewed. On the contrary, most of them considered it to be the accepted function of editing; as one chief editor observed, it was "what we are really paid for."

A third value accepted without question by film editors is that only the portions of film that fulfill the agreed-upon story should be used; film that contradicts or even appears to undercut any point in the story should be omitted. The CBS News Manual states that "the film editor should cut the pictures with a story line or general script in mind. . . . The scenes should tell the story—beginning, middle, and end—with the accompanying narration adding the related facts."

If, for example, a story concerns the integration of a school, the editor is supposed to choose footage showing black and white students together, even if the vast preponderance of footage shows either all black or all white students congregating together—a situation which often occurs, since integration is frequently token rather than real, and "integrated" schools often maintain a de facto segregation by using "track" systems. NBC producers in New York, for example, criticized the editing of a story about the integration of the Shaker Heights (Ohio) schools, since the establishing shots failed to show Negro and white students mixing. One New York producer told the field producer in Cleveland, "You need a recut to get some Negroes in there . . . You never see any signs of integration. You definitely need some Negroes in the opening scene. I'm hoping you can drop some in." The Cleveland producer replied over the telephone that there was in fact very little mixing, since "integration is just beginning here," but that he would have the film editors "put in whatever we have." However, the field editors were unable to find such footage, and the producers in New York expressed a great deal of dissatisfaction with the piece.

Further, from the total film footage available, editors presume that their jobs is to ferret out the shots which most exactly illustrate the script. This may call for shots of bearded students in a peace march, militant Afro-style black leaders in an urban riot, or clean-cut college students in a political campaign, depending on the story line. (Editors also are expected to select the appropriate background sounds from a library of tape recordings, which include such titles as "Washington Gallery Hubbub," "Arab Mumbles," "Crowd Cheering," "Crowd Chanting," "Pickets Yelling," "Noisy Riot," "Gunfire" and "Black Demonstrators.") In a very real sense, editing practices tend to reinforce existing stereotypes as well as the established stories.

Film editing can also be used to enforce the policies of producers and executives. Unlike correspondents, who at least claim some autonomy in interpreting news occurring in their presence, film editors think of themselves as working directly for the producer of a program, and their function as complying with his instructions (except where it violates the technical norms of editing). As one NBC producer said, "My final control is in the editing room." Robert MacNeil describes graphically in his book how the more gruesome shots of battle casualties in the Vietnam war were deleted in the editing room. This was an unwritten policy of the Evening News because, as one person commented, "We go on the air at suppertime." The fear among network executives was that such grisly footage would cause home viewers to switch the program off, an NBC vice-president subsequently explained to me. Film editors were thus instructed to edit out all "upsetting shots" of casualties. Similarly, profanity and obscene references, no matter how germane they may be to a story about provocation and reaction, are also cut out in the editing room.

Finally, when the edited picture track is merged with the sound track, and narration and special effects added, the process of reconstructing reality is completed. The fact that stories are reconstructed routinely according to certain established guidelines, practices and policies, tends to preform, if not determine, the resulting images of reality in a number of ways. First, since cameramen, correspondents, producers and editors all tend to favor articulate and prepared scenes over confused and spontaneous happenings—deleting inarticulate statements and any sort of distraction—viewpoints are presented as highly resolved and crisply articulated issues, and the news makers become cogent advocates of a cause. By seeking or inducing opposing viewpoints—and editing them in a point-counterpoint format—network news further adds a dimension of logic and order that often is lacking in the realm of spontaneous news.

Second, network news tends to favor pictures of action over inaction. As one NBC producer pointed out, "There is a three-stage distillation of news footage": that is, producers seek out stories with a high potential for action footage; within these stories, cameramen seek out the most "action-packed moments"; and editors then further concentrate the action. Even when an event is characterized by an unexpected low degree of activity, television can create the illusion of great activity. The relatively unenthusiastic reception General MacArthur received in Chicago during his homecoming welcome in 1951, thus appeared to be a massive and frenetic reception on television because all the moments of action were concentrated together, according to the previously cited study by Kurt and Gladys Lang. In collapsing the time frame of events and concentrating the action into a continuous flow, television news tends to heighten the excitement of any group or other phenomena it pictures, to the neglect of the more vapid and humdrum elements.

Third, since news stories tend to be constructed from those aspects of a happening that can be easily filmed and recorded, and not from the more poorly lit, softly spoken or otherwise inaccessible moments, events tend to be explained in terms of what one producer called "visual facts." One correspondent pointed out, for example, that television coverage of riots or protests at night tends to focus on fires, even if they are insignificant "trash-can fires," since they provide adequate light for filming.

Hence, urban riots tend to be defined in terms of the "visual facts" of fires, rather than more complicated factors. Visual facts, of course, cover only one range of phenomena, and thus tend to limit the power of networks to explain complex events.

Finally, the entire process of reconstructing stories tends to fulfill preconceived expectations about how various events occur. Rather than recording the actual flow of events, network news follows predetermined lines, from the developing of a story line to the photographing of selected aspects of the happening to the final editing. Since each of the participants in the process—the cameraman, sound recorder, correspondent, editor and producer —has relatively fixed ideas of what material is wanted for each type of story, the "reality" produced tends to be shaped, if not predetermined, by this web of expectations.

Chapter 6

Decisions

For two hours, a half-dozen senior people in the Huntley-Brinkley team ... debate the question of which stories are important enough to demand inclusion that night, which features should be taken from the shelf, what should come out first....
— *Robert Kintner, president of NBC*

Not all the stories filmed by network news crews are eventually used on news programs. As a "margin of safety," as one NBC executive termed it, more stories are generally assigned coverage than there is room for on the networks' limited news schedule. Moreover, almost invariably, outside news agencies offer the networks a plethora of film each day. At some point a final decision must be made as to which of the available stories will be used. The executive producer of the NBC Evening News in 1968 explained:

I have only one job on the show ... I do a rundown. I take a piece of paper and write out what's going to be on the show in what order and at what length. ... My whole day is directed towards that, and it is possible to do nothing else all day.

Even though at all three networks the executive producer of the news programs ultimately decides on this rundown —or "line-up" as it is called at ABC and CBS—the agenda of possible choices is progressively narrowed down by a series of prior decisions made by other members of the news organizations.

At each network, executives first determine how far the net will be cast for news—i.e., the cities in which news crews will be deployed, the number of correspondents, and the budget for relaying news from remote locations. Within these limits, assignment editors choose which of numerous possible stories to allocate to a limited number of network news crews; and once at the scene, the news crew itself decides which aspects of the happening will be filmed. Moreover, the number of possible stories is further reduced by each program's staff, which scans incoming films and scripts, and rejects those stories in progress which fail to meet the program's standards or otherwise seem inappropriate. By the time the producer actually does his rundown, the number of stories has thus already been routinely cut down to a limited number which meet the program's general standards. In the case of the evening news programs, for example, the fifty to a hundred stories which exist as possibilities each morning are progressively reduced to usually no more than ten to twelve by the time the rundown is prepared, and from these the producer selects six to eight for the half-hour program.

The decisions by the producer and his staff of what to include and what to reject control not only what the audience sees but also, to some extent, the direction of the future search for news. When asked in interviews why they watched network news programs, most correspondents, assignment editors, producers and news managers of affiliated stations said it helped them determine "what type of news stories were currently in demand," as one correspondent put it. Presumably, newsmen then attempt to satisfy this perceived demand for certain kinds of stories.

An example of how after-the-fact decisions feed back in the news process was given by Mike Wallace, the CBS correspondent, in an interview on public television in 1968. In explaining the heavy emphasis on bloody scenes in combat film from Vietnam in 1967, Wallace suggested: "Some of the correspondents kept a kind of scorecard as to which pieces were and were not used, and why, and it seemed as though an inordinate number of combat pieces were used, compared with some first-rate pieces in the political area or the pacification area or non-bloody stories." Similarly, according to a former NBC bureau chief in Saigon, free-lance cameramen in Vietnam had a powerful incentive to seek out and "replicate" the most frequently used types of combat scenes, since they were compensated on the basis of the amount of their film footage that was used—and presumably the types of scenes previously aired reflected the preferences of network producers. In this way the decisions to include or eliminate stories may enforce values throughout the entire news organization.

The question remains: Can such decisions be profitably analyzed? To be sure, many of the producers' decisions are based mainly on personal preferences for one subject over another, or personal opinions that one story will be more interesting to the audience than another, and choices like these can only be explained in terms of the values of the individual producer. There is, however, another class of decisions made by the subordinates of the producer as they routinely narrow down the list of possible stories, and these are based more on organizational standards than personal preferences. Indeed, the defining test of such decisions is that they can be delegated from the producer to any one of his assistants with the expectation that a similar choice will be made. Moreover, the reasons for rejecting a given story can usually be clearly articulated in critiques to members of the organization, and almost always they involve the violation of some general standard rather than a judgment about the specific "news value" of the story in question. At the very least, then, an examination of these "routine" decisions, as they are commonly called by producers, could be expected to clarify an important part of the selection process: the established rules by which certain types of news stories are pre-emptively discarded.

To approach this problem, I studied the selection process at the NBC Evening News over a ten-week period. For my purposes, a "decision" was simply defined as the elimination of a possible news story from further consideration. The point at which a story either was crossed off a producer's list or not added to a revised list was considered to be the point a decision was reached. (A positive definition of a decision as the moment at which a story was *included* on the program was less useful, since it was not usually known until the final rundown what would definitely be used, while it was known at various points throughout the day which were definitely eliminated.)

Whenever an assistant producer dropped a story from his list, I asked him for an explanation; subsequently I would also ask the deputy or executive producer—who usually had little specific knowledge about the piece—why he presumed that it had been eliminated. In cases in which there was general agreement on the standard used for eliminating a story—and this was the rule, not the exception—I assumed it to be an established criterion. I then simply counted the number of times that a criterion was used in the ten-week period, and ranked them accordingly (though, in many cases, more than one criterion was given).

Finally, to ascertain how generally these criteria were accepted as rules in network news, I asked executives and producers at the other two networks whether they would expect similar kinds of stories to be eliminated from their programs in similar circumstances (a technique which obviously has much more limited value than direct observation).

Although the more or less accepted rules are not by

any means immutable, they do reflect some of the realities of network news, and are therefore worth examining in detail.

Outside Stories

With few exceptions, film stories from outside agencies are rejected routinely, if not automatically. An assistant producer leafs through the reports of the eight to twelve films available each day from the VisNews Agency, an affiliated agency which supplies NBC News with film stories from all parts of the world; however, only rarely does he order a VisNews offering screened, or put it on his list of available films. Out of the more than six hundred VisNews films offered over the ten-week period, dealing with such diverse subjects as Soviet Fleet maneuvers in the Mediterranean, the Biafra war, the food shortage in India, and gunboat incidents in Latin America, only one short film was used. To fill "an extra fifty seconds," as the producer put it, a two-week-old VisNews film of a volcano erupting in Nicaragua was inserted in the program at the last minute. The producers all agreed that regardless of their content or subject, VisNews films tended to be inappropriate because of their form. The assistant producer in charge of reviewing this material explained that VisNews films were usually (1) too short, according to network standards; (2) "pre-edited," providing no additional footage so that network editors could revise them into the appropriate form; and (3) did not use network correspondents, which was deemed important for the purpose of audience identification with the program.

Similarly, the producer in London for NBC was routinely able to reject almost all of the six to eight films offered daily by Eurovision, a service which exchanges news stories between various European and British television stations, without consulting with the producer in

New York (which would have been difficult to do because of the five-hour time difference). Again, most of these films failed to meet network standards. They were in black-and-white rather than color; they often were not reported in the English language, or not from an American viewpoint; and in any case they tended to be "too timely," which meant they would be dated by the time they were shipped back to America. With the exception of such momentous events as the 1968 Soviet invasion of Czechoslovakia, when whatever film that is available is transmitted to New York by satellite regardless of the additional expense involved, most film stories from European news agencies are rejected out of hand. If a European story is of interest to the network producer, he will usually assign a network crew to redo it from an American perspective.

The same sort of logic applies to news stories which affiliated stations offer to the network programs. Although an assistant producer is responsible for reviewing possible affiliate offerings, which usually vary between ten and twenty a day, he usually routinely dismisses most of them without even viewing them or discussing their contents, on the assumption that they have only local interest. The only offerings that are listed for further consideration and then evaluated by telephone, according to the producers interviewed, are those which either tie in with a network story—for example, by furnishing a "peg" for a network feature-type of piece—or which contain film of strong visual interest, such as a plane crash or robbery in progress, which would otherwise not be available to the network. As in the case of foreign news, network producers would rather shoot, or at least re-edit, a story themselves than use one supplied by an affiliate. For one thing, a producer further explained, such stories rarely meet network standards or formulas. Further, since network production is geared to the amount of available time on news programs, the use of outside stories would mean displacing some network-produced stories—which producers would prefer to use. Finally, and perhaps most important, reshowing a news story supplied by an affiliate would probably mean that one segment of the audience would see the same story repeated on both the local and national news, which, an executive producer observed, "is not the purpose of network news." Indeed, out of the more than one thousand stories suggested by affiliates during the ten-week period, only eight were used on the NBC Evening News—and only sixty were even advanced on the list as possibilities.

Except for film stories supplied by the Defense Department and Communist news agencies showing otherwise unobtainable scenes of military combat in Vietnam or American prisoners, news stories from other outside agencies and free-lance cameramen rarely were even considered by producers in this ten-week period. Not only is there the presumption that outside film "cannot be trusted," as one producer suggested, but also the fear that the acceptance of such film might mean displacing network stories.

The same strong preference for network-produced over outside stories exists at the other two networks, according to their executives and producers—although, according to the logs, CBS used slightly more footage from affiliates than did NBC or ABC during this period.

Commissioned Stories

Whereas outside film tended to be routinely rejected, stories commissioned, or specifically ordered, by a program's producers were automatically advanced on the list of possibilities. Of the one hundred and ten stories commissioned during this period, none were crossed off the preliminary lists and all but a handful were eventually shown on the air. The assistant producers held that only the executive producer has the right to reject a commissioned story, since its costs are charged against the program's budget. Also, it is presumed by the staff that these stories are carefully designed to meet the program's needs and closely supervised from their inception to final editing to meet the program's standards.

Moreover, the commissioned stories are on themes hand-picked by the producer. For example, after the election in November 1968, a list of story ideas was compiled by the executive and deputy producers for commissioned pieces. Four general ideas—Violence, Narcotics, Welfare and The Peace Corps—were suggested as series; seven more, all dealing with black advancement in society through nonviolent means, came under the category of Civil Rights. Of the remaining eleven, four dealt with airplane or shipping-traffic snarls, two with restless students, two with labor problems, and three with white resistance in the South, drug addicts and the realignment of political parties. Almost all these commissioned stories dealt with "problems of a changing society," as the producer explained.

Similarly, when coverage is pooled between the networks, the resulting story is virtually always advanced to the final list and usually used, since presumably it will be shown on the other networks' programs. Aside from not wanting to appear to be scooped by the competition, an NBC producer suggested that "it never looks good to executives if we pay for a story and then don't use it."

The balance of the news stories come from the network's own general-coverage service, which assigns network crews to the events deemed, as the morning report terms it, of "principal news interest," and thus supplements the program's diet of commissioned stories. Since these general-coverage stories are reconstructed according to network standards, as discussed in the preceding chapter, they are eliminated from the list of possibilities only if they are at odds with the specific criteria of the program, which vary from time to time.

At the time of my field study, the following rules were applied in sorting out the network-produced stories, according to producers.

Correspondents. Network stories were routinely rejected or selected on the basis of which correspondent reported them. The producer's subordinates had an unwritten list of about half a dozen correspondents who were not to be used, except in the case of "earth-shattering news," as a producer put it. These particular correspondents covered news stories ranging from Congress to the space-exploration program; yet of seventy possible stories they reported, only two were not crossed off preliminary lists—if entered at all—at early stages. The reasons for blacklisting these correspondents, as the practice was known, varied, according to executive producers' offhanded descriptions, from their age ("too old") to their general appearance ("lack of sex appeal") to their presentation ("not punchy enough" or "no sense of humor").

Apart from their undesirable style, some correspondents were excluded from the program because on one or more occasions they had failed to follow a producer's explicit instructions. The blacklist thus also served as a means of exerting control over correspondents, since their continued tenure with the networks depends to a large degree on the frequency of their appearances—not to mention the additional income they receive as a "commercial fee" each time they appear on a sponsored newscast. Aware of the informal blacklist, assignment editors would go to great lengths not to assign these correspondents to stories intended to be used by the program.

Conversely, there was a small group of highly favored correspondents whose stories, regardless of subject, were almost automatically advanced to the final rundown. One producer explained: "It's simple. Some correspondents do stories the way we want them done, and some are less dependable."

At the other networks, executives do not acknowledge that news stories are rejected on the basis of the correspondent reporting them. Nonetheless, as discussed in Chapter IV, the film stories of a small group of correspondents are consistently selected and fill a large part of the evening news programs.

"Used" Stories. Network news stories were also routinely passed over as possible candidates for the evening news if they had been used on an earlier program, unless the subject had special interest for the producer. The editor responsible for reviewing for possible reuse the five to seven film stories shown each day on the *Today* show, NBC's morning news program, explained that unless a particular piece closely fits in with the news "package" planned for the evening news, it is usually discarded automatically. A notable exception, he added, is combat footage from Vietnam, which is often retained on the list until the final rundown. Of the more than three hundred stories used on the *Today* show during this ten-week period, except for combat stories, only sixteen were advanced on the list of possibilities, and of this total only four eventually were reused. "Every time we repeat a story," a producer suggested, "we run the risk that some viewers will switch channels, which is not a risk we like to take."

Local Stories. Local stories, defined by a NBC producer somewhat facetiously during a staff meeting as "news occurring outside of Washington or New York," are usually eliminated by the staff early in the narrowing-down process. In evaluating possible stories, the responding producer explained, the touchstone applied is "whether or not a story will have nationwide interest." More closely defined, a news happening occurring outside of Washington or New York City is deemed by producers to have nationwide interest if the news makers involved are both well known in most areas of the country and generally considered to be national leaders, as opposed to local ones, or if the local occurrence illustrates a national theme or "trend." Thus, news stories concerning mayors, even if they have a national following, were routinely dropped from the list.

At the time of this study, the producers interviewed said that the dominant themes included "the race problem," "the urban crisis," the threatened "collapse of the educational system," "campus unrest," innovations in "transportation," "the generation gap" and "the new politics." News stories that could be integrated with these themes were usually advanced on the list until the final rundown, while others, not apparently "relevant," were dropped. The point, the executive producer explained, was to lessen the likelihood "of duplication of stories shown on the local news."

Three exceptions were generally made in the case of distinctly local pieces. First, stories which were humorous or ironic were usually advanced on the list as possible "closers," which as a matter of policy are required to be on the "light side," according to the executive producer. Second, films which capture a highly unusual happening, such as a natural disaster, in high-quality footage were presumed to interest viewers. Third, stories about Los Angeles, especially if they purported to elucidate the California style of living, were given preference, since the executive producer considered it important to balance the bulk of New York and Washington stories with a West Coast one.

Executives and producers at the other networks also put a similarly high value on national news as opposed to local news. The producer of the ABC Evening News pointed out that most of the stories his staff selected were "packaged" around major national themes, and each of the segments of the program were devoted to a different theme. More localized stories not bearing on such themes were disregarded. Producers at CBS said they reviewed most local stories, but recommended them only if they had clear national or intrinsic interest.

Prior Decisions. In certain cases, film stories are precluded by the staff because they conflict with a prior decision or policy laid down by the executive producer or his superiors. Such policies may restrict whole categories of events. For example, as a matter of "long-standing network policy," the executive producer explained, sports stories are ruled out as a subject for the NBC Evening News except when they serve to promote a major sports event televised by the network, such as the Rose Bowl, or if they take on the importance of a national event. Therefore the staff automatically rejects sports stories.

Similarly, producers can restrict coverage of specific news makers or subjects. During the period of this study, for example, NBC producers agreed that stories which showed black militant leaders threatening violent acts against society were not desirable, and earlier two black militants, Stokely Carmichael and H. Rap Brown, had been "banned" from NBC, according to the executive producer. Moreover, fairly strict guidelines about what could not be reported in the case of riots and racial disturbances were made manifestly clear to the producers. For instance, executives at NBC News prohibited film reports which "advertised" future demonstrations or disturbances, according to Reuven Frank. The producer of the Evening News further gave instructions to avoid "inflammatory" speeches by radicals and militants.

Just as certain types of news stories are excluded at times by prior decisions, the advancement of others to the stage of the final rundown may be considered mandatory by producers. For example, any stories dealing with the space program, and any film produced by NASA could not be dropped without the specific approval of the executive producer during the period I studied the NBC Evening News. Similarly, film reports involving the President and the President-elect were automatically brought to the executive producer's attention. More frequently, the executive producer would order that a particular story, such as a mine disaster or the hunger hearings of a Senate subcommittee, be continued until he decided it was "played out," as he once put it.

Even after the staff sorts out the various stories which fail to meet the producers' standards, the remaining number almost always exceeds the available amount of time on the program. In choosing among these possibilities, producers generally give weight to those which can be expected to fulfill the requisites of the program.

Major News. Obviously, one such requisite is to carry the major news developments of the day that it can be expected the competing media will report. While what constitutes a major story is not always easy to articulate, once one is defined by producers as such, it is virtually certain that it will be selected for the program. On a typical day, however, at most only one or two stories have this status; most of the rest of the stories tend to be marginal in the sense, as a NBC producer put it, that "no one would miss them if they weren't on tonight." In deciding which of the marginal stories will be aired, the producers commonly favor those which best seem to fit in the internal requirements of the program.

Economy. It will be recalled that a network news program has a limited weekly budget for transmitting news stories from their source to New York City, where they are rebroadcast over the network, and that they are expected to keep closely to their monthly budget; if not, they are or called upon by executives for an explanation. Therefore producers at all three networks readily acknowledge that is is necessary to control carefully the money expended on marginal stories, and when there is a choice in the matter the simplest way to do this is to take stories from cheaper rather than more expensive locations.

It will be recalled that a timeless story, or one that cannot be dated by any elements in it, is as a rule cheaper than a timely story, since it can be shipped back by air freight, whereas stories in danger of being dated must usually be transmitted over special cables rented from AT&T. Of the latter stories, it is almost always cheaper to transmit those from cities in which NBC owns stations, with the exception of Los Angeles, since these four cities —New York, Washington, Chicago and Cleveland—are permanently wired for this sort of transmission, and no additional costs are charged against the program's budget. (Other major stations—notably Los Angeles—have permanent loops, and therefore the only charge incurred is the mileage charge for renting the long lines.) The transmission costs are similar at the other networks, although in 1968 the budget for remotes at ABC was greatly less than at CBS and NBC.

An analysis of the final choices at NBC during this ten-week period shows that with few exceptions, marginal stories that required little or no transmitting costs were chosen over stories that required both loop and mileage charges. To separate major from marginal stories, I excluded all the lead stories, which presumably were the major news developments, as well as any stories that producers specifically identified as major, and considered the balance as marginal stories. In the case of the lead stories, there was no clear bias in favor of the less expensive ones. For example, almost all satellite transmissions occurred in this category. Presumably these stories were selected purely on the basis of their news value.

But in the case of the marginal stories, where there were competing choices from a relatively inexpensive and expensive locale, the less expensive story was chosen five out of six times. Moreover, in the rare case where more expensive-to-transmit stories were selected, they usually featured a regular correspondent on the program—that is, one of the fifteen most often used correspondents—or else the segment concerned California news, which as a matter of policy was frequently shown on the program.

Washington News Makers. Network news is also expected by affiliates to supplement local newscasts by prominently covering the activities of government leaders, thereby relieving local stations of this responsibility. Indeed, the affiliate executives I interviewed all listed Washington coverage as a major reason for subscribing to network news. While each network features a Washington story almost every day, at NBC it is considered a "house rule," according to producers, that space be reserved for *two* Washington stories a day. Usually the Washington producer for the Evening News phones in from two to four Washington stories a day, which are then automatically listed on the final rundown, and are usually given preference over stories about non-Washington news makers.

In narrowing down the possibilities, the Washington producer said that when all other factors were equal, he would choose the news makers holding higher national office. The order he followed is, first, the President, then the Vice-President and high Cabinet officers (Defense, State and the Attorney General), presidential candidates, senators, other Cabinet officers and administrative spokesmen, and finally, congressmen. This order of preferences is roughly confirmed by my analysis of the elimination of Washington stories, which showed that the President, President-elect and their chief spokesmen were virtually never dropped by the Washington producer; Senate subcommittee chairmen and Cabinet officers were rarely preemptively eliminated; congressmen and bureau heads were eliminated three times as often as senators. (Since this analysis was made immediately after the 1968 election, there were no candidates in the news.)

"Action."   Since a major imperative of network news is to hold the attention of as many viewers as possible, producers are expected to put together a show that has continuous interest to a highly disparate audience, ranging from preschool children to the elderly. Possibly the only element of network news that is presumed to have "holding power," as an NBC producer termed the quality, for all segments of the audience is visual action, or pictures which are considered exciting. At all the networks, each morning an assistant producer is charged with evaluating film shipped to New York for its visual appeal. During the period of my field study, this evaluation carried great weight in the selection process at NBC: if the producer

characterized a film story as showing a great deal of action, it was usually advanced to the final rundown. On the other hand, if a story was depicted as lacking action, it was usually dropped—with the notable exception of Washington stories shipped to New York.

To be sure, there are limits to the extent that violent action can be depicted on the Evening News. Films that are considered excessively gory, and which might cause parents to switch channels, are usually either rejected or re-edited. In its manual, CBS News advises: "Television's intimacy and its family audience require special consideration in dealing with one type of newspaper story. The lurid, the sensational, the gruesome—or at least the details thereof—usually are not for television." Up to this limit, however, the chances of a film piece being used on network news increases with the amount of violent action it contains.

Integration. Producers generally assume that there is more chance of retaining the viewers' interest if the stories used on the program, or at least in each segment before the commercial message, seem to dovetail together, rather than appearing to be unrelated. In its manual, CBS News suggested that "a story which adds something to an organizational topic takes on some importance from the value of the over-all topic. It may outweigh the otherwise-equal stray item." The executive producer of the ABC Evening News follows a similar procedure, selecting those stories which can be "packaged" together into a single segment. Similarly, at NBC, stories which seemed to "play well" with the themes and commissioned stories the producer preselected were usually chosen over stories which could not easily be connected. (An important exception to this rule is the idiosyncratic California stories used as "closers.") Otherwise, all other things being equal, stray stories were regularly eliminated by the deputy producer as he prepared the preliminary rundown, usually with the explanation that "it doesn't seem to fit." The same principle held true with stories that appeared to contradict commissioned stories or continuing ones. So as "not to confuse the audience," an NBC producer explained, such inconsistent stories usually were cut out before the final rundown.

The Final Decision. Although the choice is narrowed down considerably by the staff applying more or less established criteria, the executive producer still must decide on the final rundown. At all three networks, the accepted practice is to choose the major story, if any is commonly agreed on that day, as the lead item on the program. If there is a second major item—which is a rarity on any given day—it usually immediately follows the lead item. According to the producers interviewed, the rationale for this order is that some viewers might switch channels if major developments are not reported early in the program. The other clear-cut choice is the closer, which is usually a humorous or "light" story. California stories, which also helped maintain the image of coast-to-coast coverage, or stories about the wilderness, which the producer claimed balanced the "tragic news," were usually chosen for this purpose. At CBS, according to the former president of its news division, Fred W. Friendly, the corporate policy was to fill the final five minutes of the evening news with " 'back of the book' news, which would include sports" in order to retain an automobile sponsor. More recently, CBS producers explained that they usually tried to end the program with a nostalgic piece from the "hinterlands," as one put it, which also served to give the program geographical balance. At ABC, the producer claimed in 1969 that the policy was less rigid, but that he attempted to close with a feature which would interest the "silent majority" audience. More recently, ABC News has followed a policy of ending with a comment by one of its two anchormen.

In selecting the film pieces for the body of the program, weight is usually given to maintaining the appearance of nationwide news. In looking at the preliminary list each day in which the stories are divided according to the city from which they must be transmitted, the producer must first decide from which cities other than New York news stories will be used that day. Depending on that decision, long lines, special equipment and technical personnel may have to be ordered from AT&T or the network's broadcast center, and a highly intricate technical schedule for "switches" between cities worked out. Since at ABC it is more or less established policy to take daily stories from the capital, and the technical connections are permanently maintained, the producer first checks the Washington stories that will be used and writes them into the final rundown. Next, a decision must be made whether to go to Los Angeles, Chicago and Cleveland, where NBC owns and operates local stations, and from which it is desirable from the organizational point of view to take stories, if only to utilize these resources fully. In making this choice, the producer commonly asked his staff the last time a story was taken from one of these cities; if it turned out that a segment had not been transmitted from one of these stations for a number of days, he was more likely to select it than if a story from there had been used the previous day.

Next, the producer must decide whether or not to take stories from more remote cities that require special facilities, which are charged to the program's budget and must be ordered in advance. Not infrequently, at this point the producer would ask the unit manager whether the program was running over budget, to help him decide whether or not a further expenditure was warranted.

Further, the producer must choose pieces that fit in with the selections already chosen. The program is divided into five segments, each punctuated by a commercial, and of a predetermined length. This means that a producer often chooses supplemental stories because he needs a piece of a certain length to complete the jigsaw of the program.

Producers are also responsible for "pacing" the program, which was defined half-humorously by an NBC producer as "not putting two long, talky pieces next to each other." In practice, when pieces were selected for pacing reasons, it almost always involved choosing a relatively short story involving a good deal of action.

After the film stories are finally selected, producers or other newsmen are assigned the job of writing lead-ins and leads, and the summary of headlines gathered from the wire services with which the anchormen tie together the final program.

In sum, the process of weeding out and selecting news stories involves a set of predecisions about the types and specifications of film pieces that fit the mold of a news program. In the case of the NBC Evening News, producers first decided in advance on what type of news stories to commission, the cities that were to be favored, the visual content, the correspondents, the focus or perspective, and the news makers to be given preference. At CBS and ABC, producers similarly attempted to shoulder responsibility by setting forth criteria and standards.

The net effect is that the news selected is the news expected. These expectations range from what is national as opposed to local news to the programs' budget for expenditures; it is shaped in part by the organizational needs of the networks, and in part by the values of the producers and correspondents intimately involved in the news process.

Chapter 7

Values

The essence of professionalism is discipline.
—Reuven Frank, president of NBC News

Since the perspectives of society that emerge
on network news are, in the final analysis,
selected and reconstructed by a small group
of newsmen, it is commonly assumed that any
particular slant that these news pictures appear to have can be best explained by examining the personal values of the newsmen
involved in the selection process. Exemplify-
ing this view, Frank J. Shakespeare, the
director of the United States Information
Agency and a former vice-president of CBS,
asserted in a speech that television news is
"clearly liberally oriented" because the "over-
whelming number of people who go into the
creative . . . and . . . news side of television
tend by their instinct to be liberally oriented." Precisely the same logic can be found
in Vice-President Agnew's public denuncia-
tion of network news, in which he argued
that it was heavily influenced by the personal
ideologies of a small "fraternity of newsmen

with similar outlooks." And in a much more sophisticated form, the same approach can also be found in the analyses of social scientists who argue that news is largely predetermined by newsmen's economic and social class, or what Marxists now call a "sociology of knowledge."

At different levels, then, a considerable portion of the research about the news media has been focused on the values and social situation of the reporter. The trouble with this approach is that it tacitly assumes that newsmen have a stable set of values or ideologies to which they are inextricably attached and which they carry with them to the news organization they work for. At the same time this theory neglects the converse possibility that newsmen take their opinions from the news organization, altering them whenever organizational needs change. The question the first assumption begs is: Which way do values run in a large organization?

While undoubtedly there is some connection between what a newsman values and what elements of an event he chooses to emphasize or ignore, these values may come from the requisites of the news organization, rather than being deep-seated individual beliefs or ideologies. Just as students of organizational behavior have found what they call an identification of values, whereby employees substitute corporate for personal preferences, newsmen may be expected to identify their values with those of their news program. Thus, Sander Vanocur wrote in *Esquire*, after resigning from NBC News as a correspondent and anchorman:

> NBC is a very paternalistic company. . . . Corporately, the image projected—at least to me—was that not of Big Brother but rather Big Mother . . . She feeds you (rather more than you need for your own good), she rewards you, and she punishes you in the sense that for years during the period of prolonged adolescence you tend to feel that you must not do anything or say anything which she will not approve. You find more and more that your journalistic behavior pattern tends more and more to be shaped

towards an expression not of what you believe but rather towards what Big Mother will find acceptable.

Some form of identification of values occurred, as Vanocur explains:

I began to realize that I had taken on the psychological trappings of THEY [the corporate executives]. And one day I asked myself, who was I? Was I Me? Or was I THEY? And if I were me, then how much of THEY had seeped into what was supposed to be me? It was then I realized the process was so subtle that for years I had taken their institutionalized fears and inhibitions and had now institutionalized them into myself.

The result, he further suggested, was that "the commentators became subordinate to the producers, who in turn were being continually second-guessed by management."

In most cases, the process is not as subtle or Orwellian as Vanocur describes it. But newsmen are supposed to conform to a certain image of news reporting, even if it means modifying their own values. Consider the situation of Chet Huntley, when he was co-anchorman, with David Brinkley, of the NBC Evening News in 1969.

The format of the program, then called "The Huntley-Brinkley Report," was intentionally designed to differentiate the style of the two anchormen, who presented the news contrapuntally from Washington and New York, according to the creator of the program, Reuven Frank. The idea of contrasting the styles of Huntley and Brinkley as sharply as possible, Frank explained, was to install "a built-in tension." Brinkley took on the role of "an antiestablishment maverick," and Huntley the role of a more conservative "defender of the status quo." No doubt both men felt comfortable in their roles to begin with, but as the program became successful it became important to maintain and accentuate the differences. The image of Huntley as a hard-line conservative was quite consciously emphasized by staff writers—and openly discussed at staff meetings I attended—to contrast with Brinkley's comments, which he himself wrote. While Huntley accepted this image, if only by reading the comments prepared for him by the staff, off the air he still considered himself to be the same staunch liberal he had previously had a reputation for in radio, where he had made a name for himself as an opponent of Senator Joe McCarthy. In fact, when I interviewed Huntley, his views on most major issues seemed remarkably similar to those of David Brinkley. Yet for the sake of providing tension for the program, he was expected to act out a different image.

Further, one of the main writers for Huntley considered himself to be extremely liberal in his own politics. However, unless they were simply statements of fact taken directly from the wire services, the scripts he prepared for Huntley conformed—without exception during the period I examined them—to the conservative image of Huntley. Like Huntley, this particular writer modified his view of the world—at least in his writing—to support an organizational image with which he often disagreed. In both cases, instead of personal views affecting the presentation of news, the reverse happened.

Even when newsmen expressed definite views on controversial subjects, it does not necessarily follow that these opinions stem from any deeply ingrained ideology, or are even sustained over any extended period of time. Opinions are often ephemeral. For example, in the last week of October 1968, I asked eight NBC correspondents which black leaders, if any, they admired. Six of these correspondents named Lou Smith, the articulate but little-known organizer from the Los Angeles area, who had been interviewed on the NBC Evening News earlier that week. A month later, immediately after the Reverend Jesse Jackson, a Chicago civil rights leader, appeared on the program, I put the same question to the six correspondents who had previously listed Lou Smith. This time Smith was not named by one of them, and Jackson, who had not previously been mentioned, was listed by four. As similar, repeated questions on other subjects seemed to confirm, correspondents' opinions, even when strongly stated, often tended to change with the content of the program they watched regularly.

Finally, even on topics in which newsmen maintain strong personal views on a subject, the influence of these values in shaping the news is limited by their ability to inject them into a newscast. More than perhaps other news media, television is a "group effort," in Reuven Frank's words, and producers—and ultimately executives —retain a measure of control over the final script. It will be recalled that as an NBC anchorman, Robert MacNeil narrated a revised conclusion to a program on gun control with which he profoundly disagreed and even considered to be dishonest, because he recognized the right of executives to revise his script in accordance with organizational needs. With only a few exceptions, the other newsmen I interviewed accepted without question the right of producers to delete their personal views or, as in the case of Huntley and his writer, to *create* views or take positions on important events.

There are also fairly strict guidelines and policies imposed by executives to which correspondents must conform, and these can be quite explicit. For example, on the subject of riots, Julian Goodman, the president of NBC, pointed out to the National Commission on the Causes and Prevention of Violence that NBC reporters are instructed to "describe a disturbance as a 'riot' or as 'racial' only after it has been officially designated as such; . . . to check all rumors of estimates of damage and crowd size with the proper authorities; to avoid reports about 'crowds gathering' in possible trouble spots; to avoid any mention of how homemade weapons are constructed; to avoid persons or groups making an obvious play for attention; and to report as early and as completely as possible the background of the disturbance." Further, they are specifically "instructed to avoid interviews with 'self-appointed leaders,' and not to label as 'leader' individuals who may be 'militants' or 'activists' operating on their own"; and certain phrases "like 'tensions mounted . . .,' 'renewed outbreaks are feared . . .,' 'the city was rocked . . .' " are not permitted at NBC News.

Lastly, most correspondents maintained that even if no controls or restrictions were imposed on them, they themselves would resist injecting personal views into newscasts, since it violated their concept of "objective reporting." While skeptical observers may doubt the effectiveness of this concept, it is relentlessly cited by executives and producers as a goal of good reporting.

Thus, the question of whether the personal values of newsmen shape the organization they work for, or vice versa, is much more complicated than some analyses suggest. By their very nature, values influence newsmen, either consciously or unconsciously, and therefore must be considered an ingredient in the selection process. However, the extent to which they give the news operation a consistent direction or slant depends on the stability and consistency of newsmen's values, the control they retain over their final product, and their willingness purposely to inject—or suppress—these preferences when given the opportunity. Hence, in examining the values of newsmen, the first question is: How deep and durable are their preferences and commitments?

Correspondents

Most network correspondents are what sociologists call upwardly mobile. The typical correspondent was born in the Depression of the 1930s in a small Midwestern city, attended a non–Ivy League college, concentrating on speech, drama or English, then worked for a local television or radio station, moved East and rapidly ascended the ladder of success, surpassing the income and educational level reached by his parents. (Older correspondents, recruited in the days of radio, followed a more varied path.) Most of the thirty-two correspondents I interviewed at length suggested in one way or another that they had severed their ties to the past when they moved to network news. More than three fourths of them were divorced or separated from their first wives, whom most of them had married early in their careers. None still reside or claim to maintain any connection with the place where they grew up; most now own their own home in the suburbs of New York City, Washington, D.C., or Los Angeles.

Although readily identifying their parents' religion (predominantly Protestant), most correspondents maintained that they themselves had no religious affiliations and commonly called themselves agnostic or non-religious. (The main exceptions were correspondents over fifty who were Catholics.) While all attended liberal arts college, correspondents generally considered their formal education inadequate, or even "useless," as one put it, and suggested that they acquired most of their useful knowledge as working journalists. Few maintained any long-standing connections with political or social organizations. More than two thirds denied ever having registered as a member of a political party, and, with only two exceptions, they had never worked in a political campaign, belonged to a political club or actively participated in a political cause. Indeed, except for voting, correspondents claimed to be almost totally nonpolitical in their pre-network careers.

According to senior executives, this claim is very much in line with the recruitment policies of all three networks. A former CBS News vice-president explained that new recruits were thoroughly screened by senior executives before being hired as correspondents. "In those days [the early 1960s] we took on only a few new correspondents a year; in each case, an enormous amount of time was spent checking their past performance, and if any trace of bias or ideology was found, they were rejected out of hand." According to this former executive, the presumption at CBS was that the qualities of being "committed," "politically involved," a "true believer," "dogmatic" or an "advocate" were mutually exclusive with those of a "professional, objective newsman." Moreover, he continued, citing a number of examples, if a newsman begins to espouse ideas strenuously, even privately, after he is hired, "he doesn't last long."

NBC follows similar procedures in evaluating candidates. By far the largest number have traditionally been recruited from other NBC owned-and-operated stations, or two affiliates—WSB-TV in Atlanta and WSDU-TV in New Orleans—which, a vice-president of the news division suggested, served as the network's "farm teams." This vice-president explained that usually candidates are closely watched by both network and local executives for more than a year before they are given an opportunity with the network. While weight is given to such positive attributes as the correspondent's on-the-air appearance, elocution, reportorial ability and general image—"youthful," "stable," "wry," and so forth—they are preemptorily rejected if they seem to be committed to some cause or otherwise show a high degree of what the vice-president termed "activism." In showing me a file of letters discussing potential black correspondents, he pointed out that all of them had been passed over, despite their favorable image, because all were in one way or another involved in a cause. "I don't object to their values; in fact, I agree with them," he continued, "but we can't afford the headaches" which might result from having an "advocate" report the news. The headaches referred to the Fairness Doctrine, complaints from affiliates, congressional critics, and internal disputes with producers and other correspondents. "It is simply not in our enlightened self-interest," another senior executive commented, "to employ reporters with too firmly fixed ideas on how the world ought to be."

The same logic also applies at ABC. Since it was created only in 1941 out of a group of former NBC stations and lacked the long tradition of radio news that existed at the other two networks, ABC recruited a relatively large number of already established newsmen, mainly from CBS and local stations. Even so, a senior executive of the news division explained, a sustained effort was made to weed out correspondents who were not completely objective, which he defined as "being able to present facts uncolored by personal opinions." ABC executives were, he continued, likely to look askance at correspondents who espoused ideas too strongly, had "closed minds" on subjects, or became "overly involved" in issues. In a word, correspondents were expected to be neutral on controversial issues. (One former ABC correspondent, Sam Jaffee, claimed that he was "eased out" of ABC News because it was suspected that he had "leftist ideas.")

Even if networks are reasonably successful in recruiting correspondents without fixed ideas, can they remain uncommitted to ideas in an occupation devoted to political issues and arguments? The notion that network correspondents are inevitably politicized by their constant contact with news makers and other newsmen does not take into account the peripatetic nature of their job. Quite literally, the network newsman is an itinerant. Unlike his counterpart on a newspaper, who covers a specific beat or locality, most network correspondents spend a large part of their time traveling from one varied assignment to another. They can be dispatched almost anywhere in the world on a few hours' notice and frequently log tens of thousands of miles a month in jet planes shuttling between stories. Quite often, especially at NBC, field producers do the basic research on stories—at times even roughing out scripts and filming interviews—before the correspondent arrives on the scene, and the segment may still be incomplete when the correspondent departs for yet another assignment. One NBC correspondent, who formerly had worked as a newspaperman, complained to me, "I seem to be in a continual state of jet lag. . . . I travel now more miles in a week than I used to all year." In fact, the dizzying pace of jet travel was a common complaint among network correspondents.

Most correspondents also find the opportunity for sustaining personal relations with politicians and news makers severely limited by their travel requisites. One reason the networks avoid developing "beats" and "specialities," it will be recalled, is because they want correspondents to remain "outsiders," as Reuven Frank put it. For the same reason, networks commonly rotate correspondents on extended stories, such as election campaigns, and generally avoid assigning correspondents to candidates who are personal friends. According to correspondents, these policies are effective: only six of the thirty-two correspondents interviewed claimed to have become friends with news makers they interviewed for television, and these were mainly from the older group of newsmen. Most correspondents said that they rarely saw news makers outside of their work.

Nor do correspondents seem to be swayed in any consistent direction by their reading habits. When asked what newspapers and magazines they regularly read, most of them named an extensive and even prodigious list. Not only did most correspondents claim to read the *New York Times*, the *Wall Street Journal*, the Washington *Post* and anywhere from two to six lesser-known regional papers every day, but also an impressive spectrum of magazines ranging from *Ramparts* to the *National Review*. One NBC correspondent said he read no fewer than twelve newspapers daily and eighteen magazines monthly, while other correspondents named magazines they seemed only vaguely familiar with as ones they read regularly.

Since I rarely observed these men reading any periodicals during the course of my field study and suspected that the lists might represent an ideal rather than actual picture of their reading habits, I also asked the correspondents whether any articles appearing in newspapers or magazines in the last month or two had impressed them favorably or unfavorably. Only two of the twenty correspondents I put this question to named a specific magazine article. Most of them named syndicated newspaper columnists (most frequently mentioning James Reston, Joseph Alsop, Tom Wicker and Nicholas von Hoffman), or articles appearing in the *New York Times* (Sunday) *Magazine* and the "Review of the Week" section. More than half of the correspondents were not able to cite a single article in either a newspaper or magazine that they considered impressive. On the other hand, almost all of them showed great familiarity with television news programs and documentaries, especially if they had appeared on their own network. Further, in discussing the relative merits of news media, most of the correspondents said that they relied more on television than on newspapers or magazines for news of current trends, and as one correspondent suggested, "changes in the national mood."

In moving from story to story, the correspondents tended to depend more on the producer for the general organizing idea on a subject they were assigned to cover than on either background reading or personal contacts. Even on issues on which they had definite opinions, they would begin their assignment by discussing with a producer how the story should be "played," and almost invariably they then took his advice. When a correspondent himself had a novel idea for organizing a story—which, given the hectic conditions under which he operated, was the exception rather than the rule—he generally sought out the approval of a producer, and if the latter replied that the approach was not the right one, the idea was thereupon abandoned.

Finally, networks maintain definite policies against correspondents expressing opinions on controversial subjects in public, on or off the air. For example, NBC policy explicitly prohibits newsmen from taking sides in any political dispute, or advocating any controversial cause in public because it might reflect on the network. An NBC vice-president who read me these policy statements said that they are taken seriously by correspondents, as well as executives, "if they are interested in advancement." In these circumstances, there is little incentive for correspondents to form deep or systematic opinions about the world they report. Interestingly enough, the only two correspondents who identified themselves as "political activists" subsequently resigned from their respective networks.

Despite the limitations imposed on them by their job and employers at any given time, newsmen generally express a clear set of preferences in private. Most of the correspondents I interviewed in 1968–1969 were against the war in Vietnam, against the election of Richard Nixon and against pollution, and approved of the Black Power movement. On the surface, such preferences are not uncommonly classified under the rubric of "liberal attitudes"; however, if the surface is scratched, they become somewhat more difficult to define, at least as systematically ordered opinions.

For example, when asked what should be done about the war in Vietnam, all the correspondents answered that the United States should "get out," or gave a response to that effect. Most claimed to be doves on the war. But in late 1968 and early 1969, the disengagement of America from Vietnam was virtually a consensus position, espoused by politicians on opposite sides of the spectrum, from George Wallace to Richard Nixon to Hubert Humphrey and President Johnson. Indeed, during the 1968 election campaign, it was hard to find any political figure openly supporting an indefinite continuation of the war. Thus, opposition to the war in 1968 was not a particularly liberal position. (Indeed, according to one poll conducted by the American Political Science Association, a larger proportion of the political right was against the war than the political left.)

When asked specifically how America should get out of Vietnam, almost all the correspondents replied "through negotiations." They divided, however, on the question of what the basis of the negotiated settlement ought to be. More than one third of the correspondents held that the United States should negotiate an honorable peace in which the territorial integrity and independence of South Vietnam was preserved—a condition which not even supporters of the Vietnam policy in the Johnson Administration called for. Another third of the reporters said that the United States should negotiate a peace which would allow the South Vietnamese to choose their own form of government through free elections—a position which Lyndon Johnson himself held in 1968. Thus, over two thirds of the correspondents, though describing themselves as doves, seemed more in agreement with the Johnson Administration on Vietnam policy than with the critics calling for unilateral withdrawal without condition. Only three correspondents, in fact, called for such an evacuation; most of them were against a precipitous withdrawal because it might lead to a "blood bath," as one put it.

The same situation occurred in the case of the correspondents' opposition to Richard Nixon. While few of them favored the nomination of Richard Nixon, even fewer favored Hubert H. Humphrey. When asked if they thought the major parties had nominated their best candidate, only three answered affirmatively in the case of Humphrey and six in the case of Nixon. Moreover, a majority of the correspondents interviewed refused to make a choice between the two candidates; typical answers were "Neither," "No difference," "Both would be equally bad" or simply "No opinion." In general, the responses seemed to be more nonpolitical than highly partisan. Indeed, the reasons given for rejecting both Nixon and Humphrey as candidates were remarkably similar: their appearance and style. Various correspondents suggested that Humphrey lacked "sex appeal," "style," "excitement," "charisma," "youth," and so on;

Nixon appeared to be "programmed by a computer," "out of touch," "insincere" or "dull." Fewer than a third of them mentioned the past performance of either candidate or their stand on issues.

On the other hand, most correspondents enthusiastically supported Edmund Muskie, the Democratic vice-presidential candidate, as "the best man running," as one put it. Again, the preference seemed based more on cosmetic considerations than partisan issues. Muskie was commonly described as resembling "Abe Lincoln," "beautiful," "sympathetic," "the only human being" and "Kennedy-like" by correspondents. In supporting Muskie, none of those interviewed cited his politics or stands on issues. Nor did the fact that a few months earlier at the Democratic convention he had successfully led the heated fight *against* a "dove" platform calling for a bombing halt over North Vietnam seem to make any difference to the correspondents who identified themselves as doves. In many cases, it therefore seemed that correspondents' preferences for candidates were not necessarily an index of their politics.

Similarly, the strong opinions correspondents voiced against pollution and hunger in 1969 (in my 1968 interviews, little interest was expressed in either subject) can be viewed as an attempt to avoid rather than to participate in partisan politics. An NBC public relations executive explained that after the criticisms of television news generated by its coverage of the Democratic convention in 1968 and the election, correspondents were encouraged in their public appearances to speak out "on nondivisive subjects like pollution." He added, "Who could be *for* pollution?" The same logic, of course, applies to hunger. When correspondents were further asked whether they thought pollution should be alleviated by decreasing employment or production, most answered negatively, suggesting that the problem should be solved through "technology"—which, like the term "negotiations," is essentially a nonpolitical approach.

Approval of the Black Power movement also turned

out in the case of most correspondents to be more nominal than substantive. Almost two thirds of those interviewed said that they thought the Black Power movement was on balance helpful to blacks, but of those who favored it, almost all defined Black Power as a psychological concept which meant only that blacks should have pride in their race and traditions: "Black is Beautiful" was the most common way of summing up this concept. (Most of the reporters who opposed Black Power defined it, however, as control of the governing institutions by blacks.) But when the correspondents who approved of Black Power were asked if they approved of Black Power leaders Stokely Carmichael and H. Rap Brown, all but two answered "No." Further, when asked if blacks should be given control over their schools, housing projects and police forces in their communities—which are goals of the Black Power movement by its leaders—nearly all of them disagreed; for instance, only one fourth of them thought that ghetto residents should have control over neighborhood schools.

The same pattern of responses persisted on other political issues. Correspondents characteristically approved of a general concept or shibboleth which could be construed as sympathetic to a cause, but at the same time rejected the political policies that were vital to implementing that cause. Furthermore, even when they held strong views, they were not always systematic or consistently in one direction. One NBC commentator classified himself as a "radical-conservative"—which was appropriate enough in view of his contradictory positions on various issues.

In an interview with *Variety* Walter Cronkite said that he was a liberal, which he went on to define as one "not bound by doctrines or committed to a point of view in advance." Only in this nonpolitical sense of not holding deep-seated positions on issues can most network correspondents be classified as "liberals," according to my interviews.

But even though the views of most correspondents cannot be neatly fitted into any readily identifiable mold or ideology, certain common perspectives on politics emerged from the interviews.

The Disparaging View of Politicians. Almost all the newsmen interviewed held politicians and public-office holders in low esteem, especially the older, more familiar ones; the only exceptions were a few new faces in national politics, such as Julian Bond and Edmund Muskie. The working hypothesis almost universally shared among correspondents is that politicians are suspect; their public images probably false, their public statements disingenuous, their moral pronouncements hypocritical, their motives self-serving, and their promises ephemeral. Correspondents thus see their jobs to be to expose politicians by unmasking their disguises, debunking their claims and piercing their rhetoric. In short, until proven otherwise, political figures of any party or persuasion are presumed to be deceptive opponents. This generalized cynicism toward politicians—who are often called "frauds," "phonies" and "liars" in the newsroom—may account for a substantial share of the on-the-air derogation, rather than any partisan politics of the correspondents.

To be sure, contempt for politicians is by no means limited to television newsmen. Edward Shils, the Chicago sociologist, has pointed out that disparagement of politicians is a deeply rooted tradition in American journalism, and can be traced back to the historic fact that freedom of the press preceded the franchise to vote in this country. In more recent times, it has been suggested by Daniel P. Moynihan that this traditional antagonism has been exacerbated by the recruitment of a more highly educated, and therefore competitive, Washington press corps, which has taken on the posture of an "adversary culture."

While this suspicion of politicians and officeholders may derive partly from a long-standing journalistic tradition,

the particular vehemence most network correspondents
expressed in their interviews with me may also come in
part from their special vantage point. Television newsmen are usually in a position to observe closely the difference between a subject's behavior on and off camera.
Since political figures constantly try to put on their best
face before the camera, by primping their appearance,
suggesting and rephrasing questions, and altering their
answers in retakes to achieve the best effect, they tend to
appear insincere in the eyes of those interviewing them.
One NBC correspondent asked rhetorically, "How can we
respect people who change their answers with every re-
take?" It is a common belief among correspondents that
politicians evade their questions in televised interviews
and instead attempt to patronize or deceive the public.
The very fact that television permits the news maker
direct access to the audience he is interested in reaching
further strains the relationship with the correspondent.
When a politician is interviewed by a newspaperman, he
presumably tries to impress the reporter with the logic
of his position so that he will write a favorable story,
but rather than attempting to impress the reporter when
he is interviewed on television, he can address the audience directly, appealing to their emotions or talking down
to their level, as he sees fit. One of the most frequent
specific complaints of correspondents, in fact, was that
politicians "used" them in this way—which, of course,
only adds to the antipathy.

Finally, the itinerant schedule most correspondents
follow leaves them little opportunity to temper their con-
tentious image of politicians. Again, newspaper reporters
with definite beats have more chance to become well
acquainted with public figures they cover than network
correspondents who are dispatched from subject to subject on an ad hoc basis. Furthermore, in the view of
some correspondents, the fact that they usually travel
and stay with their camera crews and field producers
when covering a story tends to make informal contacts

with the news makers more difficult. Nor is it viewed as necessary, since network correspondents are centrally assigned stories and not expected to uncover original intelligence. Therefore most correspondents seem able to keep their distance from—and general contempt for—politicians.

The Electoral Explanation. In my interviews, almost any governmental act was generally ultimately attributed by correspondents in interviews to a single motive: winning elections. In this view, politics is seen as a "game plan" for defeating determined opponents, rather than as a process for distributing values or resolving conflicts between interested parties. Economic programs, government reorganizations, Supreme Court appointments and foreign policy were commonly explained in terms of an officeholder attempting to attract potential voters to his side. Neither ideology nor personal commitment to substantive goals were considered to be realistic explanations for such acts. For example, when President Nixon announced a new program in 1972 which would make American ships competitive with foreign maritime fleets and create "750,000 additional man-years" of employment, an ABC correspondent wryly commented on the air that the real purpose of the program was to create "four man-years" of employment for Nixon—in other words, to help him win re-election. To most network correspondents, such interpretations of presidential acts seem so "obviously true," as one CBS commentator put it, that they are treated as axioms.

This narrow view of politics seemed to account for the surprisingly high degree of consistency I found in responses to "why" questions about the actions of public officials. For instance, when asked why they believed that President Nixon had appointed Daniel P. Moynihan, a Democrat, as his adviser on domestic affairs, all but one correspondent implied that it was for electoral reasons. Some suggested that as a minority President, Nixon was trying to attract Democratic votes for the next election, or even, as two correspondents suggested, "Irish-Catholic votes." Others suggested that if his domestic programs didn't work out by the 1972 election he wanted to be in a position to blame the Democrats for the failure and hence needed a Democrat. Only one correspondent suggested that the President chose Moynihan to muster support for his programs in Congress. The possibility that Nixon might have appointed Moynihan to develop the welfare program he had worked on in the two previous Administrations, or to take advantage of his skill in bureaucratic infighting, was not mentioned.

Similarly, correspondents almost unanimously attributed the appointment of James Farmer as Assistant Secretary of the Department of Health, Education and Welfare to Nixon's need to attract black voters, and most correspondents held that President Johnson had ordered the bombing halt over North Vietnam in November 1968 to help Humphrey win the election. In almost all cases, the President was presumed to be acting to enhance his electoral strength rather than to control his bureaucracy, implement policies or foster an ideological view.

This preoccupation with electoral pragmatics, which is by no means confined to television journalists, is closely connected to the disparaging view of politicians. The logic expressed by several network newsmen runs something like this: politicians can never be accepted at face value; therefore a self-serving motive must be sought to explain the actions they characteristically justify with public-regarding rhetoric; the motive that can be assumed common to all politicians is the desire to acquire or retain power. In the case of network television, elections take no special importance to correspondents. As one suggested, "Elections are what we do best." In election years, networks spend an inordinate amount of their news budget on covering the primaries, conventions and elections. Special research units are set up; public opinion polls are commissioned; "fact books" of electoral data are distributed to correspondents. The speechmaking, campaigning and voting are covered like major sports events, complete with well-defined opponents, rules, tactics, odds, and a clear-cut victory and loss. Since network executives prefer to give approximately equal time to the major candidates (to satisfy affiliates as well as the Federal Communications Commission), a large proportion of air time is spent on election and primary coverage. This heavy emphasis can hardly fail to reinforce the correspondents' belief in the singular importance of getting elected.

The Egocentric View of Politics. Privately almost all network correspondents expressed a strong belief in their ability to effect change in public policy through their work, if not as individuals, then certainly as a group. Some considered their self-perceived political powers "frightening" and "awesome," while others merely depicted them as a necessary part of the political process. In this view, government officials are presumed to continue in their inertial rut until confronted with the glare of public exposure; only then, to placate the public and avoid a loss of electoral support, do they take action. Needed change is thus seen as depending not on politicians or bureaucrats, but on the fourth estate, the national press.

While network correspondents differed in degree about their importance in this role—opinions varied as to whether they were merely a contributing factor or decisive in bringing about reforms—they generally agreed that they had, willy-nilly, become a force in national politics. For example, almost two thirds of the newsmen interviewed gave direct credit to network news for the enactment of civil rights laws in the 1960s. In a typical explanation, one NBC correspondent stated, "Before television, the American public had no idea of the abuses blacks suffered in the South. We showed them what was happening; the brutality, the police dogs, the miserable conditions they were forced to live in. We made it impossible for Congress not to act." One CBS commentor said, "I guess you could say we were partly responsible for the civil rights revolution. Certainly the conditions were already there, but no one knew it until fifty million Americans began seeing it on their television screens."

Similarly, correspondents commonly held that American opinion on the war in Vietnam was decisively changed through television's coverage of it—which in turn resulted in a change of policies—and Presidents. In all cases, correspondents claimed to exert control over events, not through inside information or informal contacts with government officials but by exposing to the public the visually shocking moments and dramatic contradictions of the news. In other words, their self-perceived importance in politics derives from their power to dramatically shock and alter public opinion; and politicians presumably react to this. Hence, correspondents believed both that they were outsiders and at the same time highly effective forces in politics.

While these perspectives are necessarily impressionistic and oversimplified, they seem to account for a large share of the views on politics that correspondents expressed both in interviews and news-room discussions. They do not, however, completely determine the final news product, if only because correspondents are not entirely free to shape the news from their own perspective. They must depend on technicians to reproduce the sound and pictures in their story, and they must work under the close supervision and control of producers and news editors. Neither of these groups fully shares the values, experiences or perspectives of the correspondents.

The Technicians

The cameramen, sound men and film editors, who work closely with the correspondent and producer in fashioning the final story, generally come from working-class backgrounds, and unlike the correspondents, did not depend on a formal education or eloquence to achieve their success. Of the fourteen technicians I interviewed, most did not hold college degrees and only three attended a liberal arts college. Typically, technicians went to technical schools, or had experience in film editing in the military service, and then served as apprentices to film editors for a number of years before graduating to their present positions. Their average income was between $20,000 and $25,000 a year, which is nearly as much as many correspondents earn. Almost all had families and owned their own home; all belonged to trade unions and considered themselves skilled craftsmen.

Politically, most technicians identified themselves as Democrats or Independents, but their political views were far to the right of the correspondents. More than three quarters were enthusiastic supporters of Hubert Humphrey, but one said he was for George Wallace. Almost every technician opposed Black Power, and many of them deprecated black militant leaders. Most took a hard line on Vietnam, advocating the continued bombing of North Vietnam and the preservation of South Vietnam as an independent entity. Not one identified himself as a dove. They also expressed almost unanimous contempt for student demonstrators and hippies. The majority felt that their work had made them more conservative; a good number were critical of network news for slanting events that they themselves had witnessed.

Political rhetoric or policy statements were generally viewed by the technicians as dull or meaningless, as they put it. Basically they saw their task as finding the few exciting moments in a political happening. Cameramen and sound men claimed to be able to predict within a few minutes when the actual violence or highlight would happen solely on the basis of their past experience; "They all follow the same script," one NBC cameraman suggested.

Despite these contrasting views of politics, crewmen and correspondents usually travel, dine and work as a closely knit group. In such situations, correspondents tend to moderate their views, at least in open discussions. In a sense, then, technicians serve as a check on correspondents.

Producers

Network producers and news editors have a different set of responsibilities than do correspondents or technicians. They are directly accountable to executives in their respective news organizations for every minute of news shown on the air, as well as for the resources expended to produce it. Their primary job, almost all producers agreed, is to enforce the standards of the organization for which they work. In overseeing the news operation, from the initial selection of stories to their final presentation, producers closely parallel the work of correspondents—and at times find themselves at cross-purposes. Whereas the correspondent concerns himself mainly with the particular content of an event and attempts to find the most effective way of dramatizing it or at least making it into an interesting story, the producer concerns himself with fitting individual events into a general format in a way which both fulfills the requisites of the program and avoids any violations of the network's policies. As one ABC producer put it, producers must be more attuned to "the rules of the game" than correspondents. Not surprisingly, then, producers are drawn from somewhat different backgrounds than their on-the-air counterparts.

Most network producers and news editors come from what might best be described as a cosmopolitan environment. Of the thirty-six producers and news editors interviewed, twenty-four came from either New York City or Chicago, and most of the balance came from other large metropolitan areas. A majority came from middle- or upper-class families, in which the father usually was a businessman. Twenty-one were of Jewish descent; none were black or came from lower-class backgrounds. Almost all went to public high school and then to college. Nearly two thirds attended such competitive city colleges as CCNY, NYU, Chicago, Northwestern and Columbia. One third continued their studies in graduate school, and half of these attended the School of Journalism at Northwestern University.

Most of the producers and news editors had had previous experience in large news organizations; a substantial number had worked on newspapers and magazines. None had previously been television correspondents. The common reason given for switching to television was, in a word, money. But their network job did not entail a drastic relocation in their life styles; most continued to live in the same cities and follow the same routines as before. Although they periodically traveled with correspondents as field producers, the bulk of their time was spent in the office, in close contact with the executive producer. Unlike correspondents, who saw great social significance and responsibilities in their role, producers and news editors generally regarded their position as nothing more than a fairly interesting and well-paying livelihood.

Moreover, producers and news editors tended to have a less excited and more tempered view of the world than correspondents. Although with few exceptions they identified themselves politically as Democrats, Independents, moderates and liberals—in that order—most said that their work in network news had made them more conservative, if anything. With few exceptions, they opposed the Black Power movement on the grounds that they believed an integrated society is the best alternative for blacks. In keeping with this view, they consistently opposed black control of schools, housing projects, and police precincts in the ghetto areas. In discussing social problems, they generally favored education as a solution rather than any more drastic political alternative. In listing civil rights leaders they most admired, producers and news editors, unlike correspondents, strongly favored leaders from established organizations, such as Roy Wilkins of the NAACP, as opposed to more militant leaders, such as Eldridge Cleaver of the Black Panthers. (In fact, in a number of cases, NBC producers vetoed coverage of Cleaver's speeches during the University of California dispute in 1968.)

Although all opposed continuation of the war in Vietnam, none of the producers and news editors suggested any sort of unilateral withdrawal immediately. Although opinions varied considerably, the dominant view among them was that the United States should attempt to negotiate a cease-fire, followed by a political settlement based on the present military status quo in Vietnam. In the presidential election of 1968, more than two thirds of them favored Humphrey and opposed Nixon, but many said that they would have preferred Robert F. Kennedy or Nelson Rockefeller. In news-room discussions and critiques of correspondents' reports, producers and news editors usually took a more moderate—and consistent—position.

Nor did they share the correspondents' perspectives on politics. Producers and news editors generally looked at news events from the point of view of the needs of the program—that is, from what might be described as a functional perspective. Whereas correspondents commonly evaluated politicians and officeholders in moral terms ("liars," "phonies" and "frauds"), producers and editors judged them in terms of their on-camera performance, depicting them as "dull," "gabby," "beautiful," "crafty," "Kennedy-like," "hot-headed," or other such terms associated with their performance.

Often this sort of criticism had an ulterior purpose. When a producer calls a politician dull, or otherwise uninteresting, it is generally interpreted by the correspondent as criticism of the piece—and his interviewing technique. The presumption, which is continually reinforced by producers in their critiques, is that by definition *any* news maker is interesting if handled right. As one NBC producer explained to a hopeful trainee, "They [the news makers] are the actors, we're the directors." And while most producers would not readily agree that they are in the same sort of show business as the other divisions of the network, a majority of them recognize that they are responsible for maintaining a steady flow of a product which will interest and not offend the home audience. In turn, this requires eliciting certain kinds of performances from news makers, regardless of their true inner character.

Although producers and news editors are no less skeptical than correspondents of the actions of political figures, they are less prone to accept the electoral motive as a near-universal explanation. Unlike correspondents, most producers and news editors refused to attribute Nixon's appointments and the bombing halt in 1968 to a desire to enhance his electoral chances; instead, when asked for reasons, they commonly answered that they had no idea. Admittedly, producers and editors almost always allowed simple electoral explanations in correspondents' scripts because, as one NBC executive producer put it, "It's always a plausible motive for a politician"; also as a number of other producers suggested, there is generally a preference for simple rather than complicated summaries by correspondents, if only because they are more easily comprehensible to the home audience.

Nor do producers and news editors necessarily share correspondents' views on the political efficacy of television news. Opinions here were mixed. Although almost half said that network news had been an important force in the case of advancing civil rights in the South, more than two thirds suggested that it had had little effect in changing public opinion on the issue of Vietnam. A common opinion expressed was that "people see exactly what they want to" in a news report, and that it only serves to reinforce existing prejudices. (This view may not have been unrelated to the position that network executives took, and circulated to the producers and staff in the form of memoranda and articles, when television was severely criticized after the Democratic convention in Chicago in 1968. Indeed, exact phrases from articles by Reuven Frank and others were repeated with some frequency by NBC producers in their interviews. Slightly more than one third suggested that rather than correspondents affecting politics, they were used by clever politicians. In general, most of them regarded television as reactive to politics, rather than vice versa, and felt that only an exceptionally dramatic confrontation on television could affect the course of events.

The perspectives from which producers and news editors view political issues generally coincides fairly closely with their organizational responsibilities. This is not surprising, one NBC News executive pointed out; if they had held sharply different views of how politics should be treated, they probably would not be effective producers from the networks' point of view.

Politics as a Dialogue. In news-room discussions and critiques, political issues are almost always defined by producers as a series of discussions between opposing sides. The expectation is that an issue will be presented in a point-counterpoint format. Any political report lacking this format is usually questioned by producers or news editors, who carefully review outlines and preliminary scripts before a story is completed. The notion that a matter of wide public concern might have only a single defensible side is simply not acceptable. It will be recalled that if one side of an issue is lacking in force, correspondents often are instructed to find a more authoritative spokesman for it. One NBC producer observed, "Presenting one side of an issue, even if it is obviously the right side, is a bad habit for reporters to get into." For example, even when the United States Surgeon-General

produced medical evidence indicating that cigarette smok-
ing has damaging effects on health, correspondents had to
seek opposing views from the American Tobacco Institute.

The dialogue, moreover, is limited to two sides. Whenever during my field study correspondents sought to present more than two positions, producers vetoed the idea
on the grounds that it would be "confusing," and insisted
on the formula of two contrasting viewpoints.

The Indeterminate View of Political Issues. Producers
further operated on the assumption that the obligatory
dialogue between opposing sides of an issue cannot be
resolved completely in favor of either side—at least not
by the correspondent. One NBC news editor explained
that "all we can do is cast light on issues; we can't settle
them." While not wholly successful in imposing this view
on correspondents, it is a common practice in network
news rooms, according to producers, for news editors to
rewrite correspondents' scripts in more tentative language if they reach too definite conclusions. In fact, during my study of the NBC Evening News, the most frequent complaint lodged against correspondents by producers had to do with their appearing to reach conclusions, or "to come down on one side of an issue." That this
was accepted unquestioningly as valid criticism in the
news room—it was never asked whether such a conclusion might be justified—indicates the extent to which
this view was universally shared by producers and editors.

This indeterminate view is very much in line with the
networks' interests. The alternative of encouraging correspondents to try to determine where the truth lies in a
dispute would open a Pandora's box, as one NBC News
vice-president put it. For one thing, it would turn the
trickle of complaints currently received from affiliate
managers into an unmanageable flood—each carrying
the implicit threat of blacking out network news and
revenues in his area. Every time a correspondent took an
unequivocal stand on an issue it would almost surely of-

fend an affiliate manager in some part of the country; network executives would then be called on to rectify this, which would place a very unpleasant burden on executives. Moreover, it would greatly add to the cost of producing network news, since it obviously requires more time and investigative resources to evaluate opposing positions than it does simply to present them. The assumption that issues can never be definitely settled avoids such potential problems.

The Societal Perspective. Finally, from their vantage point, network producers tended to view most happenings not as isolated incidents, but as threads of more general themes in the fabric of society as a whole. A dramatic event, though limited in time and location, is thus commonly presumed to be an indicator of a national trend or illustration of a national malaise. Through this prism, a student strike at a single college is seen as "symptomatic" (a key word in the vocabulary of this perspective) of student discontent throughout the nation; the problems of a single city represent "in microcosm" the nationwide urban crisis; a shoot-out in a single neighborhood "reflects" the increasing atmosphere of violence in this country.

Not all stories in network news are treated according to this logic; stories of great irony or human interest may be accepted as local nostalgia or quirk pieces. But when considering most serious stories, producers or news editors usually ask the question in one form or another: "What national significance does this have?" Not uncommonly, during my study correspondents and field producers were asked to rewrite, or even reshoot, stories in a way that connected them to national trends or problems. The presumption that a nexus existed between specific occurrences and societal themes was never questioned; it was accepted as an axiom of network news. In interviews, producers and editors repeatedly cited as a critical part of their task their ability to perceive the wider significance of events. Again, this is a productive view in terms of fulfilling network requisites. By converting happenings that otherwise might have only local interest into stories of national import, it helps differentiate network news programs from the local news programs, even when they treat the same subject.

Thus, the perspectives that producers and news editors have about the news help maintain certain standards. And while they do not necessarily contravene the views of correspondents, they tend to impose a certain logic and form on them.

Executives

In his classic study of the functions of executives, Chester I. Barnard found that they most effectively control large organizations not by participating in day-to-day decisions, but by inducing the necessary organizational values in their subordinates. This is also true in the case of network news executives, which includes the network news president, vice-presidents, and news managers of the various operations. While they may decide on program budgets, long-term assignments and the coverage of such major scheduled events as elections, conventions and moratoriums, they have little opportunity to intervene in most of the routine decisions involved in covering and reconstructing the day's news stories. In most cases, the speed and diversity of news events make any sort of close executive supervision virtually impossible. To run a news organization effectively, then, executives depend on producers making the same sort of judgments that they would make in similar circumstances. In turn, this requires that they recruit or inculcate producers with the "right" outlook and values for their particular job.

In practice, executives are involved in an almost continuous process of impressing certain of their views on producers. Not only are there frequent critiques of the newscasts, there are daily briefings which the executive producers or their deputies attend in the news executives' offices. For instance, at NBC the morning begins in the executive suite with a meeting of the news managers, and the producer of the NBC Evening News is expected to attend. On difficult questions, such as sending a crew overseas or coverage of a major event, producers usually discuss the matter in advance with executives.

The relationship between executives and producers is usually informal, if only because most executives in the news divisions were more often than not recruited from the ranks of producers themselves, and tend to maintain friendships. Of the eleven news executives I interviewed, eight had formerly been network producers and two others had worked as executive editors of publications. Not surprisingly, their backgrounds and careers closely resembled those of the producers as a group, though they came from more varied religious backgrounds. Most executives attended liberal arts colleges, went on to graduate school, served in the Army, and joined television as a news writer or editor. On political issues, most of the executives expressed even more moderate opinions than producers, though not necessarily conservative opinions. Their political affiliations were divided almost equally between Democrat, independent and Republican. However, almost all expressed a strong belief that politics should be separated as much as possible from the news operation.

Despite the frequent public defense of news as a "mirror of society," in private discussions most executives seemed to regard news stories as problematic constructions. Indeed, they more or less operated on the assumption that a news story could be shot, edited and narrated in a number of different ways, and that the producer was responsible for reconstructing it along lines that met the standards and policies of the network. In other words, producers could not abdicate their responsibilities with the excuse that "the news dictated a story." For example, just as single stories cannot be allowed to run for thirty minutes, one side of a dispute cannot be presented in an obviously unfavorable light. Moreover, in composing the program, no single set of stories is presumed to be ineluctably determined by news developments; producers are held responsible by executives for selecting segments which give the program the correct "mix," "texture" and "pacing"—and, over the long run, for choices that do not vastly exceed the budget of the program. As one NBC executive said, "Indispensable stories are extremely rare, in my opinion."

In sum, network news is not simply determined by the personal opinions of newsmen. The picture of events that correspondents and commentators present is constantly questioned, modified and shaped by technicians, news editors, producers and executives with quite disparate values and objectives. This inevitably creates some tension. From the executives' point of view, it would be best for the organization—and the least trouble for them personally—if newsmen had no values whatsoever. But since this is recognized as an impossible demand, the news operation is organized so as to limit the opportunities for newsmen to impose their personal views on sensitive issues for any prolonged period of time. Recruitment, training, supervision, rotation, editing controls and general policies all reinforce this purpose.

On the other hand, newsmen work in circumstances which often make complete control of their words and actions difficult, if not impossible. Correspondents often have strong preferences on the more highly charged issues, even though they may be short-lived and non-ideological, and are in a position to favor or disparage one side in a controversy through the tone, nuance and style of their presentation of the news. The fact that it may not be in the interest of the organization to slant coverage in any one direction does not always prevent correspondents from doing so, and one can always find some specific examples of their asserting personal values in their reporting. The real question is thus one of control: How effective are the networks in preventing newsmen from slanting their reports in accordance with their personal values, and under what circumstances can newsmen consistently evade network controls?

In most cases, producers have adequate tools to enforce standards: scripts can be checked, and corrected, before a piece is filmed; films and stories can be screened in advance; audio portions can be re-edited, and if necessary, redone; and even at the last moment, stories can be dropped from the program. Correspondents who repeatedly manifest strong personal values or improper attitudes on the air can be "blacklisted," or at least not assigned controversial stories. There are four situations, however, in which correspondents have considerable discretion, or in which the controls are less effective.

First of all, it is difficult for producers rigorously to supervise and control correspondents' reports when they go on the air "live." In these circumstances, correspondents can only be restrained from inserting their opinions by the threat of future sanctions or disfavor. Live coverage is, however, a rarity in network news, and confined almost exclusively to extraordinary events, such as the coverage of political conventions.

Second, correspondents are usually given considerable leeway in reporting nonserious stories on subjects that are not considered by producers to be "controversial." In fact, in the case of "feature" and "light" stories, correspondents are often encouraged to use tone, nuance and facial expressions to bring out the irony or humor of a situation. There are of course definite limits to how far correspondents can go in their interpretations even in nonserious stories, but these are usually defined by producers in terms of "bad taste" rather than "fairness."

Similarly, controls over correspondents are greatly relaxed in the case of overseas news. For one thing, the FCC's Fairness Doctrine does not apply to foreign news, and therefore there is no legal need to seek opposing viewpoints on foreign issues or avoid personal attacks on foreign leaders. Nor is it assumed by executives that affiliates would be greatly concerned with the way foreign news is handled (there are no foreign affiliates). And it is further presumed that the general viewing audience would not be familiar with the various facets of the issues. The main control that is exerted over stories from abroad by producers simply involves excluding pieces from the program that might possibly insult a significant segment of the American audience, such as derogatory stories about Israel or Ireland.

Finally, controls tend to be disregarded when executives, producers and correspondents all share the same view and further perceive it to be a view accepted by virtually all thoughtful persons. News reports about such subjects as pollution, hunger, health care, racial discrimination, and poverty fall in this category. On such consensus issues, correspondents are expected by executives openly to advocate the eradication of the presumed evil and even put it in terms of a "crusade," as a CBS vice-president suggested with respect to the pollution issue. The subjects that fall within this consensus are clearly demarcated for correspondents; in fact, they are usually "cleared" in advance by executives for use in speeches and public appearances by correspondents. At times, however, what are assumed to be commonly held values turn out to be disputed ones in some segments of the country; and when executives are apprised of this (by affiliates or others), the usual "fairness" controls are applied to the subject.

In other situations, network controls are generally considered effective by both producers and correspondents, and as Vanocur gradually discovered, network "inhibitions" are generally accepted as personal values, or "institutionalized," by newsmen. Even in political situations which excite the strongest personal emotions on the part of the correspondents, network policy is rigorously enforced. Consider, for example, NBC coverage of the 1968 presidential election campaign. Most correspondents and producers were strongly opposed to the election of Nixon, and favored his opponent, Hubert H. Humphrey; there was no support at all for George Wallace, the candidate of the American Independent Party. Network policy, however, called for both major candidates to receive equal coverage, and for Wallace to receive "half-coverage." At the beginning of the campaign, an NBC vice-president told the producer of the Evening News that the division of time between the three candidates was to be "40, 40, 20," with Wallace receiving the smallest share. Throughout the campaign, despite strong personal feelings against Nixon and Wallace, producers maintained this ratio. In the last seven weeks of the campaign (which were during the period of my field study at NBC), Nixon received 45 minutes and 40 seconds, Humphrey 44 minutes and 10 seconds, and Wallace 35 minutes and 20 seconds of coverage on the NBC Evening News. In more than 90 percent of the coverage dealing with Nixon or Humphrey, correspondents adhered to a set formula in which they introduced the piece with a brief description of the candidate's movements and closed the piece with a recap of what the candidate had said. In this formula, correspondents had only a limited amount of time—usually no more than twenty seconds—to make any sort of evaluative statement of a candidate's performance (and this was closely supervised by producers).

While the allocation of time to candidates and the formats of news reporting closely conformed to the network's standards, the degree to which the correspondents' personal values surfaced in their evaluative on-the-air comments is far more difficult to judge. An examination of the scripts for this period shows that correspondents did not openly endorse or reject any candidate or express any direct preference, but a large proportion of their comments could be interpreted as favorable or unfavorable to the candidates they were reporting on. Since almost all the correspondents and producers privately were against the candidacy of Nixon, one might expect to find a high proportion of on-the-air anti-Nixon comments from reporters *if* network controls were slack or non-existent in this area. The contention of one writer, Edith Efron, that her personal "content analysis" of this same seven-week period shows that NBC correspondents spoke only 23 favorable words about Nixon compared to 1,501 unfavorable words about him is quite interesting in this respect.

When examined closely, however, the data are far less impressive in demonstrating anti-Nixon bias. All the purportedly unfavorable words about Nixon by reporters came in only 14 of the 37 newscasts featuring a report on Nixon in this period. In 2 of these 14 reports, according to Efron's data, NBC reporters also made pro-Nixon statements, and in 4 others pro-Nixon statements by public figures are featured, which satisfies the network's standard of fairness. Thus, according to Efron's interpretation of the NBC reporting, correspondents made anti-Nixon statements without carrying any sort of pro-Nixon statement in fewer than one sixth of their reports (6 out of 37).

Miss Efron's interpretations, however, are open to question. In re-examining the "anti-Nixon" comments by reporters, I found that no unambiguous "anti-Nixon" remarks were made in 7 out of the 14 broadcasts, and at least 4 of what Efron claims are "anti-Nixon" comments by reporters might more reasonably be interpreted as pro-Nixon comments. For example, on September 20, 1968, the NBC correspondent with Nixon, Herbert Kaplow, reported that Nixon drew "large" crowds in Philadelphia compared to the crowds his opponent was drawing, and I at least presumed this to be a favorable report on Nixon. Efron claimed this to be an anti-Nixon report, despite the fact that no words were spoken against Nixon, because it did not report the "intensity" of support these crowds showed toward Nixon (Humphrey carried Philadelphia in the election by a wide margin). In other words,

Efron was classifying what she considered to be the lack of perception of the reporters, rather than what they actually reported, as being "anti-Nixon."

If one considers only what the correspondents actually reported, as opposed to what they might have omitted, only 5 of the 37 newscasts contained direct criticisms of Nixon, and 3 of these 5 newscasts also contained favorable comments on Nixon (for example, his "commanding lead"). The remarkable fact would thus seem to be that in the vast majority of their reports, correspondents were restrained from expressing their unfavorable personal opinions about Nixon, or even induced to express a favorable opinion. This, in turn, seems to indicate that the personal values of newsmen, though an important input in the news process, are not by any means decisive when in conflict with organizational values.

Part III

Outputs

Chapter 8

Pictures of Society

> *The domestic political story is the skeleton on which all news is built. It's a continuous, repetitive story ...*
>
> —*William McAndrew, former president of NBC News*

When Walter Cronkite noted that "we live in a time when almost all stories are related: Cambodia is as much a part of Kent State as Kent State is a part of the state of the nation," he was refering particularly to those stories of national import shown nightly on network news. The ways in which these stories on television are related to each other are worth considering.

In some cases, news stories are connected by a cause-and-effect relation. For example, the announcement that American troops were being dispatched to Cambodia in May 1970 was the proximate cause for the student protest at Kent State which ended in the tragic shooting of students. In other cases, however, where the nexus between different events occurring in different places is problematic, if existent at all, a relation between them can always be inferred by an interpreter of events. Indeed, any two stories can be related by being placed in a more general category, just as in geometry any two points may be connected with a line. But the relation between such stories is not ineluctably drawn; it exists in the eye of the interpreter and is shaped by the range and limits of his vision. The same logic applies to television news: if almost all stories on network news are related, as Cronkite suggests, what part of this relation is supplied by its interpreters, the news organizations, and how is the vision of these organizations shaped by the imperatives of survival in their particular business?

At perhaps the most basic level, the imperatives of network scheduling tend to impose certain common forms on essentially disparate events. Because of the networks' limited time for news programs and the economic necessity of interspersing commercials at regular intervals, news events must be truncated to fit predetermined segments of time on the program, no matter how large or small their value may be in reality. On the Evening News, for instance, segments are rarely more than five minutes long. Thus, almost all news events appear to take place in a roughly similar time frame and are explained in approximately corresponding length—usually a few minutes per story.

Moreover, the paramount need of the networks to maintain a maximum audience flow compels producers to reorganize the news into certain story formats that are presumed most capable of holding the attention of viewers, regardless of their subject or content. Since, as Reuven Frank points out, a television channel, unlike a newspaper, allows its audience no respite or selectivity in the flow of news it is watching—the only alternative being to switch channels—in theory every news report must continually interest the audience.

This presents a problem. Unlike local news, which can be expected to interest a local audience because it concerns its immediate environment, network news cannot be expected to hold the same sort of immediate interest for people dispersed across the nation. The solution found by the networks is to cast each event, which in itself might not be immediately relevant to the lives of most of those watching, into conflict stories that presumably have universal appeal. "Every news story should, without any sacrifice of probity or responsibility, display *the attributes of fiction,* of drama," Reuven Frank instructed his staff at NBC. This fictive form is to be accomplished by reconstructing all stories in a very definite order, the Frank memorandum suggests: all segments are to be organized around the triad of "conflict, problem and denouement, and to contain "a beginning, middle and end," as well as "rising action" which presumably builds to a climax, and then "falling action."

The same format was used for much the same reasons in mass-circulation magazines, as the sociologist Robert S. Park perceptively points out:

> The ordinary man, as the *Saturday Evening Post* has discovered, thinks in concrete images, pictures and parables. He finds it difficult to read a long article unless it is dramatized, and takes the form of what newspapers call a "story." "News story" and "fiction story" are two forms of modern literature that are now so like one another that it is sometimes difficult to distinguish them.

Because similar assumptions are made about the television viewer, news stories about essentially different events are given an underlying structural similarity in form.

Audience considerations also affect the content of news programs. Since almost all network research indicates that the dinnertime audience has fewer years of formal education than the population in general, as well as a relatively high proportion of children, producers generally require that stories must be self-contained in the sense that no outside information on the part of the audience is necessary to understanding them. As one CBS producer said, "We have to act on the assumption that the audience has zero knowledge about a subject." Yet only a few minutes are available for explanation in a story. This dilemma is resolved by selecting news pictures which can be expected to have "instant meaning," as an NBC film editor put it. Ideally, every picture should tell a story to everyone watching the program. To meet this requisite, news stories are illustrated with certain kinds of readily identifiable images with emotional appeal. A half-naked child is commonly used, for example, to symbolize abject poverty, just as a uniformed policeman is used to represent authority. In each case, because of his appearance or uniform, the individual is recognizable as representative of a larger group, and the emotion he engenders is expected to evoke a basic response in the audience. Thus, a network news story about the declining prices of farm commodities in the Midwest should be cast in pictures of a single heartbroken farmer leaving his homestead in tears, Reuven Frank advised, because "the highest power of television journalism is not in the transmission of information but in the transmission of experience." Since there is usually a limited repertory of such symbols favored by cameramen and producers at any given time, stories about different events are often composed of similar visual elements.

In dealing with controversial subjects, almost all news stories use similar modes of exposition, which proceed from the government regulations under which all the networks operate. The most expedient way of satisfying the Fairness Doctrine, it will be recalled, is for stories to be made up of pro and con segments (even if one side is specially solicited for this purpose), followed by a non-conclusive synthesis by the correspondent. Ideally, presenting their respective sides, spokesmen for each point of view in this format must be evenly matched in articulateness and authoritativeness, even through their arguments may not have equal validity. The more potentially controversial a subject, the more likely it is that this format will be employed. Thus, the major issues are consistently depicted and explained as dialogues between well-matched spokesmen for opposing sides, which cannot be logically resolved in favor of either.

Finally, as discussed earlier, the exigencies of affiliate-network relations require that network news be national in scope, both to differentiate it from the local news on affiliated stations and to satisfy the Federal Communications Commission. To comply with this demand, network news focuses on selected national themes. This is usually accomplished by presenting a story about a local occurrence—since every event happens *somewhere*—as an illustration of what are considered to be the dominant national stories at that time. Hence, almost any visually dramatic incidents can be used as an example of a national trend, mood, malaise, crisis or the like.

The "nationalization" of news can also be achieved by editing together events that fall into a common category, such as a number of different incidents of urban unrest in different cities. Thus, the executive producer of the ABC Evening News wrote his staff: "I believe in 'packaging' related stories into segments, ending each segment with a commercial." (At times, it will be recalled, additional stories on a theme are purposely commissioned by producers in cities where there are available camera crews to suggest a national pattern of occurrences.) At other times, the correspondent simply integrates an event with a national theme in his narrative. As Cronkite further observed, it is now considered the job of newsmen "to report events markedly significant beyond the moment, and to relate stories to each other." In short, the interrelation of stories on network news is often the inevitable product of a concept of "national" news.

Over an extended period of time, news stories on any single subject may also be related to one another by the organizational machinery that produces them. The relatively constant procedures by which networks select planned events for coverage, reconstruct them into stories and integrate them into news programs tend to give

stories on the same subject similar perspectives. Of
course, sharp differences can always be found between
individual stories, but when a large number of stories in
the same category are examined together, in what might
be termed a composite picture of a subject over a period
of time, certain background features seem to persist in
almost all the reports. In other words, while the characters and conflicts change, the setting remains constant
from story to story in many important respects. These
similarities in background, I submit, can be at least partly
explained in terms of the internal processes employed by
a network. Consider the following composite pictures of
society that appeared on the NBC Evening News over a
three-month period in 1968–1969.

California: The Bizarre Setting. Almost all stories about
California during this period were depicted as taking
place in curious, eccentric and highly unpredictable circumstances. An unpluggable oil leak erupts in someone's
patio in Los Angeles; governors on horseback and in cowboy hats ride off into the California sunset at Governor
Ronald Reagan's ranch; prisoners commute to outside
jobs from San Quentin Prison in a novel experiment, and
experience California life styles, while inmates at Fol-
som Prison furtively build an unflyable helicopter in the
machine shop; California adults become heavily involved
with war toys; California researchers advance the theory
that inherited traits which can be detected in advance account for criminal behavior, so that traditional concepts of
justice may have to be reconsidered in California; and
national politicians visiting Palm Springs are described
as being in an atmosphere that is "somewhat artificial."
Even the few events that were treated as serious news
events, such as the trial of Sirhan Sirhan and the disorders at San Francisco State University were often portrayed against a background of "kooks" and novelties.
For example, the first report on the Sirhan trial dealt
mainly with an experimental hidden television camera

that might be used to televise the trial for members of
the press for whom there would not be room in the court-
room itself, and the reports on San Francisco State
focused on such student characters as "the strolling
troubadour warning that the police were on campus . . .
or the blue meanies, as he called them." The bizarre
setting is, moreover, accentuated in most of these California reports by unorthodox camera shots, odd music and
sound effects, and by correspondents ending stories with
a smile or ironic comment.

Such stories may, of course, express some existing
reality about California, but this is not the reason that
they are consistently selected for the evening news, according to producers and executives. In treating California news, an NBC executive in the Los Angeles bureau
explained, "the basic problem is time." The three-hour
time difference between the Pacific Coast and New York
City greatly diminishes the chances of covering "hard"
news. In practice, the filming of a story must be completed before noon on the West Coast for it to be processed
and edited in time for the evening news, which originates
in New York at 3:30 P.M. Pacific Standard Time, and then
is taped and rebroadcast later on the West Coast. Since
it is usually difficult to locate events which will surely be
completed in the morning, and since network camera
crews are a scarce resource on the West Coast, assignment editors are explicitly instructed to seek out "stories
of perennial interest," as one put it, which are both un-
connected to the day's events and unlikely to be dated by
newspaper reports. These usually turn out to be feature-
type stories.

The economic logic of network news also provides a
strong incentive for covering timeless stories instead of
current ones in California. A timely story about the day's
events would first have to be transmitted to New York on
a specially rented cable, it will be recalled, which in 1969
cost about $3,000 per hour (nearly half of the program's
daily budget for relaying stories from all over the world).

On the other hand, timeless features can be transported at practically no cost by air freight—or when cables were rented by the hour for other purposes. Since a regular flow of California stories is needed to maintain the appearance of coast-to-coast news, the Los Angeles bureau executive further explained, "the least expensive way [of meeting this requirement] is by commissioning feature stories."

Finally, California feature stories can also be conveniently used to satisfy the networks' policy of ending the program with humorous or light stories. Since the appeal of features, as they are defined in the Frank Memorandum, is based on their internal irony, color or absurdity —which are also "attributes of fiction"—they are presumed to have a more universal appeal to the news audience than hard-news reports about a specific occurrence in a specific locality. To be effective, however, features usually require more time to reconstruct and edit than do regular news reports. But since producers in New York generally do not expect California stories to deal with timely subjects, crews and correspondents based in Los Angeles work under less time pressure than crews elsewhere. Besides, producers and correspondents assigned to the Los Angeles bureau commonly assumed that unless otherwise instructed, they were "to develop interesting features," as one field producer explained his job.

The search for quirks and aberrations in California life is thus rooted partly in the logistical difficulties of covering current events, and partly in the program's need for feature stories, especially as it is perceived of by members of the Los Angeles bureau.

Europe in Turmoil. The view of Europe in this three-month period was mainly one of extreme turbulence. There were anti-American protests in London; embittered Czech refugees; demonstrations, riots and repressions in Rome, Prague, Bratislava and Berlin; economic crises in Paris and Bonn; floods and bursting dams in Italy; reports of a Loch Ness monster in Scotland; civil strife in Northern Ireland—and very little else except for the peace negotiations in Paris. Most of these events were depicted in a tumultuous setting: mob actions, mass arrests, soldiers in disarray, shouting, fires and casualties. Few of the stories were more than two minutes long. Typically, the rising action led to a confrontation, then to a confused scattering of forces. The narration tended to be terse, which, if anything, heightened the drama of the conflicts.

While these scenes of turmoil may have been an important part of the news from Europe during this period, NBC News' concentration on them was virtually assured by the selection criteria then in force. One assignment editor explained that in choosing European stories, "the first rule is that overseas news must hold some interest for American viewers." Since it is generally assumed that the audience is not familiar with European news makers or politics, the stories routinely selected by assignment editors (without special commissions from producers) are limited to certain forms of visual action which presumably can be understood without any further frame of reference. These include demonstrations, conflicts between uniformed authorities and protestors, and natural disasters.

Producers also prefer action pieces that require no lengthy exposition, since they can easily be truncated to fill the available time in a segment and thus help pace the program. "No one gives a damn how you cut a foreign piece," an NBC editor observed. In turn, this discourages correspondents from attempting to cover anything more than visual action in European stories. For example, the NBC correspondent in London told the editor of *TV Guide*: "We cover Northern Ireland, and the stuff that gets on the air is the rough stuff. If there's something fairly peaceful or something that involves their parliament, it's hard to get it on."

China: Pomp and Ceremony. The only news pictures available from China during this period depicted Chinese leaders against a backdrop of massive rallies, bunting, parades and wildly enthusiastic supporters. There was a simple reason for this constant picture. Because American newsmen were not allowed into China at the time, NBC openly took its footage directly from Chinese television, which can be monitored in Hong Kong by means of a kinescope—that is, film of the television image. And since Chinese television is used for political purposes, NBC's coverage of it tended to reflect a panorama of popular enthusiasm. The decision to cover China at all was made by an NBC News executive who explained to me that he considered it important that NBC appear to have "world-wide coverage."

Similar constraints exist, of course, in other areas in which the networks are primarily dependent on government-controlled agencies for their film. For example, the news pictures of the Soviet Union which are shown on American television, but which are necessarily filmed by Soviet technicians, are almost exclusively of parades, weaponry and government accomplishments of some magnitude, staged against a background of stark technological efficiency. Similarly, the news film of U.S. achievements in exploring outer space, which is supplied to the networks by the National Aeronautic and Space Agency, is also set against a background of smoothly operating computers, efficient technicians and seemingly complete control over all contingencies.

Vietnam: The Mechanical War.   During the survey period, the war in Vietnam was almost invariably depicted as a routine series of American patrols, none of which seemed connected with the others or with any overall strategy. Helicopters whirl their rotors, hover and ascend into the sky; armored launches slowly cruise along rivers, with their searchlights scanning the shores and machine guns rotating back and forth; jet planes, with their arsenals of rockets mounted under their wings, take off from runways and aircraft carriers; a company of American soldiers disembarks from helicopters and walks single file along a trail; artillery on a hilltop fires at regular intervals round after round of shells at an unseen enemy in the far distance. The stories often contained a brief climax of visual action—soldiers firing their weapons, rockets lighting up the sky, bombs and napalm from planes exploding—but even these moments seemed to be routine operations, unprovoked by any direct enemy action or other stimulus. In terms of the repetitive visual images, both the machines and the soldiers seemed to be moving circuitously through difficult terrain.

While these scenes reflect some of the realities of this particular kind of warfare, other images could certainly reflect other aspects of the war, such as the strategic plans for isolating the Vietcong or the deprivations suffered by the Vietnamese people. But as the previously cited memorandum from Av Westin to the ABC Saigon bureau amply demonstrates, the particular reality that network news chooses to focus on is determined by network personnel. In this sense, the NBC portrayal of a routine, mechanical war can partly be traced to certain organizational requirements.

In the first place, since executives deemed it too expensive to transmit daily Vietnam stories back to New York by satellite—and, moreover, direct "satelliting" of film gave producers less opportunity to control the contents of news reports by editing—NBC requested its correspondents and free-lance cameramen in Vietnam to avoid filming actions which would date the story, and instead to concentrate on timeless stories which, as one producer suggested to a correspondent preparing to go to Vietnam, "illustrate the techniques of the war." Routine operations, such as search-and-destroy operations, helicopter airlifts, river patrols and artillery firings suited this purpose better than did major actions whose outcome might be reported in the press days before the film reached New York.

Second, in a policy decision made by news executives in

New York, news coverage was mainly limited to American units. As an NBC News vice-president explained, "It's not a Vietnamese war, it's an American war in Asia, and that's the only story the American audience is interested in." Hence, according to producers, correspondents were instructed to avoid stories about Vietnamese policies, South Vietnamese army units or casualties inflicted on South Vietnamese without advance clearance from New York.

Third, in covering American units, correspondents were restricted by the military Public Affairs Office, on which they were dependent for both information and transportation, as to the types of stories they could film. ("The main source for hard news is the daily briefing given by the Joint United States Public Affairs Office," ABC advised its correspondents in 1966.) In late 1968 the Army apparently wanted to discourage coverage of certain aspects of the war. For example, in the case of United States Marines trying to dislodge North Vietnamese units from the demilitarized zone, an NBC correspondent advised New York in a memorandum of a "new USMACV [Military Assistance Command, Vietnam] rule . . . no correspondent will be allowed into DMZ. They want as little publicity about the confrontation as possible." On the other hand, a former press officer in Vietnam pointed out that it was generally considered desirable from the Army's point of view to direct television coverage, whenever possible, toward "military hardware."

Finally, in early November 1968 (as was discussed earlier), the producer of the Evening News decided that the main emphasis of reporting about Vietnam should be on the search for peace through negotiations in Paris, and that it would only serve to confuse the audience if combat stories which aimed at military victories were also included on the program. To enforce this decision, it will be recalled, he simply rejected most of the combat pieces of this kind for the Evening News, though a year earlier such stories had been in heavy demand. In turn, this gave correspondents and free-lance cameramen little incentive to take risks and seek out more volatile situations.

The Congress: An Investigative Agency. Most of the news pictures about Congress during this period concerned Senate investigations of consumer products. Typically, senators sitting in a courtlike atmosphere heard testimony about automobile defects, dishonest credit practices and nutritional deficiencies. Most of the remaining news film of Congress featured critiques and exposés of Administration policies by a small group of senators— Edward Kennedy, Eugene McCarthy, Edmund Muskie, George McGovern and William Fulbright. Other elements of Congress were much less visible: members of the House of Representatives, with few exceptions, rarely appeared in the news pictures, and the legislative process itself—the passing of laws and approval of appropriations—was almost completely neglected.

To some degree this limited view of Congress is shaped by procedural considerations. For one thing, since the rules of the House of Representatives prohibit the filming or televising of any of its sessions or of the proceedings of any of its committees or subcommittees, the activities of this branch of the legislature can only be effectively covered in film by interviewing individual congressmen outside the official proceedings. This usually results, one Washington producer for NBC explained, in "talking heads, and unrecognizable ones at that, discussing some complex issue in a crowded corridor." On the other hand, it will be recalled, the Senate allows committee hearings —though not the proceedings in the Senate itself—to be televised at the discretion of committee chairmen. Since the built-in conflict of hearings are perhaps the most dramatic available stories on Congress—and certainly the most predictable ones—committee chairmen have considerable influence over what issues are covered by network television. Chairmen who desire coverage on an issue and permit cameras in the hearing room are obviously more likely to be covered by the networks than those who, for one reason or another, shun exposure.

The assignment criteria discussed in Chapter 4 also tend to narrow coverage to a few subcommittees and individual senators. As there are usually more subcommittee hearings in a given day than there are network camera crews available, a choice must be made fairly early in the morning which hearings will be assigned coverage. Of the open hearings, those chaired by nationally known senators are given routine preference over committees chaired by less recognizable figures. The senators presumed by assignment editors to be most identifiable to a national audience are those who are candidates—or even "noncandidates"—for President or Vice-President; hence the concentration on Kennedy, Muskie, McGovern and McCarthy, who had all either been candidates for the 1968 Democratic nomination or were potential candidates for 1972. These candidates also might be expected to be most critical of Administration policy. In cases where there are no recognizable national figures involved, full committees are given preference over subcommittees.

The producer of the Evening News further focused his selection on investigation of consumer products—automobiles, credit practices and nutrition—because he assumed that these were most relevant to his audience. In choosing between two Senate hearings, he would generally select the one which, as he put it, "more people would care about." Thus, one role of the Senate tended to represent symbolically all of Congress, just as the flag might represent the nation.

The Mystique of the President. The President is virtually always presented in dignified and controlled surroundings. Usually the setting is a White House office, podium or official reception; the background is stationary and darkened, and the emblematic eagle is conspicuously displayed on the desk or lectern. The President almost never enters, moves about or leaves a room; an unseen voice generally announces his presence, and suddenly he appears in a close-up, poised and prepared, and begins to speak. Rather than an interview or discussion, the format is typically a declaration of purpose, an announcement of an event, or a symbolic act such as lighting the White House Christmas tree.

The networks have scant alternative but to present the President in this light. The policy at NBC and at the other networks is that the President is to be covered whenever possible. But he and the White House staff determine the times and circumstances when coverage will be permitted. This is tantamount to control over the setting, since the accepted ground rules of the White House press corps, as well as security regulations, make it nearly impossible for television crews to cover the Chief Executive when he wishes to avoid it, or even in impromptu circumstances. And the White House staff, which has a strong interest in enhancing the President's image, can hardly be expected to schedule coverage of situations which might detract from the President's dignity or popularity. In the case of Nixon's trip to Europe in February 1969, for example, NBC prepared, with the assistance of the White House press office, a 26-page advance schedule for television coverage which included such details for his arrival at the Brussels airport as "The King will greet Nixon two or three times. . . . Mr. Nixon will respond once."

Moreover, the networks themselves have an interest in not unduly embarrassing the President or showing him in unfavorable light. In their relations with their affiliates, networks are heavily dependent on the government and its leading spokesmen placing a high value on network news. One justification for the coverage of such Presidential events as his trips abroad is the good will it may gain for the networks. From this point of view, any sort of coverage that undermines White House good will would be questionable. Even before Vice-President Agnew's public criticism of network news for, among other things, "instant analysis" of presidential statements (which served to change the format from the customary one of presidential speeches to one of debate), NBC producers were extremely sensitive to the problem of "decorum," as it was called in the news room, when presenting the President on television.

The Apocalyptic Battle on the Campuses. One of the major continuing stories on NBC during this three-month period was student strife; news pictures depicted bloody melees between two sharply drawn sides spreading from campus to campus. The story usually began with mounting protest, a confrontation, the climactic battle, then a tapering off of the action. In their televised interviews, leaders of the opposing sides attributed the strife to deep-seated differences and irreconcilable demands. The correspondents' narration further stressed the rational "causes" for the violence. In most cases the theme was the same: a purposeful struggle between students seeking to expand their freedom and authorities seeking to maintain the status quo, which inevitably led to conflict.

During these same months, there were hundreds of student actions which neither led to bloody confrontation with the police nor illustrated the theme of an apocalyptic war on the campuses. The nature of these were more varied: hunger strikes over university policies; silent vigils over Vietnam; boycotts of pollutants; sleep-ins at women's dormitories; polemic struggles among factions of the New Left; efforts to change the curriculum, and so on. But despite the variety of student protests, a dozen incidents on five campuses, all on a single theme, were shown on the NBC Evening News. In part, the emergence of this particular picture of the campuses can be traced to certain procedures and policies then in force at NBC. For one thing, the choice of which kinds of student stories would be covered at all was predetermined to a large extent by assignment-desk criteria. As a rule, assignment editors would not assign a camera crew to a student protest unless the police had already been called in or a violent riot was already in progress. They explained that this was not only because network crews are a scarce resource and usually assigned to scheduled events, but also because network policy prevented them from dispatching a crew to a situation in which it might either precipitate a riot—as a camera crew on campus conceivably might do —or where it would advertise a planned protest. "Our duty is to report the story when it develops, not to promote it," NBC policy states; "we should no more predict violence than we would a bank run." In effect, this meant that only one type of campus story was routinely covered: the confrontation between police and students (though producers can, of course, commission a story on other student subjects).

Policy guidelines also dictate the way in which stories will be reconstructed by cameramen, correspondents and editors. In 1968, NBC policy for riot situations and civil disorders specifically ordered: "Edit all film and tape with particular care for deletion of obscenity, profanity or slander." This also effectively deleted many of the less rational and unplanned moments that might provoke violence, such as insults and flare-ups of temper. Moreover, while policy limits the filming of immediate provocations to violence, it requires the reporters to attempt to connect any incident of violence to root causes, stating that "the news function is not served unless violence is related to its background." To comply with this policy, correspondents need to suggest in their summaries that long-term conditions (that is, "background") are responsible for the outbreaks of violence, rather than any sort of irrational act on the part of individuals.

Finally, producers prefer stories that illustrate themes familiar to a national audience. This both allows reports of disruptions at various universities to be "packaged" together in the same segment, since they can be presented as part of the same theme, and for essentially local happenings to be integrated into a national story. The stories that the NBC producer specifically commissioned for his program thus concerned potentially bitter confrontations between sharply drawn sides.

Such themes, once established, tend to become self-perpetuating. In July 1970 the NBC Evening News developed a report from an unattributed source on another network that two presidential advisers on student unrest, Alexander Heard, chancellor of Vanderbilt University, and James Cheek of Howard University had reported to President Nixon that the University of California's Berkeley campus and Columbia University were in serious trouble. Beginning the program with the dramatic statement, "Two college officials, appointed by President Nixon to advise him, are about to advise him that numerous colleges and universities may not even be able to open this fall," David Brinkley reported that Heard and Cheek were about to give Nixon a report that "says the University of California at Berkeley, as an institution of freedom and learning, is dead . . . [and] Columbia University is faltering badly and may be dead within a few years." The next night this apocalyptic theme was illustrated with specially commissioned filmed interviews of students commenting on the imminent death of their universities. As it turned out, the speculation was untrue. Heard and Cheek denied ever reaching such conclusions, or making such a report to the President, and NBC acknowledged its error some weeks later. An NBC producer explained that the initial story about such a presidential report was accepted without a source and translated into a series of filmed reports because it seemed so "believable" in the light "of all the other reports of the campuses about to explode."

These pictures of society are meant to be neither exhaustive or immutable; they are given simply as illustrations of the principle that over a period of time, organizational imperatives shape the portrayal of a given subject on network television. If this principle is accepted, then it follows that network news can be partly explained in terms of the relatively stable procedures, criteria and values by which it is gathered, selected, reconstructed and presented on television. And if it is further accepted that these procedures, criteria and values derive in large part from the structure of commercial television, then it is possible to conclude that the selection of reality that a national audience sees on television as news will follow certain consistent directions.

Chapter 9

Versions of National News

News is essentially protean in character. Any happening can be reported in a multitude of different forms and takes on radically different appearances in different news media. Nor is there necessarily one correct way of reporting an event. Alternative ways always exist for organizing information, and events themselves do not ineluctably determine the forms in which they are reported. Yet in examining the product of a news organization, one may find striking similarities in the ways in which the news is presented and the direction it takes. What accounts for these consistent directions and news forms is the central question that this study attempts to answer, or at least to clarify in the case of network news organizations.

The main finding of this study is that the pictures of society that are shown on television as national news are largely—though not entirely—performed and shaped by organizational considerations. To maintain themselves in a competitive world, the networks impose a set of prior restraints, rules and conditions on the operations of their news divisions. Budgets are set for the production of news, time is scheduled for its presentation, and general policies are laid down concerning its content. To satisfy these requirements—and keep their jobs—news executives and producers formulate procedures, systems and policies intended to reduce the uncertainties of news to manageable proportions. The timing, length, content and cost of news thereby becomes predictable. Since all the networks are in essentially the same business and compete for the same or similar advertisers, affiliates and audiences, under a single set of ground rules laid down by the government, the news product at each network is shaped by very similar requisites. The basic contours of network news can thus be at least partly explained in terms of the demands which the news organizations must meet in order to continue operating without crises or intervention from network executives. In this respect, four critical demands structure the scope and form of network news.

First, there is the budgetary requisite set by the economic logic of network television. The prevailing assumption among network executives, it will be recalled, is that increasing the budget of a news program for news gathering or production past a certain point will not bring about a commensurate increase in advertising revenues, and that the point at which these diminishing returns set in is located immediately beyond the budget necessary to produce the minimum amount of news programing of adequate technical quality to fill the news schedule. These assumptions proceed from the audience-flow theory that network news programs, unlike entertainment or local news programs, inherit most of their audience from the preceding programs. In other words, national news does not attract its own audience to any significant extent. Therefore, the logic goes, increased expenditures for the scope and quality of the news effort will not necessarily increase the size of the audience—or of the advertising revenues, which are dependent on the size of the audience.

Whatever the merits of this theory, the fact that network executives commonly accept its implications profoundly limits the news operation. Because budget levels are fixed with an eye toward filling a specific number of minutes of news programing a week, the allocation of funds for the unseen parts of news gathering tends to be held to a minimum. For one thing, there is no economic incentive to spend money on searches for original information, or intelligence gathering, since it is not presumed that scoops, exclusives or original reporting significantly increase the audience, and hence the revenue, for network news. Instead, for advance notice of news events, the networks rely heavily on the wire services, the *New York Times* and other secondary sources. Similarly, investigative reports requiring a large amount of field work and research are a luxury which cannot be justified in terms of economic returns. Networks therefore simply do not maintain the research facilities and staff which would be necessary to support investigative reporting on a regular basis; instead, select subjects are occasionally explored in depth by a documentary or special-events unit, which also must meet network requisites.

Further, since there is no economic reason regularly to employ more film crews than is necessary to produce the daily quota, coverage is generally limited to a dozen or so selected events. This, in turn, requires that the events which are selected for coverage are highly predictable and almost certain to produce a usable news story. Though they would extend the range of coverage to less definite and more risky events, additional crews would not be economically justifiable under the assumptions of this theory. Also, because direct information is not always available about the precise news content of planned events—what will emerge, for example, in a scheduled hearing or speech—producers and assignment editors must rely routinely on certain broad-gauged criteria to narrow down the field of possibilities. Consequently, there tends to be a repetition of certain types of story situations and news makers over long periods of time, or what Walter Lippmann would have called a "repertory of stereotypes."

Moreover, since it is less expensive to take a film story from some cities than from others, according to the budgetary accounting practices of the networks, the filmed news tends to be skewed toward certain geographic areas of the country—specifically, New York, Washington and, to a lesser extent, Chicago. The societal themes depicted on network news thus tend to be illustrated with a disproportionate number of visual examples taken from a few cosmopolitan centers with special problems.

Finally, the economic logic tends to focus attention on a relatively small group of news makers who are actively engaged in conflicts or contests for office. Since there is no economic justification in overcoverage, according to the accepted rationale, assignment editors tend to ration the camera crews among news makers that can be relied on with a fair degree of certainty to produce usable happenings. For this purpose, it is generally assumed that high-ranking figures of authority involved in heated conflicts or challenges to their authority are more likely to produce news than news makers who are explicating developments or policies in a complex world. The more heated the dispute or challenge, the more certain the news story.

A second basic requisite that network news divisions are expected to meet is that their programs maintain—or at least not significantly diminish—the networks' "audience flows." While it is presumed that network news cannot *attract* large numbers of new viewers to a channel, no matter how high the quality of its coverage, executives also generally believe that "visually unsatisfactory" news, as one NBC vice-president put it, can cause a significant number of viewers to change channels. Since any noticeable reduction in a network's audience flow during the dinnertime news seriously affects the ratings of the entire prime-time schedule—programs begin with a smaller "base" audience—network executives insist that the news be presented in its most visually satisfactory form, no matter how complex or difficult to comprehend the subject is. The effectiveness of the visual presentation is measured by a low "turn-off" rate among viewers. The logic of audience maintenance can thus be extrapolated from analyses of audience studies.

The first assumption made by news executives and producers is that viewers' interest is most likely to be maintained through easily recognizable and palpable images, and conversely, most likely to be distracted by unfamiliar or confusing images. This has special force in the case of the dinnertime news, when, according to studies, the audience has fewer years of formal education than the population at large—and a large proportion of viewers are children. In practice, therefore, cameramen, correspondents and editors are instructed to seek out and select pictures that have an almost universal meaning. Hence, stories tend to fit into a limited repertory of images, which explains why so often shabbily dressed children symbolically stand for poverty; uniformed police symbolically stand for authority; fire symbolically stands for destruction, and so forth. Since television is regarded as a medium for the "transmission of experience" rather than "information," complex issues are represented in terms of human experience; inflation, for example, is pictured as a man unable to afford dinner in a restaurant. Of course, the repertory changes, but at any given times, images, especially emotional ones, which are presumed to have the broadest possible recognition, are used to illustrate news events.

A second assumption in this logic of audience maintenance is that scenes of potential conflict are more interesting to the audience than scenes of placidity. Virtually all executives and producers share this view. Situations are thus sought out in network news in which there is a high potential for violence, but a low potential for audi-

ence confusion. News events showing a violent confrontation between two easily recognizable sides in conflict—
for example, blacks versus whites, uniformed police versus demonstrators, or military versus civilians—are pref-
erable to ones in which the issues are less easily identifiable. However, even when the conflict involves confusing
elements, it usually can be reconstructed in the form of a
two-sided conflict. Therefore network news tends to present the news in terms of highly dramatic conflicts
between clearly defined sides.

A third closely related assumption is that the viewer's
span of attention—which is presumed to be limited—is
prolonged by action, or subjects in motion, and sharply
reduced by static subjects, such as "talking heads." As
has been previously discussed, the high value placed on
action footage by executives leads to a three-step distillation of news happenings by correspondents, cameramen and editors, all of whom seek the moment of highest
action. Through this process, the action in a news event,
which in fact may account for only a fraction of the time,
is concentrated together and becomes the central feature
of the happening. This helps explain why news on television tends willy-nilly to focus on activity.

It is further assumed in this logic that news reports are
more likely to hold viewers' attention if they are cast in
the form of the fictive story, with narrative closure. For
this purpose, it will be recalled, stories are generally
edited so that there is a discernible beginning, middle and
end; rising action, a climax, then falling action; conflict
and then apparent resolution. This self-contained form
tends to "lock" an audience into a news story, an NBC
vice-president for audience research suggested. The net
effect is that most events on network news are presented
as miniature documentaries with similar plots: two opposing sides confront each other, the tension builds to a
climax, and then there is an apparent denouement. As
Reuven Frank instructed, news is thus given "all the
attributes of fiction."

Affiliates place a third basic requisite on network news in requiring that it be *national* news. The stations affiliated with a network, it will be recalled, substitute the half-hour network news for their own local programing, which is generally highly profitable, because they are expected by the FCC to provide some coverage of national as well as local issues. To meet this expectation, producers must solve the problem of converting local happenings—since all news happens in *some* locality—into national stories. The "nationalization of news," which is commonly regarded by network producers as the crux of their operation, is accomplished by using reports about particular events as illustrations of national themes. Almost any event can be subsumed under a universal category. The opening of a municipal heating plant in a single city was, for example, utilized by CBS to illustrate its on-going "Can the World Survive?" theme. Since producers can easily "commission" stories about happenings which illustrate themes that are presumed to be of national interest or simply concentrate their coverage on news makers associated with national causes, the precommitment of network news to an agenda of national themes and causes is virtually assured.

Finally, government regulation of television sets a fourth basic requirement for network news: it must conform to certain outside standards of fairness in the presentation of controversial issues. Since the Federal Communication Commission defines fairness simply as the presentation of opposing views on an issue, network news commonly has satisfied this requisite by soliciting views from spokesmen of two opposing sides in a controversy—and then editing the opposing views together as a "dialogue." To avoid any apparent disparities in the presentations, equally articulate spokesmen are usually selected to present the arguments on each side. Complicated issues thus appear to be merely a point-counterpoint debate between equally matched opponents.

Nor is this framework of fairness conducive to questioning the arguments presented, or exposing the weakness or superiority of one or another side in a controversy. For even to appear to favor one side might be construed as an unfair presentation by network executives who closely monitor the news. Quite inadvertently, the fairness standards encourage rhetoric and even demagoguery, at least to the degree that spokesmen in a controversy are aware that their arguments are not likely to be questioned. Moreover, the networks' vulnerability to government regulation—which includes antitrust action as well as the FCC—requires a firm policy of neutrality in the view of key network executives. This entails recruiting correspondents without fixed views on political subjects, frequently rotating those who cover sensitive subjects, and not encouraging them—if only by not making sufficient time or resources available—to attempt to resolve controversial issues in favor of one side or another by conducting their own investigations. In a very real sense, then, the network policies of fairness and neutrality limit, if not define, the style of journalism on network news.

To be sure, network news cannot be entirely explained in terms of organizational requisites. The personal opinions of newsmen color newscasts to some degree, no matter how stringent a network's controls; also, reporting and editorials in other news media, especially the *New York Times* and *Time* magazine, help crystallize issues and heavily influence the producers in their selection of news. Nonetheless, the organizational imperatives of network news, and the logics that proceed from these demands, irresistibly shape the pictures of society in consistent directions, and therefore produce a very particular, perhaps unique, version of national news. In this version, all local events tend to be transmuted to great national themes, with the inevitable loss of their local and specific character. Since the events that are used to illustrate the national themes tend to be taken from large cosmopolitan centers, which are economically and geographically the most convenient sources of news, the themes tend to follow the line of conflict in such cities as New York, Washington and Chicago. To maintain the interest of the audience, happenings involving visual conflict are routinely selected over less violent ones, and ones involving recognizable figures of authority are selected over less identifiable images.

The loci of these demands are situations involving challenges to authority. Since the amount of time that can be allotted to a story is limited to a few minutes, both because of network scheduling and the need to separate commercial messages, it is generally not possible to present all the reasons for the challenge. Nor, given the networks' fairness standards, is there an incentive to evaluate the validity of the challenge, though the very fact that challenges are prominently featured as news gives them some presumption of legitimacy. By comparison, the legitimizing myths of authority, which depend on complex historical analogies and cannot easily be illustrated by current news happenings, suffer for want of explanation. Unlike print journalism, which can state such historical concepts as, say, the "balance of power" rationale in foreign policy, the need for visual images of action makes network news oriented toward the most immediate aspects of an event.

Moreover, the requirement to present conflicts as disputes between no more than two equally matched sides tends to reduce complex issues, which may have a multitude of dimensions, to a simple conflict between protesters (or nonauthorities) and authorities. When this is presented in the usual story form of rising action, confrontation and denouement, the visually presented issue becomes simply one of the protesters' right to protest or the authorities' right to suppress the protest. In this version of the news, change always seems relatively easy to accomplish, since the more complex reasons for tempering change—such as economic feasibility, minority interests and possible consequences in other areas—are neglected by a purely visual presentation.

The process of nationalizing the news further requires elevating most problems to a level of universal concern. Viewers everywhere must be made to feel that even events occurring in distant locations are part of wider problems that directly concern their well-being. Diffuse and random happenings, which are an accepted part of local news, thus become elements in apocalyptic, can-the-world-be-saved types of national themes. (Nonproblems, such as the gradual rise in per capita income in the United States, rarely manifest the visual conflict necessary for a news happening, and thus rarely appear in the network rendition of news.) Moreover, to integrate and balance these nationalized stories, spokesmen are selected on the basis of their ability to dramatize a desired theme. Rather than representing any local viewpoint, such spokesmen usually must have a world view encompassing the present and future state of society in order to illustrate how local events fit into the wider scheme of things. For instance, such spokesmen for Black Power as Stokely Carmichael and H. Rap Brown were able to tie together into a nationally symbolic theme a myriad of essentially local protests over the deprivation of civil rights for blacks occurring in widely separated places. By synthesizing momentary flashes of conflict in specific localities into sustained national themes, articulated by national spokesmen, which aim at a universal level of concern, the networks produce a form of original news.

This version of the news is not the product of a group of willful or biased or political men, but of an organization striving to meet the requisites needed to survive in a competitive world. While other critiques, starting from very different premises about news, have reached similar conclusions about the version of the news that television presents, the organizational approach produces a different set of causes and implications. For example, perhaps the most common critique made of television news by other journalists—and faculty members of journalism schools —is that it is superficial in the sense that it affords only scant coverage of news events, lacks depth or sufficient

analysis of events, and engages in only a minimum amount
of investigative reporting. The main thrusts of such
criticism are that television newsmen lack journalistic
credentials, and that producers and executives are lax or
indifferent toward their responsibilities—or else lack
public spirit. For example, in examining the deficiencies
of television news, the Alfred I. Dupont–Columbia University *Survey of Broadcast Journalism* suggested:

> This might give the impression that all broadcast-
> ers are assumed to be evil men. This is obviously far
> from true. There are in broadcasting as elsewhere in
> our society the public-spirited along with the mean.
> At the moment, unfortunately, the latter seem to
> prevail.

The implication that runs through this type of critique
is that the level of journalism is set by the magnanimity
of broadcasters, and that more enlightened or public-
spirited broadcasters can remedy the insufficiencies in
network news. It then follows that changing or educating
the broadcasters will improve the news product. The organizational approach suggests, however, that the level
of journalism in network news is more or less fixed by
the time, money and manpower that can be allocated to it,
and that these resources are ultimately determined not
by "mean" or public-spirited broadcasters, but by the
requisites which the news divisions must meet in order
to maintain their operations. And these requirements imposed on the news divisions are not arbitrary; they flow
from the logic and structure of network television. As
the previously discussed case of Fred W. Friendly illustrated, an executive, no matter how public-spirited, who
over time fails to meet these requirements will be replaced, or his responsibilities in the organization will be
changed. Any substantial improvement in the level of
network journalism, such as expanding coverage of
events to a truly nationwide scale, would therefore require a structural change in network television which

would effectively reorder the economic and political in-
centives, rather than merely a change of personnel.

Alternatively, consider the conservative critique which
holds that network news is politically biased in favor of
the causes and leaders of the liberal-left faction. In this
critique, the liberal-left bias of television is generally attributed to a small clique of newsmen in New York and
Washington who share the same perspectives on politics,
report preponderantly the same kinds of challenges to
established authority, and then shape the news to fit their
own political commitments. What emerges is seen as a
consistently distorted view of a small minority which is
falsely represented as the beliefs of a majority of Americans. Since in this critique network news is presumed to
be highly politicized by the men who select and report it,
the remedy most often suggested is to employ conservative newsmen to balance the liberal viewpoints. Again,
the implication is that a change of personnel will substantially change the journalistic product.

The organizational approach accounts for some of the
same manifestations in less political terms. While most
of the domestic news on the network programs does, in
fact, come from a few cities—New York, Washington,
and Chicago—it is because news is less expensive and
more conveniently available from these cities, not because of the political preferences of any small fraternity
of newsmen, as Vice-President Agnew suggested. Moreover, since a considerable portion of the efforts to change
the distribution of political values and services were concentrated in Washington, New York and Chicago during
the 1960s for a complex of reasons, network news reported, willy-nilly, a disproportionately large share of
these activities. And since the logic of audience maintenance favors conflict between easily recognizable
groups, network news almost irresistibly focuses on challenges to established authority. Lastly, the requirement
that news be nationalized, though it is foisted on the networks by generally conservative affiliate-owners, further

adds to the impression that network news is advancing radical causes. For in elevating local disputes to national proportions, newscasters appear to be treating them with uncalled-for importance.

In short, the tendency of network news to focus their attention on certain causes to the comparative neglect of others proceeds more from organizational problems than from the political biases of individuals.

Similarly, it is worth considering the radical critique that argues that network news neglects the inherent contradictions in the American system. In this view, network news focuses not on substantive problems but on symbolic protests. By overstating the importance of protest actions, television news invites the audience to judge the conduct of the protesters rather than the content of the problem. This creates false issues. Popular support is generated against causes which appear on television to rely on violent protests, while underlying economic and social problems are systematically masked or ignored. Broadcasters can be expected to help continually perpetuate "the system," it is argued, because they are an important part of it. Thus, one commentator writes: "The media owners will do anything to maintain these myths. . . . They will do anything to keep the public from realizing that the establishment dominates society through its direct and indirect control of the nation's communication system."

The organizational approach provides a quite different explanation for the same observable outcome. The tendency to depict symbolic protests rather than substantive problems is closely related to the problem of audience maintenance. Protests can be universally comprehended, it is presumed, if they are presented in purely symbolic terms: one group, standing for one cause, challenging another group and cause. On the other hand, substantive problems usually require contextual knowledge about the circumstances in which the problem occurs. Moreover, the sort of detail that would be necessary to clarify economic and social issues is not easily translated into visual terms, whereas the sort of dramatic images that can be found in violent protests have an immediate impact on an audience. Newsmen therefore avoid radical arguments not because they are politically committed to supporting "the system," but because they do not satisfy the audience requisites of network news.

Finally, in what might best be called the social science critique, network news is commonly criticized for presenting a picture of society that does not accurately correspond with the empirical data. To wit, spokesmen selected to represent groups in society tend to be statistically atypical of the group they are supposedly speaking for. For example, militant students may appear to be in the majority on college campuses in America because of the frequency with which they are selected to represent student views, when in fact data collected by social scientists might reveal that they constitute only a small minority. It is generally argued that such discrepancies stem from a lack of readily usable data rather than any intent on the part of journalists to misrepresent situations. The clear implication in this critique is that if network news had the techniques of social scientists, or employed social scientists as consultants, they would produce a more realistic version of the claims and aspirations of different segments of society.

The problem with this approach is that spokesmen are selected to represent sides in controversy at least partly because they fit in with the organizational needs of the program. It is assumed that spokesmen must be articulate, easily identifiable and dramatic in order to hold the interest of viewers to whom the subject of the controversy may be of no interest. Since the "average" person in a group cannot be depended on to manifest these qualities—as Reuven Frank pointed out, "Most people are dull as far as their television image is concerned"—producers are expected to select spokesmen who are capable of retaining the audience's interest, even if they are not what social scientists would consider to be representative. Moreover, in a very real sense the nationalization of news requires that the selection of spokesmen be based on "thematic" criteria, which aim at finding individuals capable of illustrating the major themes in society, rather than modal criteria, which aim at finding the statistically typical unit. Given the organizational needs to illustrate news stories with both dramatic and thematic spokesmen, the pictures of society that network news presents cannot be expected to conform to that delineated by social scientists, no matter how much data and technical skills they supply.

If the version of the news presented on network television is fixed to a large extent by organizational requirements, the prognosis for change is severely limited. The systematic distortions of events which journalistic critics, conservatives, radicals and social scientists point to will not be remedied by more enlightened executives, the education of journalists, different personnel, the politicization of recruitment—which, ironically, both conservative and radical critics advocate—or the availability of data from the academic world. As long as the requisites remain essentially the same, network news can be expected to define American society by the problems of a few urban areas rather than the entire nation, by action rather than ideas, by dramatic protests rather than substantive contradictions, by rhetorical dialogues rather than the resolution of issues, by elite news makers rather than economic and social structures, by atypical rather than typical views, and by synthetic national themes rather than disparate local events.

The implications of this finding are not that the organizational structure of television needs to be radically altered—a different set of requisites might simply mean that the contours of network news would be propelled in different directions—but that alternative sources of national news are necessary for balance. Presumably, different news media with different organizational requirements would produce different versions of the news. Local television stations, which are not compelled either to nationalize their news or to select stories which are not of immediate interest to their audience, can be expected to produce a different version of reality in which news of other cities plays a comparatively minor role. Public television, if it is allowed to develop into a news medium, has very different audience maintenance requirements from commercial television, and can be expected to produce a journalistic product less dependent on visual appeal. Radio, which has much lower production and transport costs, can be expected to furnish still different versions of national news. Further organizational studies of other news media, such as local, public and cable television, radio, newspapers and magazines, would greatly clarify the relation between the news organizations and news renditions, and provide a test of the general applicability of the hypotheses advanced in this necessarily limited study.

The point is not to change news, but to understand its limitations. Like map making, news cannot realistically hope to produce a model which perfectly represents all the contours and elevations of reality, but at least the basic distortions in any given mode of projection can be clarified.

Source Notes

PAGE	LINE	*Preface*

xi **14** Walter Lippmann, *Public Opinion* (New York: Free Press, 1965), p. 101.

xi **20** *Ibid.*, p. 203.

xii **7** For examples of the former, see Bernard C. Cohen, *The Press and Foreign Policy* (Princeton, N.J.: Princeton University Press, 1963); Leo C. Rosten, *The Washington Correspondents* (New York: Harcourt, Brace, 1937); Douglass Cater, *The Fourth Branch of Government* (Boston: Houghton Mifflin, 1959); Dan D. Nimmo, *Newsgathering in Washington* (New York: Atherton, 1964); William L. Rivers, *The Opinion-Makers* (Boston: Beacon Press, 1965), and James Reston, *The Artillery of the Press* (New York: Harper & Row, 1966).

xii **27** Kurt Lang and Gladys Engel Lang, *Politics and Television* (Chicago: Quadrangle, 1968), pp. 36 ff. In England, James Hallorohan of the Mass Communications Center in Leicester conducted similar experiments during the 1969 protests at the American embassy in London. A more indirect method of comparing the behavior of individuals not exposed to an event on television with that of television viewers was used by Herbert A. Simon and F. Stern, "The Effects of Television Upon Voting Behavior in Iowa in the 1952 Presidential Election," *American Political Science Review*, XLIX (June 1955), 470–78.

PAGE LINE

xiii   5   Edward C. Banfield suggests that journalism differs from political science by focusing on the atypical rather than the typical. *Political Influence* (New York: Free Press, 1961), p. 11.

xiii   16   Robert K. Merton, *On Theoretical Sociology* (New York: Free Press, 1967), pp. 1–38.

xiii   22   For example, Warren Breed, "Social Control in the Newsroom: A Functional Analysis," *Social Forces*, XXXIII (May 1955), 331.

xiii   32   See Paul Weaver, "The Metropolitan Newspaper as a Political Institution" (unpublished Ph.D. dissertation, Government Department, Harvard University, 1968), preface.

xiv   14   This approach is perhaps most clearly developed in Chester I. Barnard, *The Functions of the Executive* (Cambridge, Mass.: Harvard University Press, 1966), pp. 139–60, and *passim*.

xv   12   Roper Research Associates, *A Ten-Year Attitude toward Television and Other Mass Media: 1959–1968* (New York: Television Information Office, 1969).

xv   18   Exceptions include Fred W. Friendly's illuminating book, *Due to Circumstances Beyond Our Control* (New York: Random House, 1967); Harry J. Skornia's more general appraisal of television, *Television and the News* (Palo Alto, Calif.: Pacific Books, 1968); and Norman Swallow's *Factual Television* (New York: Hastings House, 1966), which is more descriptive of local television than network news.

Chapter 1

3   Epigraph: Reuven Frank, Memorandum, p. 1.

4   2   A. C. Nielsen estimates for October 1969.

5   2   Reuven Frank, Memorandum, p. 20. Cf. Robert E. Park, "The Natural History of a Newspaper," in *On Social Control and Collective Behavior*, edited by Ralph H. Turner (Chicago: University of Chicago Press, 1967), p. 107.

PAGE LINE

5   9   Frank, Memorandum, p. 17.

5   21   *Ibid.*, pp. 18, 20.

5   35   Walter Lippmann, *Public Opinion* (New York: Free Press, 1965), p. 59.

6   5   *Ibid.*, pp. 3–20.

6   24   Public Broadcasting Laboratory, "The Whole World's Watching," December 22, 1968, 8 P.M. (transcript, p. 57).

6   31   An examination of the role that this fear has played in American history can be found in Edward Shils, *Torment of Secrecy* (New York: Free Press, 1950), pp. 23–50. Compare, for example, Vice-President Agnew's complaint: "The American people would rightly not tolerate this concentration of power in government. Is it not fair and relevant to question its concentration in the hands of a tiny, enclosed fraternity of privileged men elected by no one and enjoying a monopoly sanctioned and licensed by the government?" (*New York Times*, November 14, 1969, p. 24).

7   31   *New York Times*, November 14, 1969, p. 24.

8   10   William Small, *To Kill a Messenger: Television News and the Real World* (New York: Random House, 1970), p. 263.

9   15   The study referred to is Roper Research Associates, *A Ten-Year Attitude towards Television and Other Mass Media: 1959–1968.*

9   32   Small, *op. cit.*, p. 3.

9   36   Frank, Memorandum, p. 3.

10   4   The belief in the efficacy of television as a medium of communication, it should be noted, is based more on intuitive than empirical evidence. Social science has not been able to make a definitive link between television and public opinion, if one indeed exists, because of all the other intervening variables that cannot be completely accounted for—other media, the influence of peer group, education, etc. The problems of different approaches

PAGE LINE

can be seen in William Y. Elliot, *Television's Impact on American Culture* (East Lansing, Mich.: Michigan State University Press, 1956), *passim*.

10 7 Sig Mickelson, quoted in the *New York Times*, March 19, 1970.

10 23 Richard C. Wald, Memorandum, September 9, 1968 (transcript, author's files).

10 37 NBC News, "From Here to the Seventies," October 7, 1969.

11 24 Huntley-Brinkley Report, October 7, 1969.

11 33 *Ibid.*

13 18 National Commission on the Causes and Prevention of Violence (NCCPV), *Testimony*, December 20, 1968, p. 4.

13 22 *Ibid.*, October 17, 1968, p. 1608.

13 26 Reuven Frank, "The Ugly Mirror," *Television Quarterly* (Winter 1969), pp. 89, 91.

13 29 *Ibid.*, p. 90.

13 32 NCCPV, *Testimony*, December 20, 1968, p. 218.

14 1 U.S. House of Representatives, *Deceptive Programming Practices*, Hearings before the Committee on Interstate and Foreign Commerce, 90th Cong., 2d Sess., 1968, p. 176. The mirror metaphor is also used to describe newspaper journalism. For example, the *New York Times* has stated about itself: "A newspaper, to stay vital, mirrors and is influenced by the world" (A. M. Rosenthal, managing editor, *New York Times*, March 20, 1970). The general manager of the AP, Wes Gallagher, also said in a speech in 1969: "The task of the journalist is to hold a magnifying mirror before our society to show warts and all" (quoted in Small, *op. cit.*, p. 10).

14 5 "The American Congress and Television," speech to the Inter-Parliamentary Union, Geneva, Switzerland, December 6, 1968 (transcript, p. 27).

14 8 CBS Sunday News, December 21, 1969.

PAGE LINE

14 13 *New York Times*, August 13, 1967, quoted by Elmer W. Lower in speech to Sigma Delta Chi, Buffalo, New York, September 21, 1967 (transcript, p. 23).

14 23 Myron Abrams, *The Mirror and the Lamp: Romantic Theory and Critical Tradition* (New York: Norton, 1958), p. 34.

14 29 Sig Mickelson, *The Electric Mirror* (New York: Dodd, Mead, 1972).

15 10 William Allen White Lectures, University of Kansas, February 10, 1969 (transcript, p. 8).

15 16 Public Broadcasting Laboratory, *op. cit.*, p. 26.

15 27 Analysis, September 19, 1968–January 18, 1969.

15 30 *Ibid.*

15 33 CBS and ABC Evening News Logs, December 1968.

16 3 Quoted by William R. McAndrew, *Television Age* (September 26, 1966), p. 35.

16 7 Huntley-Brinkley Film Logs, and analysis, September 1, 1968–February 1, 1969.

16 9 CBS Logs, ABC Logs, December 1, 1968, and January 20, 1969.

16 27 Reuven Frank, speech at Television Award Dinner, Omaha, Nebraska, January 12, 1970 (pp. 20–21).

16 36 See Karl W. Deutsch's definition of "will" in an organization as "the internally labelled preference for predecision messages over post-decision ones." *Nerves of Government* (New York: Free Press, 1966), pp. 5–6.

17 5 Letter from Howard Monderer to FCC (undated [1968]), reprinted in *Television Quarterly* (Winter 1969), pp. 97 ff.

17 10 Frank, "The Ugly Mirror," p. 87.

17 16 NCCPV, *Testimony*, December 20, 1968, p. 108.

18 13 Network News Logs, April–June 1969.

18 23 Huntley-Brinkley Logs, November 1968–January 1, 1969.

PAGE LINE

18   25   *Ibid.* See also, Huntley-Brinkley Logs, November 1967–
         January 1968.

18   37   Frank, Memorandum, p. 15.

19   9   Karel Reisz and Gavin Millar, *The Technique of Film
         Editing* (New York: Hastings House, 1968), pp.
         194–96.

21   10   Script, Huntley-Brinkley Report, October 4, 1968 (au-
         thor's files).

21   32   Small, *op. cit.*, p. 39.

22   11   U.S. House of Representatives, Subcommittee on De-
         partment of Agriculture and Relating Agencies Ap-
         propriations, 91st Cong., 1st Sess., 1969. Part 5, "Con-
         sumer and Marketing Services," pp. 59–61.

22   14   "The Selling of the Pentagon: A Postscript," March 23,
         1971 (transcript, p. 7).

22   26   CBS Evening News, June 30, 1970.

22   30   James Russell Wiggins, a former editor of the Wash-
         ington *Post*, has, in respect to news photographs, said
         in a speech to a journalism class in North Dakota, "It
         has been said that the camera does not lie, but the
         camera does lie. It is a notorious, compulsive, unashamed
         and mischievous liar," and provided a list of examples.
         Quoted in Small, *op. cit.*, p. 286.

23   25   Huntley-Brinkley Report, April 8, 1968.

24   2   *New York Times*, April 10, 1968.

24   3   "April Aftermath of the King Assassination," *Riot
         Data Review* (August 1968), p. 41.

24   4   *New York Times*, April 10, 1968.

24   6   The data are supplied in a letter from W. D. Swift of
         the American Insurance Association, September 5, 1969
         (author's files).

24   17   *New York Times*, April 5, 1968. See also Gloria Steinem
         and Lloyd Weaver, "The City on the Eve of Destruc-
         tion," *New York* (April 22, 1968), pp. 32a–32c.

PAGE LINE

24 25 Memorandum from David Schmerler to Richard Wald, December 18, 1968 (author's files).

25 32 Talcott Parsons, *Essays in Sociological Theory* (New York: Free Press, 1967), p. 372.

26 36 Colloquium on Network News, Yale University, New Haven, Conn., February 17, 1970 (transcript, p. 33).

27 4 *Ibid.*, pp. 10–11.

28 28 *Newsweek*, December 1, 1969, p. 56–57.

28 34 William Allen White Lectures, *op. cit.*, p. 8.

28 39 NCCPV, *Testimony*, December 20, 1968, p. 245.

30 31 Frank, Memorandum, p. 21.

30 34 *Ibid.*, pp. 22, 24.

31 34 Huntley-Brinkley Film Logs, September 1969–January 1969.

31 36 NBC Content Analysis for Violence Commission, prepared by David Schmerler, December 18, 1969 (author's files).

32 29 *The* (Montreal) *Gazette* (December 13, 1968), p. 10.

32 32 *New York Times*, January 4, 1969.

32 34 *Ibid.*

33 6 Huntley-Brinkley Report, December 26, 1968.

33 8 *Ibid.*, January 3–4, 1968.

33 11 Huntley-Brinkley Logs, September–December 1968; CBS and ABC Logs, November 1968–January 1969.

34 26 Comparison of Huntley-Brinkley Reports and the *New York Times*, September 1968–January 1969. See also Alfred I. duPont–Columbia University, *Survey of Broadcast Journalism: 1968–1969* (New York: Grosset & Dunlap, 1969), p. 82.

35 6 Personal interviews with producers and correspondents involved in the story. January 8–11, 1969.

36 25 George H. Quester, "Israel and the Nuclear Non-Pro-

PAGE LINE

      liferation Treaty," *Bulletin of Atomic Scientists* (June 1969), p. 45.

38   8   Analysis of ABC, NBC and CBS Film Logs, December 13, 1968–January 25, 1969 (with "news analysis," such as Eric Sevareid, excluded).

38 27 *New York Times*, December 2–6, 1968.

39 22 Huntley-Brinkley Report, December 6, 1968.

39 37 Frank, Memorandum, pp. 3, 6, 10.

40 36 Colloquium on Network News, *op. cit.*, pp. 23–24.

42 14 Frank, Memorandum, p. 2.

42 24 Lippmann, *op. cit.*, p. 214.

42 26 *Ibid.*, p. 216.

Chapter 2

44   Epigraph: Fairness Doctrine Hearings, March 6, 1968, p. 35.

45 15 *Newsweek* (December 1, 1969), p. 82.

45 22 James M. Herring and Gerald C. Gross, *Telecommunications* (New York: McGraw-Hill, 1936), pp. 238 ff. Also, National Broadcasting Company v. U.S., *319 US 190*, pp. 210 ff.

46   6 Communications Act of 1934 (47 U.S.C.).

46 11 FCC v. Sanders Bros. Radio Station, *309 US 475*.

46 35 George Gillingham, "Broadcast Primer," in *Broadcasting Yearbook: 1969* (Washington, D.C.: Broadcasting Publishing, 1969), pp. C48 ff.

47   4 U.S. House of Representatives, Committee on Interstate and Foreign Commerce, *Network Broadcasting*, 85th Cong., 2d Sess., 1958, H. R. 1297, pp. 124–43. (Hereafter referred to as *Network Broadcasting*.)

47 26 *319 US 190*, pp. 215–16.

48 11 FCC, "Editorializing by Broadcast Licensees," Docket No. 8516, June 1, 1949, p. 4.

PAGE LINE

48   17   *326 US 1*, p. 20. Also, FCC, Office of Network Study, "Television Network Program Procurement," Docket No. 12782, May 8, 1963, p. 21. (Hereafter referred to as "Television Network Program Procurement.")

48   21   Associated Press v. U.S., *326 US 1*, p. 28 (quoting Judge Learned Hand).

48   26   *Ibid.*

49   2   *Network Broadcasting*, pp. 124 ff.

49   5   FCC, "Report and Statement of Policy re Commission En Banc Programming Requirements," FCC 60-970, Mimeo. 91874 (July 29, 1960), Exhibit 7, p. 13.

49   31   William Small, *To Kill a Messenger: Television News and the Real World* (New York: Random House, 1970), p. 265.

50   8   *Network Broadcasting*, pp. 82–83, 100.

50   14   *319 US 190*, p. 191.

50   23   A congressional investigation concluded: "In recent decisions, the Commission has tended to *favor* applicants with other broadcasting facilities on the basis of their past experience and past programming performance providing the most reliable guide to capacity to serve the public interest. Hence, in certain comparative hearings, the diversification factor has been treated by the Commission in such a way as to reach the conclusion that less than the maximum possible competition will constitute an overall net gain in the public interest. Maximum competition is therefore not always sought." (Emphasis added.) *Network Broadcasting*, p. 105.

50   35   Irving Bernstein. "The Economics of Television Film Production" (New York: Screen Actors Guild, 1960 [mimeo.]), p. 19.

51   9   *319 US 190*, pp. 197–98.

51   19   "Television Network Program Procurement," pp. 35 ff.

51   22   *Ibid.*, p. 43.

52   1   *319 US 190*, p. 206.

PAGE LINE

52   24   *Ibid.*, pp. 190–91.

53   9   Quoted in Small, *op. cit.*, p. 264.

54   3   Newton N. Minow, *Equal Time* (New York: Atheneum, 1964), p. 118.

55   18   Memorandum by Richard C. Wald, originally written for publication but never published, November 1969 (author's files).

55   24   *New York Times*, December 9, 1969.

55   28   *Broadcasting* (December 15, 1969), p. 22.

56   3   *Network Broadcasting*, p. 136.

56   9   Wald, Memorandum, p. 3.

57   6   Les Brown, *Television: The Business Behind the Box* (New York: Harcourt, Brace, 1971), pp. 199–204.

57   20   Fred Freed, "Television and the Academic Community: Some Observations and Suggestions for Cooperation," n.d. [1967] mimeo (author's files).

58   27   Huntley-Brinkley Field Study, November 15, 1968.

59   12   *Broadcasting*, July 13, 1970, pp. 44–45.

59   29   FCC, "Editorializing by Broadcast Licensees," pp. 1 ff.

60   1   Minow, *op. cit.*, p. 152.

60   6   *Ibid.*, p. 118.

60   18   W. Theodore Pierson, "The Need for Modification of Section 326," *Federal Communications Bar Journal*, XVIII (1963), 21.

61   3   U.S. Senate, Subcommittee on Communications of the Committee on Commerce, *Fairness Doctrine*, 90th Cong., 2d Sess., 1968, p. 80. (Hereafter referred to as *Fairness Doctrine*.)

61   25   *Ibid.*, pp. 22, 28, 30.

61   31   A recent exception was the finding of an FCC hearing examiner that television station KHJ-TV in Los Angeles, estimated to be worth more than $20 million, was not fulfilling the public-interest requirement partly

because it devoted too small a proportion of its time to news and public affairs and too high a proportion to entertainment fare. Donahue thus found in favor of the challenging applicant, and the license was revoked, pending appeal. FCC 69D-43, Docket No. 16679–80, August 13, 1969.

62   3   Pierson, *op. cit.*, p. 20.

62   22   Robert E. Kintner, "Television and the World of Politics," *Harper's Magazine* (May 1965), p. 132.

62   36   *Fairness Doctrine*, p. 79; also Minow, *op. cit.*, p. 118.

63   22   Robert Paul Wolff, *The Politics of Liberalism* (Boston: Beacon Press, 1969), pp. 11 ff. Also, for example, *319 US 190.*

63   33   "Television Network Program Procurement," p. 22.

64   21   *Fairness Doctrine*, p. 12.

64   30   The recent exemption by Congress of the electoral campaigns of the President and Vice-President from this rule, however, is of far less consequence to the networks than other aspects of the Fairness Doctrine.

64   38   FCC, "Application of the Fairness Doctrine in the Handling of Controversial Issues of Public Importance," *Federal Register*, Vol. 29, No. 145, Part II (July 25, 1964), p. 10416.

65   14   *Ibid.*, p. 10417, and *Fairness Doctrine*, pp. 57 ff. Also, interviews with FCC members.

66   7   *Fairness Doctrine*, p. 103.

66   18   *Ibid.*, pp. 104–5.

66   22   Robert K. Baker and Sandra Ball, *Violence and the Media: A Staff Report to the National Commission on the Causes and Prevention of Violence* (Washington, D.C.: U.S. Government Printing Office, 1970), p. 220.

66   24   *Fairness Doctrine*, p. 110.

66   31   "Racial Stress and the Mass Media," speech at Buffalo, N.Y., September 21, 1967 (transcript, p. 20).

66   36   Kintner, *op. cit.*, p. 128.

PAGE LINE

67 29 *Broadcasting* (December 15, 1969), p. 22.

68 3 One of the few fairness complaints against the networks which has been upheld by the FCC came about because an NBC report on air traffic in Miami convincingly presented the case of the commercial pilots and concluded that pilots of private aircraft added to the safety hazard in congested airports. After NBC was in effect ordered by the FCC to present the "other side" (i.e., the views of the pilots of private aircraft), an NBC executive complained to me that although he agreed with the reporter, who felt strongly that the "other side" was "false" and "confusing," under the Fairness Doctrine he had no choice but to reprimand the reporter. See also, *Broadcasting* (May 4, 1970), p. 9.

68 14 Robert MacNeil, *The People Machine* (New York: Harper & Row, 1968), pp. 268–70.

69 3 *Ibid.*, pp. 270–71.

69 35 FCC Rules and Regulations, 73.679, 32; *Federal Register*, pp. 10305–6, as amended at p. 11532 (1967).

70 2 *Fairness Doctrine*, pp. 47–48.

70 36 U.S. Court of Appeals for the Seventh Circuit, September 10, 1968, pp. 11–12.

71 8 *Fairness Doctrine*, p. 80.

71 16 Letter to Senator John O. Pastore, June 20, 1967; reprinted in *Fairness Doctrine*, p. 106.

71 28 Richard W. Jencks, "Equal Time, Fairness and the Personal Attack Rules: A Comparison," paper given at seminar, New York, June 22, 1968, p. 19.

72 2 Personal interviews with producers. Also see, Edward Jay Epstein, *Counterplot* (New York: Viking, 1968), pp. 107–8.

72 16 Address by Frank Stanton, New York City, November 25, 1969 (transcript, p. 10).

72 22 The so-called "50-50 Rule," passed in 1970, forbids licensees from taking more than three hours of programs

PAGE LINE

produced, owned or distributed by networks between the hours of 7 P.M. to 11 P.M. Since the networks had previously supplied programs for three and a half to four hours during this period, it represented a substantial reduction in time that they could sell national advertisers. *Broadcasting* (April 6, 1970), p. 102.

72   27   *Variety* (October 22, 1969), p. 43.

73   5   *Broadcasting* (April 6, 1970), p. 102.

73   29   MacNeil, *op. cit.*, p. 261.

74   15   Quoted in *ibid.*, p. 245.

74   37   Robert E. Kintner, "Broadcasting and the News," *Harper's Magazine* (April 1965), p. 52.

75   9   Baker and Ball, *op. cit.*, p. 220.

75   26   Letter from Reuven Frank to Roger Wilkins, December 8, 1967.

75   30   Baker and Ball, *op. cit.*, pp. 220–21. CBS also accepted the suggestion made at the conference that a television camera be stationed permanently in the "ghetto," and made this a regular feature, or "beat," on the CBS Morning News with Joe Benti.

76   14   NBC Logs, January 1969. Personal interview with Reuven Frank.

76   34   Public Broadcasting Laboratory, "The Whole World's Watching," December 22, 1968 (transcript, p. 68).

Chapter 3

78   Epigraph: *New York*, January 25, 1971, p. 20.

79   2   U.S. House of Representatives, *Broadcasting Ratings*, Hearings before the Subcommittee of the Committee on Interstate and Foreign Commerce, 88th Cong., 1st Sess., 1963, Part I, p. 82 (testimony of Werner). (Hereafter referred to as *Broadcasting Ratings*.)

79   7   *Ibid.*, p. 88.

79   10   Emmanuel Gerard, "The Television Industry," unpublished report (1966), p. 1.

PAGE LINE

79   25   *Broadcasting Ratings*, pp. 37, 39.

79   28   *Ibid.*, p. 119.

79   34   Gerard, *op. cit.*, p. 1.

80   14   *Broadcasting Ratings*, p. 117.

80   27   *Network Broadcasting*, p. 207. (See note for p. 47, l. 4, Chapter 2.)

80   39   Personal Interviews with Steve Flynn, vice-president, NBC News.

81   12   *Network Broadcasting*, pp. 285–88.

82   15   *Broadcasting Ratings*, p. 45.

82   23   *Broadcasting Yearbook: 1969* (Washington, D.C.: Broadcasting Publishing, 1969).

82   32   A. C. Nielsen, January 1969.

82   37   Gerard, *op. cit.*, Appendix on UHF.

82   40   *Network Broadcasting*, pp. 207 ff.

83   35   *Fairness Doctrine*, p. 77.

85   32   Memorandum, January 1962, p. 6 (author's files).

86   6   *Ibid.*, p. 7.

87   9   Paul Klein, "Local News Lead-In to Network News: Top Twenty Markets," unpublished memorandum, March 1969.

88   5   CBS Budget (author's files). Sales figures estimated from Broadcasting Advertising Research.

89   2   Frank, Memorandum, p. 6.

89   8   *Ibid.*, p. 22.

89   11   *Ibid.*, pp. 21–22.

89   14   Klein, Memorandum, p. 6.

89   22   Analysis of CBS, NBC and ABC Logs, December 5–21, 1962, 1968.

PAGE LINE

90   1   Fred W. Friendly, *Due to Circumstances Beyond Our Control* (New York: Random House, 1967), p. 264.

90   31   Klein, Memorandum, p. 8; also, personal interviews with Klein.

91   2   *Ibid.*

92   2   Statement by William R. McAndrew before the FCC, January 1962, Docket No. 12782, p. 10.

92   21   A. C. Nielsen Reports, January 1969.

92   24   Personal interviews with William Fricke (and research done by McCann-Erickson).

93   7   Gerard, *op. cit.*, p. 24.

94   16   *Broadcasting Ratings*, p. 38.

94   34   A. C. Nielsen Ratings, February–March 1969 (McCann-Erickson Tabulations).

96   4   The same point is illustrated in "Research Evaluation of Network News," pp. 17–18.

96   26   Klein, Memorandum, p. 14.

98   18   Memorandum from Klein to Goodman, March 18, 1968.

98   33   Untitled study by Statistical Research, Inc., for NBC (author's files).

98   36   *Ibid.*, p. 12.

99   17   U.S. House of Representatives, Committee on Interstate and Foreign Commerce, *Staging of Marijuana Broadcast: Pot Party at a University*, 91st Cong., 1st Sess., 1969, Report No. 91–108, p. 5.

101   4   Data in author's files, 1968–1969.

102   9   Study of Huntley-Brinkley Film Logs, September 1968–January 1969.

103   31   Memorandum dated March 14, 1969.

103   35   Memorandum dated March 21, 1969.

104   30   Memorandum dated May 1, 1969.

105   3   Frank, Memorandum, p. 21.

PAGE LINE

107   12   Friendly, *op. cit.*, p. 305.

109   1   Analysis of Huntley-Brinkley Film Logs, September 1968–January 1969.

109   26   *New York Times*, November 14, 1969.

109   35   Analysis of NBC Evening News Film Logs, September 1968–January 1969; analysis of CBS and ABC Logs, December 1968–January 1969.

110   1   Huntley-Brinkley field study.

110   20   Shooting script, author's files.

110   29   Friendly, *op. cit.*, p. 306.

111   37   Nicholas Johnson, *How to Talk Back to Your Television Set* (Boston: Little, Brown, 1970).

112   5   For a further discussion of this refutation, see Edward Jay Epstein, "The Commissioner," *Commentary* (June 1970).

112   19   Friendly, *op. cit.*, p. 109.

117   30   Friendly, *op. cit.*, pp. 219–20.

118   4   Personal interviews with Fred Friendly; also *ibid.*, p. 222.

118   10   Personal interviews with Fred Friendly.

118   18   Friendly, *op. cit.*, p. 220.

118   23   *Ibid.*, p. 221.

119   5   *Ibid.*, p. 223.

119   15   *Ibid.*, p. 225.

119   19   *Ibid.*

119   29   *Ibid.*, p. 226.

119   31   *Ibid.*, p. 227; p. 226.

119   36   *Ibid.*, p. 230.

120   9   *Ibid.*, p. 232.

120   15   *Ibid.*, p. 233.

PAGE LINE

120   19   *Ibid.*, p. 250.

120   23   *Ibid.*, p. 239.

120   28   *Ibid.*, pp. 191, 225.

120   33   *Ibid.*, p. 272.

121   7   *Ibid.*, p. 186.

121   17   *Ibid.*, p. 195.

121   25   *Ibid.*, p. 196.

121   38   *Ibid.*, p. 243.

122   17   *Ibid.*, pp. 217–18.

122   30   *Ibid.*, p. 244.

123   12   *Ibid.*, p. 261.

124   25   *Ibid.*, pp. 225–26.

125   3   Personal interview with Reuven Frank.

125   9   *Ibid.*

125   19   *Ibid.*

127   21   Friendly, *op. cit.*, p. 164.

128   16   *Variety* (September 3, 1969), p. 3.

128   28   *Ibid.*

129   5   *Ibid.* See also Sheldon Zalaznick, "The Rich, Risky Business of Television News," *Fortune* (May 1, 1969), p. 97.

129   11   *Variety* (September 3, 1969), p. 3.

129   22   Fred Freed, "Television and the Academic Community" (n.d. [1967] mimeo, author's files), p. 10.

130   29   Zalaznick, *loc. cit.*

Chapter 4

133   Epigraph: Public Broadcasting Laboratory, transcript, December 22, 1968.

PAGE LINE

134   18   Daniel J. Boorstin, *The Image: A Guide to Pseudo-Events in America* (New York: Harper Colophon, 1961), p. 11.

135   13   Testimony before the National Commission on Causes and Prevention of Violence, December 20, 1968 (transcript, p. 245).

137   10   Frank, speech at Yale University, February 17, 1970 (transcript, p. 12).

137   19   Correspondence between Reuven Frank and Roger Wilkins, November 11, 1967–December 8, 1967.

138   26   CBS News Logs, and "opposition news logs," December 12, 1968–January 26, 1969.

139   25   Field Study.

140   7   Robert MacNeil, *The People Machine* (New York: Harper & Row, 1968), p. 36.

140   24   A. John Adams, "Proposal for a CBS News Research Unit," undated [1967] memorandum, p. 3.

141   18   ABC Promotion Air about Ted Koppel broadcast, December 26, 1970 (Boston).

143   8   MacNeil, *op. cit.*, p. 36.

143   16   Field Study, November 1968.

145   11   *Fairness Doctrine*, p. 25.

147   2   *New York Times*, August 18, 1969; CBS Logs, August 17, 1969; also, personal interviews with assignment editors.

150   28   NBC Logs, December 17, 1968–January 17, 1969.

Chapter 5

152   Epigraph: Elmer Lower quoted in the New York *Post*, June 21, 1972, p. 91.

153   20   Frank, Memorandum, p. 20.

154   30   *Ibid.*, p. 9.

PAGE LINE

155   24   *Ibid.*, p. 16.

155   28   Field Study, October 7, 1968.

156   4   "Correspondent's Handbook: A Guide to the Operating Practices of ABC News" (1966), p. 203 (author's files).

156   18   Frank, Memorandum, p. 10.

157   2   September 19, 1968 (transcript, author's files).

157   38   Frank, Memorandum, p. 7.

158   9   *Ibid.*, p. 9.

158   26   February 23, 1971 (transcript, p. 16).

159   2   Prepared statement by Bruce Cohn during inquiry into alleged rigging of television news programs. Hearings before the Special Subcommittee on Investigations of the Committee on Interstate and Foreign Commerce, House of Representatives, 92nd Cong., 2nd Sess., May 17, 18 and 23, 1972, p. 182.

159   16   FCC letter to networks (No. 69–19227767), February 28, 1969, p. 9.

159   22   *Ibid.*

159   34   *Ibid.*, p. 12.

160   17   U.S. House of Representatives, Committee on Interstate and Foreign Commerce, *Deceptive Programming Practices: Pot Party at a University*, 91st Cong., 1st Sess., 1969, pp. 6 ff.

160   22   *Ibid.*, p. 7.

160   24   *Ibid.*, p. 11.

161   18   Frank, Memorandum, p. 13; CBS News Manual, entitled "Television News Reporting" (New York, 1958); and Correspondent's Handbook: A Guide to Operating Practices of ABC News (1966).

161   40   CBS News Manual, p. 64.

162   10   Frank, Memorandum, p. 13.

162   30   *Ibid.*, p. 17.

PAGE LINE

163   2   CBS News Manual, p. 64.

163   6   Frank, Memorandum, p. 20.

163   12 CBS News Manual, p. 28.

163   35 Robert MacNeil, *The People Machine* (New York: Harper & Row, 1968), pp. 65 ff.

164   13 Memorandum from Harry McCarthy to Nick Archer, October 13, 1964.

164   23 Frank, Memorandum, p. 33.

164   28 Walter Lippmann, *Public Opinion* (New York: Free Press, 1965), p. 59.

165   20 Personal interviews with Reuven Frank.

167   9   ABC, "Correspondent's Handbook," pp. 251 ff.

167   31 *Ibid.*

168   18 *Ibid.*, pp. 265–66.

170   31 NBC, August 26, 1970.

175   1   Karel Reisz and Gavin Millar, *The Technique of Film Editing* (New York: Hastings House, 1968), p. 194. (Note: "For example the Nazi propaganda film, 'Victory in the West' and the American propaganda film, 'Divide and Conquer,' used exactly the same footage of fleeing French refugees to make completely different points. In the first film, the footage to symbolize a German victory, and in the American film as evidence of the French spirit of resistance" [p. 196]).

175   38 CBS News Manual, p. 77.

176   35 NBC Evening News, September 23, 1969.

177   11 CBS News Manual, p. 77.

177   27 Field Study, November 19, 1968.

178   21 MacNeil, *op. cit.*, pp. 65–66.

178   23 *Ibid.*

179   25 Kurt Lang and Gladys Engel Lang, *Politics and Television* (Chicago: Quadrangle Books, 1968), pp. 36 ff.

Chapter 6

181   Epigraph: *Harper's Magazine*, 1965.

181   18   Public Broadcasting Laboratory, "The Whole World's Watching," December 22, 1968 (transcript, p. 15).

183   11   *Ibid.* (transcript, p. 11).

185   19   NBC Evening News, November 21, 1968.

187   25   CBS Logs, November 8, 1968–January 10, 1969.

188   19   Robert J. Northshield, Memorandum, November 12, 1968.

196   14   CBS News, *Television News Reporting* (New York: McGraw-Hill, 1958), p. 94.

196   26   *Ibid.*, p. 112.

196   29   John O'Connor, *New York Times*, November 15, 1971.

197   27   Friendly, *Due to Circumstances Beyond Our Control*, p. 195.

Chapter 7

200   Epigraph: Frank, Memorandum, p. 8.

200   13   Speech to the Radio and Television News Directors, September 26, 1969, reprinted in *New York Post*, November 29, 1969, p. 27.

201   5   For example, Vilfrado Pareto held that "the chief element in what happens is in fact the order or system, not the conscious will of individuals." The only individual who could be exempted from this form of "non-logical action" was the social scientist. *The Mind and Society* (New York: Harcourt Brace, 1935), edited by Arthur Livingston and translated by Andrew Bongiosno. See especially para. 2254. For a full discussion of the "sociology of knowledge," see Karl Mannheim, *Ideology and Utopia*, translated by Louis Wirth and Edward Shils (New York: Harvest Books, 1936), pp. 264 ff.

PAGE LINE

201   8   Leo C. Rosten, *The Washington Correspondents* (New York: Harcourt, Brace, 1937); William C. Rivers, *The Opinion-Makers* (Boston: Beacon, 1965); Bernard C. Cohen, *The Press and Foreign Policy* (Princeton, N.J.: Princeton University Press, 1963; Theodore E. Kruglak, *The Foreign Correspondent: A Study of Men and Women Reporting for the American Information Media in Western Europe* (Geneva: Librarie E. Droz, 1955); and Bernard A. Weisberger, *The American Newspaperman* (Chicago: University of Chicago Press, 1961).

201   25   Herbert A. Simon, *Administrative Behavior* (New York: Free Press, 1965), pp. 198 ff.

202   2   Sander Vanocur, "How the Media Massaged Me," *Esquire* (January 1972), p. 82.

202   13   *Ibid.*

202   16   *Ibid.*, p. 148.

203   16   December 1, 1968–January 15, 1969.

204   18   Robert MacNeil, *The People Machine* (New York: Harper & Row, 1968), pp. 270 ff.

205   5   Testimony before the National Commission on the Causes and Prevention of Violence, December 20, 1968 (transcript, pp. 219–20).

211   2   NBC Policies and Procedures (a collection of network policy statements circulated among producers).

211   38   Quoted in Edith Efron, *The News Twisters* (Los Angeles, Nash Publishers, 1971), p. 63.

212   10   Lyndon B. Johnson, *The Vantage Point* (New York: Holt, Rinehart & Winston, 1971), pp. 473 ff.

212   14   *Ibid.*

214   20   Stokely Carmichael and Charles V. Hamilton, *Black Power: The Politics of Liberation in America* (New York: Vintage Books, 1967), see Chap. III.

214   35   November 4, 1970. Quoted in Ephron, *op. cit.*, p. 198.

215   30   Edward Shils, *Torment of Secrecy* (New York: Free Press, 1956), p. 23; also pp. 36–45, 109 ff.

PAGE LINE

215   35   Daniel Patrick Moynihan, "The President and the Press," *Commentary* (March 1971).

216   10   Compare Erving Goffman's discussion "on face-work" in his *Interaction Ritual* (Garden City, N.Y.: Doubleday, 1967), pp. 5–45.

217   13   For alternate definitions of politics, see Harold P. Lasswell, *The Future of Political Science* (New York: Atherton, 1963), pp. 15–18.

217   26   ABC Evening News, January 4, 1972.

219   25   In the case of the Washington press corps, the "confrontation model" is trenchantly analyzed by Moynihan, "The President and the Press."

226   8   Reuven Frank, "The Ugly Mirror," *Television Quarterly* (Winter 1969).

227   3   ABC, NBC and CBS Evening News, January 11, 1972.

229   16   Chester I. Barnard, *Functions of the Executive* (Cambridge, Mass.: Harvard University Press, 1966), pp. 233 ff.

229   24   For examples of such extraordinary interventions, see Les Brown, *Television: The Business behind the Box* (New York: Harcourt, Brace, 1971), p. 221.

234   18   September 16–November 5, 1968.

235   9   Efron, *op. cit.*, p. 349.

235   18   *Ibid.*, pp. 266–67 (pro-Nixon); pp. 284–86 (anti-Nixon).

235   29   Broadcasts on September 16, 20, 1968; October 9, 14, 1968.

236   9   Broadcasts on September 23, 1968; October 11, 16, 18, 1968; November 1, 1969.

Chapter 8

239   Epigraph: *Television Age*, September 11, 1967, p. 30.

239   7   Walter Cronkite, *Eye on the World* (New York: Cowles, 1971), p. ix.

PAGE LINE

239 16 President's Commission on Campus Unrest, *Report* (New York: Avon Books, 1970), pp. 233 ff.

240 35 Reuven Frank, "The Ugly Mirror," *Television Quarterly* (Winter 1969).

241 9 Frank, Memorandum, p. 20. (Emphasis added.)

241 15 *Ibid.*

241 26 Robert E. Park, *On Social Control and Collective Behavior* (Chicago: University of Chicago Press, 1967), p. 107.

242 21 Frank, Memorandum.

243 22 Westin, Memorandum, March 21, 1969.

243 30 Cronkite, *loc. cit.*

244 14 Field Study, October 28, 1968–January 19, 1969.

244 19 November 18, 1968.

244 21 December 6, 1968.

244 25 November 29, 1968; December 6, 1968.

244 26 December 8, 1968.

244 29 December 17, 1968.

244 31 November 26, 1968; December 6, 16, 1968; January 2, 1969.

245 6 January 8, 1969; November 19, 1968; December 2, 1968.

246 35 October 28–December 12, 1968.

246 36 November 4, 6, 8, 11, 20, 29, 1968; October 28, 29, 31, 1968; December 12, 1968.

246 37 November 19, 29, 1968 (Paris and Bonn).

246 37 November 29, 1968; December 12, 1968 (Italy).

247 1 December 18, 1968.

247 2 November 7, 1968.

247 35 Merrill Panitt, "To Let Europe See Us As We Are," *TV Guide* (February 12, 1972), p. 49.

PAGE LINE

248   2   For example, December 3, 13, 1968.

248   22   For example, November 7, 1968; January 14–16, 1969.

248   27   For example, November 12, 28, 1968; December 11, 23, 1968.

248   33   October 30, November 28, December 3, 1968; January 2, 1969.

248   35   December 5, 1968; January 7, 1969.

248   37   November 6, 1968; January 2, 1969.

249   2   December 3, 9, 1968.

249   4   November 13, December 17, October 30, 1968.

250   13   Howe McCarthy, a former press officer in Vietnam, sheds some light on this form of control in his Senior Honors Thesis at Harvard University, "Viet Nam Press Coverage" (Department of Government, 1971).

250   16   *The ABC Newsmen's Saigon* (privately printed, June 6, 1966), p. 5.

250   25   Memorandum from Bob Jones, December 17, 1968.

250   29   Personal interview with Howe McCarthy.

251   8   December 3, 5, 1968.

251   9   December 11, 1968 (credit).

251   9   January 8, 10, 11, 1969 (nutrition).

251   12   October 29, December 16, 1968; January 3, 1969 (Kennedy).

251   12   January 13, 1969 (McCarthy).

251   12   December 30, 1968 (Muskie).

251   13   December 17, 1968; January 11, 1969 (McGovern).

251   13   January 17, 1969 (Fulbright).

251   16   The most notable exception was the unseating of Congressman Adam Clayton Powell from the House Education Committee, over which he had presided. January 3–4, 1969.

PAGE LINE

252   1   December 23, 27, 1968; January 16, 17, 1969.

253   8   December 16, 1968.

253 19   Personal interview with Al Schneider, January 16, 1969. Mr. Schneider was then adviser to the President on television communications.

254 15   November 14, 18, 20, 1968; December 2, 3, 9, 1968; January 6, 8, 11, 17, 1969.

254 17   *Ibid.*

254 31   Lemberg Center for the Study of Violence, Brandeis University, Reports, October–December 1968. Also, NBC Morning Reports for this period.

255 13   ABC Interdepartmental Correspondence, June 11, 1968 (author's files).

255 23   *Ibid.*

255 30   *Ibid.*

256 34   For a fuller account of this incident, see James Keogh, *President Nixon and the Press* (New York: Funk & Wagnall, 1972), pp. 121–23.

Chapter 9

261   3   Walter Lippmann, *Public Opinion* (New York: Free Press, 1965), p. 59.

262 29   Frank, Memorandum, p. 3.

263 30   *Ibid.*, p. 20.

263 38   *Ibid.*

264 18   CBS Evening News, April 18, 1972.

267 23   Network news is, of course, not the only news media which chooses spokesmen who can generalize from local occurrences: the *New York Times*, the Washington *Post* and other national periodicals used the highly exaggerated charge of "genocide," made by a spokesman for the Black Panther Party to tie dramatically together a number of shooting incidents between police and Panthers which in fact happened under widely different

PAGE LINE

        circumstances in different cities. See Edward Jay Epstein, "The Black Panthers," *The New Yorker* (February 13, 1971), pp. 45 ff.

268   2   For example, Alfred I. Dupont-Columbia University, *Survey of Broadcast Journalism 1968–1969*, ed. by Marvin Barrett (New York: Grosset & Dunlap, 1969). Or, for an example of newspaper criticism, see Jack Gould, "The Camera Never Lies—But It Doesn't Ask Questions Either," *New York Times*, August 3, 1969, p. 17.

268 14 Barrett, p. 4.

269   5 This criticism is perhaps most forcefully articulated by Vice-President Agnew, for example. See also, James Keogh, *Nixon and the Press* (New York: Funk & Wagnall, 1972), and Efron, *The News Twisters*.

269 17 Frank Shakespeare, speech to the Radio and Television Directors, September 26, 1969, reprinted in the New York *Post*, November 29, 1969, p. 27.

269 31 For a description of the activities of the 1960s, see William L. O'Neill, *Coming Apart* (Chicago: Quadrangle Books, 1971), *passim*.

270 11 For example, see Robert Cirino, *Don't Blame the People* (Los Angeles: Diversity Press, 1971).

270 27 *Ibid.*, p. 221.

271 21 Freed, seminar on Television.

272   1 Frank, Memorandum, p. 17.

Bibliography

Public Documents

United States, Federal Communications Commission. *Network Broadcasting.* Staff Study Published by the House Committee on Interstate and Foreign Commerce. 85th Cong., 2d Sess., 1957.

——. "Editorializing by Broadcast Licensees." Docket No. 8516. June 1949.

——. "Report and Statement of Policy re Commission En Banc Programming Requirements." No. 91874. July 1960.

——. "Application of the Fairness Doctrine in the Handling of Controversial Issues of Public Importance." *Federal Register,* Vol. 29, No. 145, Part II. July 1964.

——. Letter to Networks. No. 69-19227767. February 28, 1969.

——. "Television Network Program Procurement." No. 12782. May 1963.

United States, Senate, Subcommittee on Communications of the Committee on Commerce. *Fairness Doctrine.* 90th Cong., 2d Sess., 1968.

United States, House, Committee on Interstate and Foreign Commerce. *Hearings on Deceptive Programming Practices.* 90th Cong., 2d Sess., 1968.

United States, House, Committee on Interstate and Foreign Commerce. *Hearings on Broadcast Ratings.* 88th Cong., 1st Sess., 1963.

―――――. *Hearings on Network Broadcasting.* 85th Cong., 2d Sess., 1958.

―――――. *Hearings on Staging of Marijuana Broadcast: Pot Party at University.* 91st Cong., 1st Sess., 1969.

Books

Abrams, Myron. *The Mirror and the Lamp: Romantic Theory and Critical Tradition.* New York: Norton, 1958.

Arlen, Michael J. *Living Room War.* New York: Viking, 1969.

Baker, Robert K., and Ball, Sandra J. *National Commission on the Causes and Prevention of Violence: Staff Report, Violence and the Media.* Washington, D.C.: U.S. Government Printing Office, 1969.

Banfield, Edward C. *Political Influence.* New York: Free Press, 1961.

Barnard, Chester A. *The Functions of the Executive.* Cambridge, Mass.: Harvard University Press, 1966.

Boorstin, Daniel J. *The Image: A Guide to Pseudo-Events in America.* New York: Harper's Colophon, 1961.

Brown, Lester L. *Television: The Business Behind the Box.* New York: Harcourt Brace Jovanovich, 1971.

Barret, Marvin (ed.). *The Alfred I. Dupont-Columbia University Survey of Broadcast Journalism: 1968–1969.* New York: Grosset & Dunlap, 1969.

CBS News. *Television News Reporting.* New York: McGraw-Hill, 1958.

Cater, Douglass. *The Fourth Branch of Government.* Boston: Houghton Mifflin, 1959.

Cirino, Robert. *Don't Blame the People.* Los Angeles: Diversity Press, 1971.

Cohen, Bernard C. *The Press and Foreign Policy.* Princeton, N.J.: Princeton University Press, 1963.

Cronkite, Walter. *Eye on the World.* New York: Cowles, 1971.

Deutsch, Karl W. *Nerves of Government.* New York: Free Press, 1966.

Efron, Edith. *The News Twisters.* Los Angeles: Nash Publishing, 1971.

Epstein, Edward Jay. *Counterplot.* New York: Viking, 1968.

Fagen, Richard R. *Politics and Communications.* Boston: Little, Brown, 1966.

Fang, Irving. *Television News.* New York: Hasting House, 1968.

Friendly, Fred W. *Due to Circumstances Beyond Our Control.* New York: Random House, 1967.

Gillingham, George (ed.). *Broadcasting Yearbook: 1969.* Washington, D.C.: Broadcasting, 1969.

Goffman, Erving. *Interaction Rituals.* Garden City, N. Y.: Doubleday, 1967).

Herring, James M., and Gross, Gerald C. *Telecommunications.* New York: McGraw-Hill, 1936.

Johnson, Lyndon B. *The Vantage Point.* New York: Holt, Rinehart and Winston, 1971.

Johnson, Nicholas. *How to Talk Back to Your Television Set.* Boston: Little, Brown, 1970.

Kendrick, Alexander. *Prime Time: The Life of Edward R. Murrow.* Boston: Little, Brown, 1969.

Keogh, James. *Nixon and the Press.* New York: Funk & Wagnalls, 1972.

Kruglak, Theodore E. *The Foreign Correspondent: A Study of Men and Women Reporting for the American Information Media in Western Europe.* Geneva: Librarie E. Droz, 1955.

Lang, Kurt, and Lang, Gladys Engel. *Politics and Television.* Chicago: Quadrangle, 1968.

Lippmann, Walter. *Public Opinion.* New York: Free Press, 1965.

MacNeil, Robert. *The People Machine.* New York: Harper & Row, 1968.

Mayer, Martin. *About Television*. New York: Harper & Row, 1972.

Merton, Robert. *On Theoretical Sociology*. New York: Free Press, 1967.

Mickelson, Sig. *The Electronic Mirror*. New York: Dodd, Mead, 1972.

Minow, Newton N. *Equal Time*. New York: Atheneum, 1964.

Nimmo, Dan D. *Newsgathering in Washington*. New York: Atherton, 1964.

O'Neill, William. *Coming Apart*. Chicago: Quadrangle, 1971.

Opotowsky, Stan. *The Big Picture*. New York: Collier, 1962.

Parsons, Talcott. *Essays in Sociological Theory*. New York: Free Press, 1967.

President's Commission on Campus Unrest. *Report*. New York: Avon, 1970.

Reisz, Karel, and Miller, Gavin. *The Technique of Film Editing*. New York: Hastings House, 1968.

Reston, James. *The Artillery of the Press*. New York: Harper & Row, 1966.

Rivers, William L. *The Opinion-Makers*. Boston: Beacon Press, 1965.

Roper Research Associates. *A Ten-Year Attitude Study Towards Television and Other Mass Media: 1958–1968*. New York: Television Information Office, 1969.

Rosten, Leo C. *The Washington Correspondents*. New York: Harcourt, Brace, 1937.

Shils, Edward. *Torment of Secrecy*. New York: Free Press, 1956.

Simon, Herbert A. *Administrative Behavior*. New York: Free Press, 1965.

Skornia, Harry J. *Television and the News*. Palo Alto, Cal.: Pacifica Books, 1968.

Small, William. *To K¹ll a Messenger: Television News and the Real World*. New York: Hastings House, 1970.

Swallow, Norman. *Factual Television.* New York: Hastings House, 1966.

Turner, Ralph H. (ed.). *On Social Control and Collective Behavior.* New York: Free Press, 1967.

Weisberger, Bernard A. *The American Newspaperman.* Chicago: University of Chicago Press, 1961.

Whale, John. *The Half-Shut Eye.* New York: St. Martin's, 1969.

Wolff, Robert Paul. *The Politics of Liberalism.* Boston: Beacon Press, 1969.

Articles

Breed, Warren. "Social Control in the Newsroom," *Social Forces,* XXXIII (1955), 326–335.

Coase, R. H. "The F.C.C.," *Journal of Law and Economics,* Vol. II (1959).

Epstein, Edward Jay. "The Commissioner," *Commentary,* June 1970.

———. "The Black Panthers," *New Yorker,* February 13, 1971.

Frank, Reuven. "The Ugly Mirror," *Television Quarterly,* Winter 1969.

Kintner, Robert E. "Broadcasting and the News," *Harper's Magazine* (3-part series), April, May, June 1965.

McAndrew, William. "Return News in Review," *Television Age,* September 26, 1966.

———. Statement before the FCC, January 1962, Docket No. 12782.

Moynihan, Daniel Patrick. "The President and the Press," *Commentary,* March 1971.

Panitt, Merrill. "To Let Europe See Us As We Are," *TV Guide,* February 12, 1972.

Pierson, W. Theodore. "The Need for Modification of Section 326," *Federal Communications Bar Journal,* Vol. XVIII (1963).

Pool, Ithiel de Sola, and Shulman, Irwin. "Newsmen's Fantasies, Audiences and Newswriting," *Public Opinion Quarterly,* XXIII (1959), 145–158.

Quester, George H. "Israel and the Nuclear Non-Proliferation Treaty," *Bulletin of Atomic Scientists*, June 1969.

Simon, Herbert A., and Sterm, F. "The Effects of Television upon Voting Behavior in Iowa in the 1952 Presidential Election," *American Political Science Review*, Vol. XLIX (June 1965).

Vanocur, Sander. "How the Media Massaged Me," *Esquire*, January 1972.

Weaver, Paul. "Is Television News Biased?," *The Public Interest*, Winter 1972.

Zalaznick, Sheldon. "The Rich, Risky Business of Television News," *Fortune*, May 1, 1969.

Unpublished Material

ABC News. "Correspondent's Handbook: A Guide to the Operating Practices of ABC News." New York, 1966.

————. "The ABC Newsmen's Saigon." 1966. (Mimeo.)

Adams, A. John. "Proposal for a CBS Research Unit." Undated [1967]. (Mimeo.)

Bernstein, Irving. "The Economics of Television Film Production." New York: Screen Actors Guild, 1960. (Mimeo.)

Cronkite, Walter. William Allen White Lecture, University of Kansas, February 10, 1969.

Frank, Reuven. Memorandum on the Half-Hour NBC Network News Program. 1966. (Mimeo.)

————. Speech at the Television Award Dinner, Omaha, Nebraska, January 12, 1970.

————. Speech at the Colloquium on Journalism, Yale University, New Haven, Conn., February 17, 1970.

Freed, Fred. "Television and the Academic Community: Some Observations and Suggestions for Cooperation." Undated [1967]. (Mimeo.)

Gerard, Emmanuel. "The Television Industry." 1966. (Mimeo.)

Jencks, Richard W. "Equal Time, Fairness and the Personal Attack Rules: A Comparison." Paper presented at a seminar in New York, June 22, 1968.

Klein, Paul. "Local News Lead-In to Network News: Top Twenty Markets." March 1969. (Mimeo.)

————. "Research Evaluation of Network News in Prime Time." January 1962. (Mimeo.)

Lower, Elmer. "The American Congress and Television." Speech at the Interparliamentary Union, Geneva, Switzerland, 1968.

————. "Racial Stress and the Mass Media." Speech at Sigma Delta Chi, Buffalo, New York, September 21, 1967.

McCarthy, Howe. "Vietnam Press Coverage." Unpublished honors thesis, Department of Government, Harvard University, 1971.

NBC. "NBC Policies and Operating Procedures." (Mimeo. Loose-leaf collection of policy statements.)

Stanton, Frank. Speech to the International Radio and Television Society, New York, November 1969.

Statistical Research, Inc. Untitled study of the news audience. 1969.

Weaver, Paul. "The Metropolitan Newspaper as a Political Institution." Unpublished Ph.D. dissertation, Department of Government, Harvard University, 1968.

Index

About the Author

EDWARD JAY EPSTEIN was born in New York City in 1935, received his B.A. and M.A. from Cornell University, his Ph.D. in political science from Harvard University, and has taught political science at Harvard and at M.I.T. He frequently writes for *The New Yorker* on subjects of political interest and journalism, and divides his time between Amagansett and New York City.

VINTAGE POLITICAL SCIENCE AND SOCIAL CRITICISM